BREAKING SUDAN

The Search for Peace

BREAKING SUDAN

The Search for Peace

Jok Madut Jok

ONEWORLD

A Oneworld Book

First published by Oneworld Publications, 2017
Copyright © Jok Madut Jok 2017

ISBN 978-1-78607-003-6
eISBN 978-1-78607-004-3

Typeset by Tetragon, London
Maps © William Donohoe
Printed and bound in Great Britain by Clays Ltd, St Ives plc

Oneworld Publications
10 Bloomsbury Street
London WC1B 3SR
England

CONTENTS

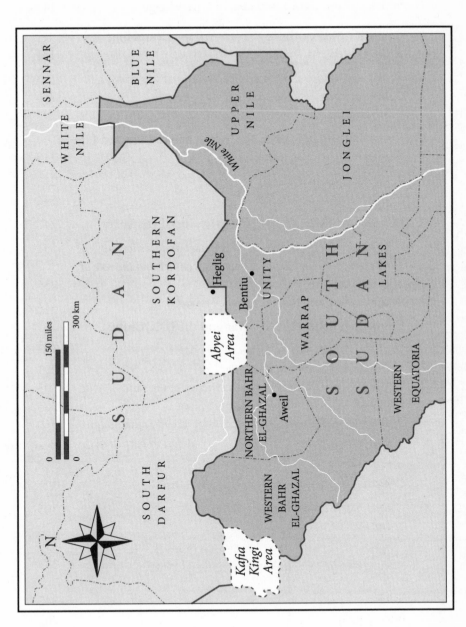

The new international border dividing Sudan and South Sudan

Incidents of violence in South Sudan, 2013 (Source: USAID)

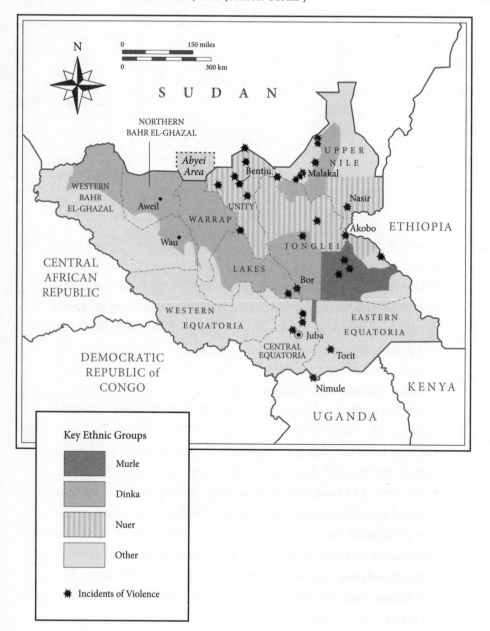

PREFACE

Research for this book, and all the plans to write it, have been overtaken by events year after year since I was offered a senior fellowship at the United States Institute of Peace (USIP) in 2011. Everyone who works on Sudan and South Sudan knows very well that nothing prepares one for the rapidly occurring political events, war dynamics and ethnic relations that are around the corner, nor how the lives of the people in Sudan and the new breakaway state of South Sudan evolve minute by minute.

Events in the new state of South Sudan, which was established in 2011 after an overwhelming southern vote in favor of separation, have unfolded at a speed that has made it difficult to update and finalize this book. Completion has been delayed for many years, as I have tried to keep the book up to date in the face of rapidly unfolding situations, from the implementation of the Comprehensive Peace Agreement (CPA), to the preparation for the referendum on unity versus break-up in what was southern Sudan, to independence and the challenges of creating a new state and a new nation from the ashes of the brutal liberation wars that have occurred throughout the sixty years since Sudan's independence from British colonial rule.

Relationships between the two new Sudanese states have long been defined by a history of acrimony, mutual suspicion and accusations and counter-accusations that spans the 192 years since Sudan was annexed to the Ottoman rule by Muhammed Ali, the Ottoman Sultan's viceroy in Egypt in 1821. Since the break-up, there have been more shifts in their relationship, mainly concerning border relations, economic rivalries and demands for mutual cooperation, with each state trying to get the better of the other. The new state of South Sudan has faced many challenges, starting with a civil war that began in 2013, a mere two years into independence. The new state was also confronted with rampant insecurity, economic problems resulting from the war and the acrimonious relationship with Sudan and issues of the capacity of institutions to run the state. The new country faced serious questions of national unity and, above all, problems of meeting the expectations of the South Sudanese people, who had pegged their aspirations for prosperity to independence.

In 2015, a peace agreement was signed in Addis Ababa, Ethiopia, under the auspices of the East African regional bloc, the Inter-Governmental Authority on Development (IGAD). Implementation of the agreement started in April 2016 but it has yet to bear fruit in terms of stabilizing the country after the deadly ethno-political conflict of 2013. But the most shocking plunge in the rollercoaster of Sudan's break-up was the fighting that broke out in Juba on July 7, 2016, between the parties to the Agreement on the Resolution of Conflict in South Sudan (ARCISS); an agreement that was supposed to end the civil war in Africa's youngest nation. The South Sudanese had hinged renewed hopes on this agreement and it was devastating to see fresh fighting just as the world was ready to help South Sudan out of its continuous and seemingly unending mayhem.

Therefore I decided that I had to stop somewhere, and produce whatever information I had obtained and analyzed, rather than waiting for a seminal moment that might never come. Therefore, this book will not account for every strand of the story of South Sudan, of how it came to be an independent state, how it nearly collapsed soon after and how its leaders grappled with turning it into a nation-state and failed. This book is a mix of reflection on sixty years of Sudanese history, an ethnographic study of how people lived with and in war for so long, what that history has done to their social fabric and how they speak of it today. It is a personal story of interactions with the South Sudanese over many years, as an aid worker, a participant researcher, a respondent to my own questions, a former government official, a director of a local think tank, and a public intellectual.

My hope has been to report that the country I call home has succeeded, proving wrong those doomsayers who write off South Sudan as a failed, useless, violent and corrupt state that no one should bother with. It is a story of how the two Sudans' leaders have toyed with the lives of the Sudanese people and how the citizens of the two Sudanese territories remain hostage to the aspirations of their political and military leaders. It is a story of the spectacular failure of South Sudanese leaders to transform their new country into a nation that its citizens can relate to, be loyal to, be proud of, respect and love.

As the South Sudanese, and other Sudanese living on the margins of state power and alienation from national resources, have had to live with the new political environment produced by the break-up of Sudan, they have had to find ways to live, move, trade, graze cattle, fight with each other, talk to each other and find peace in the midst of chaos, I cannot help but try to lend them a voice through this book. I shall attempt to document, analyze and problematize the relationship between Sudan and South Sudan, which might look like a matter of national policy, but are essentially issues of the life and death of human beings.

The book offers an alternative perspective on the euphoria of independence in South Sudan and how its leaders were unwilling or unable to read the writing on the wall, to see that independence alone could not be the solution to the suffering that the South Sudanese had endured for decades. Meaningful independence comes with significant responsibilities; the citizens of South Sudan felt betrayed by leaders who readily accepted those responsibilities but failed miserably to live up to them.

I shall attempt to expose the untruths behind the façade of homogeneity in the rump state that the government of Sudan has peddled since the break-up. The fact that South Sudan had to walk away from the union should signal to Khartoum's Islamic movement that the remaining Sudan is at risk; the breakaway of southern Sudan does not mean a more perfect and homogenous Sudan, a more perfect Arab and Islamic union, as Omar Ahmed Hassan al-Bashir declared in the wake of South Sudan's breakaway.

I hope to contribute to the debate among the Sudanese people about the new agreements, rules and regulations that govern population movement, citizenship, cross-border trade and social networks across the new international border between the two states. Can these relationships be maintained in a way that recognizes the political transition, the fact that there are now two states, while maintaining historical, social and economic links between the two new nations? The consequences of ignoring these historical social connections could be detrimental to both sides, states and peoples.

This book focusses on the period after the political settlement of Sudan's prolonged second civil war (1983–2005), but also reflects on the post-colonial era after the British left. It has been argued that the political happenings of the 1960s became the foundation for southern Sudan's quest to break away and the reason behind the continued high level of discord between southern and northern

Sudan. As the book is about the break-up of Sudan, it is important to note that the terms "southern Sudan" and "northern Sudan", as well as "northern Sudanese" and "southern Sudanese", are used for the period before the 2011 break-up. "South Sudan" and "Sudan" refer to the two new republics that came out of the CPA.

Facts presented here about national politics, war, society, economy and culture in both Sudans are very likely to be contested. I have therefore confined myself to analyzing and interpreting what the Sudanese people in both countries have said about these topics and refrained from drawing objective conclusions. Perceptions are just as good as fact when it comes to how people make decisions in their daily lives.

ACKNOWLEDGMENTS

This book would not have been possible without the help of very many individuals and institutions and they all deserve a word of thanks for their assistance with research, discussions, reviews and commentary, and for research grants. USIP deserves a special mention for its generosity, for much of the formulation of the ideas for this book was done during my tenure there as a senior fellow in 2010–11. The book would not have been accomplished without USIP funding. I particularly want to thank Jonathon Temin, Lynda Bashai and Stephanie Schwartz for their commentary and guidance and sharpening my ideas on Sudan.

In both the research phase as well as the development of the manuscript, I have gained a great deal from my colleagues at the Sudd Institute. Their friendship, guidance, critique and assistance with research were very valuable and this book would not have seen the light of day without them. Particular thanks go to Augustinao Ting Mayai, Abraham Awolich and Zachariah Diing Akol.

I am especially indebted to my home institution, Loyola Marymount University, both for grants that have facilitated many trips to South Sudan and for the extended leave of absence that made it possible for me to spend long periods of time in South Sudan, during which time I was able to work as under-secretary in the Ministry of Culture and Heritage in the new government of southern Sudan just before independence, and to co-found the Sudd Institute.

I would be remiss if I ended this preface without mentioning the tremendous assistance, friendship and accommodation accorded to me by South Sudanese and Sudanese in the course of research for this book. The devastating stories they have shared with me, their sense of humor about extremely sad experiences and their willingness to share them, have all injected life into this monograph.

I also owe thanks to the two anonymous reviewers who provided really valuable insights into both the substance and the structure of the book. I am most indebted to them for this, and to my publisher, Oneworld Publications, for their commitment to produce this book in such timely manner. But while I sincerely thank all of these friends, workmates, family and acquaintances, I must quickly add that any errors contained in this book are ultimately my own.

ABBREVIATIONS

AI	Amnesty International
ANC	African National Congress
ARCISS	Agreement on the Resolution of Conflict in South Sudan
AU	African Union
AUCISS	African Union Commission of Inquiry for South Sudan
AUHIP	African Union High-level Implementation Panel
CCM	Chama Cha Mapinduzi-Tanzania
CMC	Crisis Management Committee
CPA	Comprehensive Peace Agreement
DDPD	Doha Document on Peace in Darfur
DDR	Disarmament, Demobilization and Reintegration
DPA	Darfur Peace Agreement
DUP	Democratic Unionist Party
EPRDF	Ethiopian People's Revolutionary Democratic Front
EPLF	Eritrean People's Liberation Front
FTA	Financial Transfer Arrangements
GoS	Government of Sudan
GoSS	Government of Southern Sudan

GRSS	Government of the Republic of South Sudan
HRW	Human Rights Watch
ICC	International Criminal Court
ICRC	International Committee of the Red Cross
IDPs	Internally Displaced Persons
IGAD	Inter-Governmental Authority on Development
IMF	International Monetary Fund
JEM	Justice and Equality Movement
JMEC	Joint Monitoring and Evaluation Commission
LRA	Lord's Resistance Army
MDTF	Multilateral Donor Trust Fund
MOFEP	Ministry of Finance and Economic Planning
MSF	*Médicins sans frontières*/Doctors without Borders
NCP	National Congress Party
NDI	National Democratic Institute
NGO	Non-Governmental Organization
NIF	National Islamic Front
NPC	National Popular Congress
NISS	National Intelligence and Security Services
NLC	National Liberation Council
OAU	Organization of African Unity
PDF	Popular Defense Force
SAF	Sudan Armed Forces
SALW	Small Arms and Light Weapons
SANU	Sudan African National Union
SLA/M	Sudan Liberation Army/Movement
SPDF	Sudan People's Defense Forces
SPLA/M	Sudan People's Liberation Army/Movement
SPLA-N	Sudan People's Liberation Army North
SPLM/DC	Sudan People's Liberation Movement/Democratic Change

SPLM/A-IO	Sudan People's Liberation Movement/Army – in Opposition
SPLM-N	Sudan People's Liberation Movement– North
SRF	Sudan Revolutionary Front
SRSG	Special Representative of the Secretary General
SSDA/M	South Sudan Democratic Army/Movement
SSDF	South Sudan Defense Forces
SSLM/A	South Sudan Liberation Movement/Army
SSNPS	South Sudan National Police Service
SSP	South Sudan Pound
SSR	Security Sector Reform
SSU	Sudan Socialist Union
TFA	Transitional Financial Arrangements
UK	United Kingdom
UN	United Nations
UNDP	United Nations Development Program
UNHCR	United Nations High Commission for Refugees
UNICEF	United Nations Children's Fund
UNISFA	United Nations Interim Security Force for Abyei
UNMISS	United Nations Mission in South Sudan
UNPOL	United Nations Police
UNSC	United Nations Security Council
UPDF	Uganda People's Defense Force
USA	United States of America
USAID	United States Agency for International Development
USIP	United States Institute of Peace
WHO	World Health Organization

INTRODUCTION

THE "NEW SUDAN": HOW SUDAN'S BREAK-UP PREPARED THE GROUND FOR MORE WAR

The term "New Sudan" was the brainchild of John Garang de Mabior, founding chairman and commander in chief of the Sudan People's Liberation Army/Movement (SPLA/M). "New Sudan" was a project that aimed to bring about transformative unity in the Sudan, a country in the process of being torn apart by struggles between its disparate peoples over identity, diversity, control of resources and political power and state authority. The term "New Sudan," and how it was used in the recent history of the country, formed a major break in how the southern Sudanese had reacted to the northern Sudanese's systematic marginalization of the peripheries of the old Sudan. John Garang, unlike his predecessors in the struggle for southern rights, wanted unity, not an independent south. However, the complex dynamics of the protracted conflict between north and south ended with most southern Sudanese favoring the secession of South Sudan. Africa's largest country broke up, and two states were created from a long history of acrimony.

Southern Sudan had long taken the role of victim in the colonial anomaly that was Sudan. It saw itself as the victim of a racist
northern Sudanese minority regime that controlled the resources
of the country, totally excluding the peripheries. Having failed to
persuade both the colonial authorities and the northern Sudanese
élite to create a confederal or federal state in the wake of the
independence of Sudan from British rule, the struggles of the
south always aimed either to transform Sudan in a major way or
to break away.

There came a time in the history of Sudan when many of the
people of the peripheries concluded that the northern Sudanese
were unwilling to compromise their monopoly of power, the exclusion of the rest of the country from the distribution of resources
and the non-representation of the nation's multiple identities. The
aggressive promotion of an Islamic identity for the whole country
was particularly dangerous to the unity of the country, as non-
Muslims and moderate Muslims saw it as antithetical to the concept
of unity in diversity. But the drive to strengthen the Islamic identity
of the country by the radical Islamists who controlled the apparatus
of the state was unrelenting. That obduracy brought wars; the long
and extremely violent and destructive north-south war was just one
of many. Two major civil wars and multiple episodes of political
violence, mostly fought within southern Sudan, besmirched most
of the sixty years after the end of colonial rule in 1956, and brought
devastating consequences to the people of the region. The wars,
often allegedly fought to enforce the unity of the country not only
caused further disunity but also wrecked relationships among the
various ethnic groups, wasted an immense amount of resources,
deprived millions of services the state had promised to provide
and destroyed the nation's infrastructure. Sudan became one of the
world's largest recipients of humanitarian assistance, beginning with
the 1984 famine in Darfur,[1] the 1988 repeat of disastrous famine and

1998 famine in Bahr el Ghazal.² Today, man-made humanitarian crises persist, even after the break-up.

The southern Sudanese became so frustrated by these exclusionary practices that many saw secession as the only solution but John Garang came up with a different way of thinking. During the second round of the wars, which started in 1983, he simply stated that the issue of exclusion of the southern Sudanese from power, and from their share of national resources, could not be resolved by fighting for a breakaway but only by uniting with the rest of the country's marginalized communities to press for a transformation of Sudan from an Arab minority-dominated political entity to a democratic society in which all citizens were equal. This philosophy drew droves of fighters to the SPLA from all corners of the country except, for the moment, from Darfur.

The earliest members, Yousif Kwa Makki and Abdel Aziz Ahmed Adam Al-Hilu from the Nuba Mountains, Malik Agar Ayir from Blue Nile, Yasir Arman from Khartoum and Daoud Yahya Bolad from Darfur, either returned to their home areas or sent back envoys to recruit members for the SPLA. Yahya Bolad was captured and tortured to death in 1992, by security forces loyal to the then dictator of Sudan, the Islamist leader Omer Hassan al-Bashir. But all these fighters, from all corners of the country, fought for the right to equal citizenship, for political transition, for the recognition of ethnic and cultural diversity, for power and resource sharing and for a new political dispensation. For them, this was the essence of the "New Sudan." Many of them, and the fighters they attracted to this war, joined the fight not just from conviction about the appeal of the "New Sudan" philosophy, but also to express local grievances of a different nature from those of national politics.

Not all the fighters really understood what "New Sudan" entailed, but pointing their guns at Khartoum in such a concerted effort was convincing, desirable and central to why they joined the SPLA. The Dinka of northern Bahr el Ghazal and Upper Nile and the Nuer and the Shilluk of Upper Nile were angered by the violent raids of Arab tribesmen, the Baggara of the north-south borderlands. The Nuba were there to fight against the racism of the riverain tribes that had excluded them from the distribution of the national cake and the appropriation of their agricultural lands for the benefit of Arab farmers. The Nubians of the far north, the Ingessina of Blue Nile, the Darfuris of western Sudan and the Beja of the Red Sea Hills all had grievances over Khartoum's role in local property rights and other state-driven politics of discrimination and exclusion. All found the call for a New Sudan, and a periphery–center explanation of Sudan's woes, to be a different and appealing approach to a new statecraft.

Both the SPLA and the disparate communities found a common cause and saw an opportunity in the call for the restructuring of Sudan. Both had much to gain from a unified front with the SPLA transforming local concerns into part of a national project and local communities seeing the SPLA as a source of weapons and a credible voice in international diplomacy. The result was Africa's longest and most deadly conflict in more than a generation; a conflict that spread to much of the country; a conflict in which all the disaffected peripheries gradually and increasingly saw the value of putting their weight behind the "New Sudan."

John Garang challenged anyone who prided themselves on being a Sudanese nationalist to think about the rewards of a united Sudan, Africa's biggest country, a country of abundant resources, whose cultural, racial and religious diversity was a great asset, not the liability that the riverain Arab élite had long made it. Thinkers and activists from all corners of Sudan, many of whom might have found it impossible to reform Sudan in the past, saw that the "New Sudan," at least the way John Garang explained it, was the most viable option if the country were to keep its territorial integrity and the unity of its diverse peoples.

Over several years, from the late 1980s to the early 1990s, the conflict was re-imagined and articulated as a confrontation between the periphery and the center. During this time the conflict took twists and turns; new political and military alliances emerged among opposition groups and the oppositions split under the weight of the central government's well-planned and extremely violent, racialized and religiously based counter-insurgency tactics.[3] From 1985, multiple attempts at peace negotiation, ceasefire deals and peace agreements traversed the war period, many of which were as quickly dishonored as they were inked. The wars of Sudan were complex, with serious implications for ethnic relations, racial and religious ideologies, which made the likelihood of a peaceful resolution and future coexistence extremely remote.[4] The sentiment of mistrust had built up over the more than sixty years since independence from British colonial rule. The government in Khartoum in the post-colonial period had frequently changed hands among various political forces in northern Sudan, with each political force promising to bring about the desired transformation but all too often ending in disappointment for the people of the peripheries.

In the meantime, war raged in the bushes of southern Sudan, in the Nuba Mountains of central Sudan, in Southern Blue Nile, the Red Sea Hills and in the major garrison towns throughout southern Sudan. These conflicts had devastating consequences both for the population in these areas and for the economy of the country; the cost of the war was estimated to be about a million dollars a day for twenty years.

This was a different kind of war. People from the geographic north fought alongside southern Sudanese for the first time, the children of prominent families in the north died on far-away war fronts in the south and some northern Sudanese spoke in defense of the south, bringing the war much closer to the northern élite than in the past. The global image of the country suffered immensely. Sudan received more humanitarian aid than any other country since the post-World War II Marshall Plan and the country was written off and put under sanctions as a pariah state, dubbed as a state sponsor of terrorism since 1998.

The unity of the country also suffered, as the people of the peripheral areas, excluded from resource distribution, became ever more bitter about their exploitation by the center, leading to diminished pride in their "Sudanese" nationality, identity and belonging. This condition ended with the 2005 Comprehensive Peace Agreement (CPA), one of the most celebrated feats of peace-making diplomacy in Africa and one that involved African actors as mediators.

The hope, both of the Sudanese people and the mediators, was that the CPA would end Sudan's multiple wars, especially the prolonged second civil war in the south, if not the other wars in the other peripheral areas of the country. It was also hoped the agreement would commit the Sudanese élite to reform, national dialogue, constitutional review and above all to the relinquishing of the use of Islam for political gain, in favor of a more secular and democratic society. The option of secularism had become a viable concept in the otherwise Islam-dominated political structures in Khartoum, as had citizenship as the only basis of qualification for inclusion in all the state's responsibilities for the welfare of its citizens. Without these, the territorial integrity of Sudan was very much in jeopardy. Sadly, or gladly, as southern Sudanese saw it, the latter came to pass. The CPA forged ahead with a determination to end Sudan's enforced unity.

The CPA was a compromise to end one of the world's most deadly and destructive conflicts since World War II, to pave the way for a referendum in southern Sudan and to allow for the possibility of the country splitting into two. In return, the Sudan People's Liberation Movement (SPLM) promised not to challenge its CPA partner, the ruling National Congress Party (NCP) and its theocratic hold on power in northern Sudan. The SPLM also compromised on the application of Islamic *sharia* law in northern Sudan, so long as southern Sudan was exempt from it, including southerners living in the north. The SPLM compromised on a number of other issues, including the fight for the democratic transformation of Sudan.

The deal ended Africa's longest civil war (the first round lasted from 1955 to 1972 and the second from 1983 to 2005) between the north and the south of what used to be Africa's biggest country. But with the military victory of either side looking more and more elusive, despite the brutal violence that the Sudanese state inflicted on Sudan's marginalized peoples, and with an increasing number of South Sudanese beginning to wonder about the unitary approach that the SPLM espoused, in the 1990s it became increasingly evident that peaceful negotiations might be the only option. With that recognition came the possibility that each side would most likely have to let go of their ideological positions: the SPLM would cease its pursuit of secularism and the NCP would relinquish the control of the south.

So, even though "New Sudan" made much more sense and was more practical, the possibility began to grow that the southern Sudanese were probably going to fall back to their original secessionist position. That is, either the northern Sudanese élite would commit to democratization and secularization of all Sudan or the south would opt out of the union. Increasingly in the late 1990s, the southern Sudanese appeared to suggest that the "New Sudan" philosophy, practical and tactically brilliant as it might be, was merely a strategy to bring the war closer to the centers of power in the north. But if the north remained committed to the policies of marginalization, and if it came down to a choice between continued marginalization versus break-up, the southern Sudanese would forgo this otherwise neat philosophy in favor of total separation.

As the South and its SPLM leadership veered towards secession, the SPLM policy, previously dominated by the call for the democratic renewal of all Sudan (the "New Sudan" vision) focused more squarely on southern issues. In the wake of the tragic death of its leader John Garang in July 2005, just a month after his swearing-in as vice-president of Sudan and president of the would-be Government of Southern Sudan under the CPA, the differing visions within the party, between secessionists and "New Sudan" supporters, came into sharper focus.

The secessionists eventually prevailed, and over time most of the others were convinced, as the familiar NCP politics of intransigence increasingly diminished hopes of national reform and the dream of unity based on equality. As the SPLM increasingly disengaged from northern Sudanese internal political squabbles, from the effort to end the Sudanese Islamic theocratic state and from the push for democratization, "New Sudan" began to fade from the party's agenda. The southern view of the CPA focused on the referendum on unity or separation to be held six years after the signing of Sudan's most fateful political accord. The negotiators of the CPA facilitated the south's desire to chart its separate course but reasoned that unity should be given a chance to save the country's territorial integrity, hence the six-year gap before the referendum.

The referendum was held in January 2011. It had earned the CPA most applause from the southern Sudanese since the main protocols were signed in the Kenyan town of Machakos in July 2002, the protocols that eventually became the cornerstones of the CPA. The premise of the CPA was to prepare the Sudanese people, and the governments on both sides of the north-south divide, to either work for a genuine, just and sustainable peace if the country were to remain united, or allow it to break up if that would end the bloodshed and bring stability to the tortured country and the whole of the eastern and Horn of Africa.

The CPA recognized the southern Sudanese right to political decision as well as the provision of "making unity attractive," a program aimed at encouraging unity by investing in infrastructure in southern Sudan during the time before the referendum.[5] But if the people of the south still chose to break away, either due to Khartoum's failure to honor the unity project or because it could not convince the southerners, then the creation of two viable states, existing in peace and harmony could be a more viable solution.[6] In other words, the CPA was a political compromise, providing a choice between the age-old northern Sudanese determination to maintain the unity of Sudan, even at the risk of keeping the country perpetually at war, and the break-up of the country, a grossly undesirable option for the north but an acceptable price to pay for peace in the south.

The notion of "New Sudan" changed its meaning. Those, including some important Pan-Africanist liberation movements, who saw it as a drive for the transformation of Sudan from an Islamic and Arab élite-centered nation into a democracy that recognized the ethnic diversity both within Sudan and across Africa, were disappointed that the philosophy did not save the unity of Sudan.[7] Those who were skeptical about its viability could be content that having two Sudans formed a kind of New Sudan, as long as peace within and between the two countries could be maintained. Most South Sudanese, as the referendum would later show, were tired of war and the arrogance of the northern élite. Even though many of them knew that Sudan would be stronger whole than broken, that separation would have many shortcomings and that historical connections between ordinary people would remain a source of strong bonds between the two countries, they reasoned that there was no need to insist on an unworkable and destructive unity.[8]

For the proponents of "New Sudan" and other unity-minded Sudanese and Africans, the CPA was a sad affair. The leaders who were charged with its implementation or, more appropriately, who charged themselves with the task, could be judged to have failed in their mission to destroy sectarianism in favor of nationalism, of "continentalism," so to speak. They neither prevented the dis-integration of the country nor created two viable states that lived in peace with each other and were stable within their territories. Instead, after a near-unanimous southern vote in favor of separa-tion the country proceeded to break into two. The declaration of independence in July 2011, the cause of jubilation for the people in the southern third of the country and great disappointment and sadness in the north, produced neither the peace nor stability that were attached to this political dispensation.

There was only loss in both cases; no unity and no peace.[9] Although the CPA had ended that war, it was heavily encumbered by the many issues it left unattended, issues that have come to haunt both the independent Republic of South Sudan and the rump state, the Republic of Sudan. The most debilitating development is that both countries have continued to experience increased violence inside their new boundaries. This most insidious kind of violence continues both to threaten the two countries from within, and leave the possibility of continued or renewed wars between the two as time passes.[10]

Despite the promise of peace, the two countries remained on the brink of war with each other. In 2012 they fought a pitched battle at Panthou,[11] a contested oil-rich border town between South Sudan's Unity State and Sudan's South Kordofan. They have also continued to fight civil wars within their borders. Sudan has been challenged by long-standing rebellions in the western region of Darfur, in South Kordofan and Southern Blue Nile; South Sudan has confronted widespread ethnically based political violence and resource wars between its various diverse ethnic communities.[12] South Sudan has also faced widespread violence emanating from multiple factors related to its long and torturous liberation journey, some from the dark days of the liberation wars and others triggered anew by the deadly competition for power between the politico-military élite that led the liberation struggle.

These political rivalries and power contests reached a climax in 2013, plunging the young country into a new civil war, pitting the government of President Salva Kiir Mayardit against rebellion movements, the most significant led by former vice president, Riek Machar Teny. After being removed from office by the president in July 2013, Riek waged a war for his seat, first by launching scathing criticism of the president in an attempt at a more civil and democratic means of removing Salva Kiir and then, when that did not materialize, through armed rebellion. Though he cloaked it in the language of reforms and establishment of democracy, Riek's rebellion was clearly a quest for a return to public office, either as president or something close to it.[13]

Why and how did such a highly celebrated peace agreement, the CPA, so spectacularly fail to end political violence? Why and how did it become more of an entrenchment of violence than a solution to devastatingly prolonged violent conflicts? Is it too harsh to suggest that the CPA legitimized the continuation of war and violence, at least within each of the two countries, if not between them? A significant part of the answer to these questions lies in the way African civil wars are conducted and how mediation, negotiation and peace accords are approached. Negotiated political settlement has almost become a tradition, and remains a widely trusted and practiced method in Africa but it has not yet been vindicated as the most viable approach to the resolution of conflict.

A combination of the nature of African wars and how their resolution is approached seems to set up hope for a negotiated solution but often ends in failure, due to the complexity of the conflicts or the unsuitability of the neoliberal approach to peace-making. One of the most ubiquitous characteristics of civil wars in Africa is that they are multi-layered; smaller conflicts happen within the shadow of larger conflicts, opposition groups splinter into factions or dis-agreements within the national governments create rifts between regime diehards and those interested in reform. Some conflicts take on ethnic colors, escalating into ethnic wars and warlordism that drives many men into desperate acts of violence against opponents, real or imaginary enemies, civilians and combatants.

This results in at least three issues. First, the multiplicity of factions makes it extremely difficult for conflict to be mediated or resolved in ways that address its root causes, diverse interests and, with long-term vision, provide people-centered constitutions, reconciliation and investment in national unity and the suprem-acy of the rule of law. As the various actors hardly ever agree on unified negotiating platforms, the governments of the day often takes advantage of divisions within the opposition and use them in a calculated process to bar opponents from the negotiating table, increasing the rewards to the government and reducing the gains of peace to the opposition forces.[14] The case of the old Sudan directly attests to this observation, but another more recent development is the situation in Burundi, where the government of President Pierre Nkurunziza has flatly refused to negotiate with exiled opposition leaders, preferring to deal with opposition within the country, in a bid to disunite the opposition and weaken their resolve to unseat him.

Second, the Sudanese state has always taken advantage of the divisions within the opposition armies, both in terms of using some to gain the military upper hand and also to escape its responsibility for citizens' welfare and delivery of services to areas affected by war, often on the pretext that development cannot be undertaken in war zones and services are difficult to deliver there. In a sense, the state is blaming the populations of the war zones for their suffering; implying that if they could only stop supporting the rebellion they would receive the services denied to them by conflict.[15] National resources are therefore concentrated on augmenting the ruling élite's hold on power, financing its small support base in the capital, and security, intelligence and the army. The line between the autocracy of the ruling élite and the claims of national security protection was blurred by Khartoum's politics of divisiveness. James Ferguson refers to such governments as "governments of the capital city," in the sense that the ruling élite simply invests in the city to placate its support base, leaving the rest of the country to rot in misery.[16] People living in areas under the control of the opposition were, often indiscriminately, stigmatized as supporters of the armed opposition, regardless of the fact that they often did not have a choice.

Third, such conflicts leave stubborn legacies that live on long after the main war is over. Strained ethnic relations, sex-based and communal violence, failed and inequitable justice systems, destruction of service infrastructure, an undisciplined military and the wide availability of small arms are but some of the most important consequences of such wars, consequences which remain years after the main conflict has been settled. These legacies are not often amenable to peace agreements; the mere silencing of guns by means of an accord between the main warring parties (in the language of political settlements usually referred to as principal stakeholders), does not often translate into peace at the communal or ethnic level.[17] Instead, the legacies remain in place and trigger other rounds of violence and war down the road.[18] These legacies, the built-up mistrust, the wrecked ethnic relations and the sweeping of war-time atrocities under the rug during the peace talks, explain why the CPA was not the panacea for Sudan's political woes that it appeared and instead became another driver of conflict, an example of how disaffected people and communities choose violence so that their voices can be heard. This pattern has been observed in many African countries that have experienced prolonged civil wars.[19] The continuing conflicts in the Democratic Republic of the Congo, Somalia, earlier wars in Liberia, Sierra Leone, Uganda, Burundi and even liberation wars in colonial times exhibited these characteristics.[20] But nowhere has the situation been more pronounced than in what used to be Sudan.

This was the climate that made Sudan's north-south war Africa's longest-running conflict and the world's deadliest confrontation since World War II. The final phase caused the death of close to three million people in South Sudan alone.[21] It also made the negotiation of the peace deal between north and south Sudan more protracted, very costly and daunting and frustrating to the mediators and Sudanese citizens alike. The eventual compromise was the exclusion of some ethno-political groups and geo-political areas from the peace process, and consequently future troubles.[22]

The resolution of Sudan's conflict, on all its multiple layers, was very difficult. The agreement that settled it was only possible through the compromise of allowing the possibility of breaking up Africa's largest country. The CPA offered the people of southern Sudan the possibility of an independent state, a demand that, as history showed, the southern political class was not going to compromise on, at any cost. The referendum caused the southern Sudanese to ignore their political and ethnic differences for the duration of the north-south war.[23] However, while a protracted conflict such as the one that took place in Sudan may be resolved at a political level between the main warring parties, due to the nature of the country's political, ethnic, economic and social complexity, some factions are inevitably excluded from the negotiations, leaving the smaller wars outside the process and debarred from the negotiation. This exclusion creates a legacy that makes the resolution of the main conflict almost irrelevant to the aspirations and lived experiences of the majority of rural and small town people who lived in and with war.[24]

The impact of war, and how to help war-affected societies deal with the burden of prolonged civil wars, is often excluded from the negotiations and from the final deal. Accountability for war crimes is another victim of political settlements, save ones where justice is prioritized from the start. The people, and their war-related issues, become the sacrificial lambs with which the main warring parties bless their compromises, their negotiations into office and the distribution of spoils that accompanies their ascent to power, while at the same time negotiating their way out of any responsibility, refusing to acknowledge their roles in war-time atrocities and doing everything possible to avoid the obligation to mend the wounds of the war. These failures, the exclusion of politico-military or regional entities from peace talks and the absence of enforceable commitments to justice turned the CPA into a process of violence entrenchment, rather than the peace enforcer that most people had hoped, or thought, it would be.

This book aims to weigh the challenges that have faced the two Sudans since the CPA was signed, especially since the split in 2011. The Republic of Sudan has continued to fight the old wars of the periphery-center divide that have plagued it for decades, wars that are related to crises of governance, distribution of national resources, political confrontations over access to power at the center and the contest over the religious and racial identity of the country. The continued ethno-political violence within Sudan is also linked to the many layers of north-south war that the CPA brushed aside or tackled badly, as I will show.

Sudan also confronts new wars, linked to the socio-economic realities that emerged as a result of the north-south splinter and the realignment of military groups. For example, parties that were allied to the south found themselves cut into the north and having to continue to fight for causes that were excluded from the CPA or provisions that were not implemented during the CPA interim period.[25]

This book will provide a glimpse into how the Sudanese of the post-CPA era live with war and how, for better or worse, their daily lives have or have not changed. The CPA raised hopes for a moment, only for the Sudanese to quickly realize that it had cemented the NCP's grip on power and emboldened the government to continue to opt for a military solution over dialogue, now the SPLA/M was no longer available to give military backing to the northern Sudanese opposition.

South Sudan is beleaguered by a combination of the intense and daunting challenges of crafting a new state, of building institutions, of creating a sense of collective nationhood for its multitudinous ethnicities and of forging a collective national identity. Some of the most overwhelming burdens of its independence included the question of how to meet the high expectations that every citizen thought would follow independence, as well as the challenges of turning the new state into a cohesive and stable nation. Having failed in that project, or at least been slow in embarking on it, the country imploded in 2013, a tragedy that had been in the making since the implementation of the CPA. Having been unsuccessful with regard to national cohesion, the new state descended into chaos within two years of independence, raising a rather facile debate about whether the country was ready to become a state in the first place. This is a simplistic debate because it overlooks the treacherous journey to South Sudan's statehood and disregards the historical reality that new countries stumble at first but often find their footing in the end and at their own pace.

Between 2005 and 2011, the CPA interim period, the time when the region was preparing for the referendum and independence, South Sudan faced tremendous challenges, with rampant violence spurred by the agreement itself, as the implementers of the accord ignored the promises it made to those people who had suffered so tremendously from the war and who had pegged so many of their aspirations to the implementation of the deal. The euphoria brought on by the prospect of "freedom at last," as people chanted at independence, was unmistakable, though often accompanied by a sense of foreboding and suspicion that their leaders would not live up to the monumental challenges of statecraft and nation-building, of meeting the citizens' expectations and managing the risks and fragilities of the post-conflict era. That sense of foreboding was strengthened by memories of how the "liberators," the men and women who were now taking the helm of state power, had conducted themselves during the war, when some took a free hand over people's lives. The question of whether or not South Sudan was ready to be a viable state was not really about the country itself. It was essentially a question about the willingness and capacity of the liberators to do right by their new country and its people.

Considering whether the country did or did not live up to its people's expectations is part of this book's endeavor. In other words, how was the government trying to weigh expectations against state capacity, what did the citizens think the state was capable of, and where did they think the state would find the resources to meet their expectations, aspirations and demands?

The late John Garang was the first to ask this question, in the simple and common sense manner with which he was usually known to tackle the liberation effort. In a lecture he gave to a crowd of his SPLA fighters, he asked how they thought the state could offer anything to the people if the people themselves were disempowered and poor. "If people are poor the state would be poor, if people are working and making income then they would be the ones funding the state, and the state would in turn invest that funding in the welfare of the people," he concluded. Unfortunately, many of his great civic ideas stayed in his head and in his notebooks and computers, but his militarist ideas were internalized by many generals. The legacy of those militarist ideas was partly responsible for the demise of the SPLM and the welfare of the country it is ruling.

The burden left behind by the liberation wars quickly began to manifest itself across South Sudan in the form of heightened expectations that both the interim period and eventual independence would lift the war-time suffering, relieve the injustices that had accumulated and mitigate the sense of utter insecurity that had prevailed during the twenty years of the latest phase of north-south war. Liberation wars dating back fifty years left in their wake serious scars on ethnic relationships, the state-citizen relationship and on people's confidence in the promise of liberation. Revisiting and addressing these issues in the context of the CPA was the peace dividend that the people had intensely yearned for and expected. But when no sign of this kind of reflection was forthcoming, when the SPLM was largely rated to have lost its vision, when violence and insecurity continued to ravage communities right under the noses of the liberation veterans and when the state, the guarantor of security, was increasingly absent from rural areas, disappointment set in.

Citizens relied on their own security and self-protection mechanisms, which often meant arming themselves. When everyone took responsibility for their own security, when there was no monopoly of force by the state and when it was plain that justice was ever more difficult to attain, there was no security for anyone.[26] More guns means more gun-related deaths: even in countries where there are no active wars, the fallacy of gun ownership for self-protection is all too evident, as accidents proliferate, drunks can easily kill, mentally ill gun-owners rampage and people become too quick to use guns to settle minor disputes. The world has learnt this from the gun slayings and mass shootings in major cities of developed countries such as the United States of America.

Furthermore, as revenues began to flow into South Sudan during the interim period, the promise of independence was more assured and the new state became more evidently in the grasp of the southern leadership, and the state quickly began to be contested more vigorously by the politico-military élite that had struggled for its independence. The more valuable the state was seen to be, the more intense the competition for power became, as competing forces tried to capture the state machinery. State power, state resources, and the liberators' sense of entitlement to them sparked an intense competition for public office. This led to ghastly corruption, with clientism and nepotism reinforcing sectarian divides. With ubiquitous consumption and visible greed for quick riches came the loss of the vision that had driven the commitment to liberation that spanned several decades. The civil war that began in 2013 was at least partly rooted in the short history since the CPA. It was also a culmination of the history of violence that had engulfed South Sudanese communities during the liberation wars and in the waste that these wars laid to ethnic relations, all of which the CPA had promised to mend and reconcile but did not.

The CPA has become the classic example of the dilemma of negotiated political settlements. On the one hand, the negotiated settlement that culminated in the CPA proved a desirable and less deadly way to end wars but, on the other, it emboldened socio-politically aggrieved sections of the population to see militarized violence as a legitimate means of registering their grievances, seeking inclusive peace processes and gaining political concessions. The CPA, despite being celebrated for having ended the protracted north-south war and having granted the South Sudanese their wish, a very momentous political dispensation, has further entrenched violence within and between both countries. It has also legitimized violence as a tool for achieving political goals and a means of asserting state authority as well as being a way to govern.[27]

SUDAN AFTER THE CPA

Many years since the country broke into two, it seems that Sudan is further from reaching any peaceful settlement of its conflicts than it was at the start of the period of CPA-related promises. The continuing wars in Darfur, South Kordofan and Southern Blue Nile, although rooted in deep historical grievances of exclusion from state services, were essentially triggered by the realization that the CPA would exclude Darfur from the negotiations, power-sharing, wealth distribution and post-war reconstruction programs that were worked into the peace process. The Darfuri leaders realized that the suffering of their region and the massive injustice it had endured for decades would be ignored in the north-south deal. This was the moment when the people of the northern peripheral regions, Darfur above all, realized that the peace agreement would be confined to the overall north-south conflict, to a compromise between the ruling Islamist NCP and the south-based SPLA/M, sacrificing the other aggrieved peripheral regions. It was an open secret that Darfur, despite suffering hugely since the mid-1980s in famines related to exclusion from national resource-sharing policies, was once again to be relegated to the realm of the unimportant, its grievances treated as local tribal feuds and not genuine political and economic grievances against the Sudanese state.

The CPA offered a moment when many groups could rally support for political and military action to register their call for inclusion in the process. The Sudan Liberation Movement (SLM) and the Justice and Equality Movement (JEM) quickly formed and war broke out against Khartoum in 2003, almost on the eve of the CPA. Despite the long history of marginalization, confiscation of land and Khartoum's politics of divide and rule, it was the realization that Darfur was to be excluded from the CPA that finally prompted the Darfuris to open warfare in a quest for political visibility.

This war eventually raised global warnings about state-sponsored genocide and saw the indictment of President Omer Hassan al-Bashir in 2009, the first incumbent head of state to be wanted at the Hague-based International Criminal Court (ICC), on charges of genocide, war crimes and crimes against humanity. This war would kill an estimated 300,000 people in two years, ravage Darfur to unprecedented levels, destroy property and wreck ethnic and race relations, particularly between Arabs and non-Arabs. This war gave rise to the much-feared government-sponsored Janjaweed Arab militias, who fought on behalf and alongside the government and wreaked havoc across Darfur.[28] Yet Darfur is not Sudan's only continuing civil war, though covering much more of the country and just as deadly as ever. There are wars in Southern Kordofan, specifically the Nuba Mountains and Southern Blue Nile, which broke out on the eve of South Sudan's independence. Together, these wars have collectively drained the country's economy, led to immense suffering for the Sudanese people and laid waste to areas of the country remote from the center of power in Khartoum.

These are wars with which the Sudanese government continues to grapple, at times promising to end them by crushing opposition militaries, something it has not accomplished since 1983, and at others attempting to stitch the country back together by announcing a "constitutional conference" or a "national dialogue" among all the Sudanese political forces but without any real commitment to either route.

These wars, and the viciousness with which the government and its proxies have pursued military options to end them, and the frustrations they have caused among the people of the peripheral regions, have renewed the question of the viability of Sudan, as did South Sudan.[29] In other words, what was the point of Khartoum agreeing to the CPA, the referendum and the split of the country, if these were not enough to save the unity of even the remaining Sudan? The specter of Sudan's peripheral regions following the example of South Sudan and breaking with the Sudanese union became all too real.

The continuation of the conflict in these regions is rooted both in the ambiguity of the CPA with regard to the status of these areas within the agreement, and in the failure of the premise on which the country's break-up was built: letting go of South Sudan and sacrificing the unity of the country in exchange for peace and to save the remaining part of Sudan from splintering further. Their status in the agreement was not just one of exclusion from their physical presence at the talks but also a question of how substantively inclusive the whole peace process was. The fact that certain regions and populations of Sudan were insufficiently involved in the search for the compromises in the name of peace, and the fact that the factors that had caused them to set up war fronts, were not even acknowledged.

Many Sudanese now jokingly refer to these regions, all falling on the southern border of the rump state, as "the new south." Now that South Sudan has broken away, these provinces have become the southernmost regions of Sudan. "The new south" is a phrase often used in jest, but makes a poignant point, asserting that Khartoum's current wars against Southern Kordofan and Southern Blue Nile, "the two areas," as they are known in the CPA lexicon, the atrocities committed, the contempt shown towards the people of these areas, and the disdainful language used by Khartoum in the media, resemble the attitudes the north used to have toward South Sudan. Attitudes that resulted in disintegration and could provide fodder for a more prolonged destabilization in the future, if not further splintering of the remaining Sudan.

The weakness of the CPA provisions for "the two areas" has called into question not only the concept of comprehensiveness invoked in the accord, but also generated a theoretical debate about how, in a country with such a complex political, social and cultural history as Sudan, a negotiated political settlement to end a pro- tracted conflict should be approached. The CPA has now become a lesson to be referenced widely with regards to other conflicts in the Horn of Africa. Few other searches for political settlement have offered peace-brokers more dilemmas than the quest for an end to the Sudanese conflict. On the one hand, the temptation to focus on the main parties to produce a quick settlement was almost unavoidable, but this risked excluding other important actors, who might become potential spoilers of peace or victims of further violence if the agreement failed. On the other hand, there was intense pressure on the mediators to press for representation of all stakeholders, and to ensure that mechanisms of institutional reforms, accountability, restitution, justice and reconciliation were built into the peace agreement. These issues were at the root of the conflict and the necessary ingredients for a durable peace, one to which all citizens could subscribe and commit to its success, but such wide representation would have risked causing the main power contenders, the men with guns, to keep away from the negotiating table.

These two questions – of broad-based peace talks that include the root causes and the grievances that had sparked the conflict in the first place and of a comprehensive process that involves more than just the primary power contenders – have recently attracted the attention of conflict resolution and peace-building analysts.[30]

Sriram and Young vehemently argue that focusing the negotiation on issues of power-sharing and wealth distribution, simply reduces the peace process to a question of dividing the anticipated peace dividends between the primary contenders, merely patching over the mistakes of the warring parties and ignoring the root causes and failing to create mechanisms for the repair of social relationships wrecked by war. Without instruments to address them, such grievances can intensify during peacetime, due to the high expectations often raised by a peace deal. And when these expectations are not met, or are delayed, a return to violence or the collapse of the accord become all too likely.

Throughout the CPA negotiations, a period characterized by internal political stresses and military pressure from all the peripheral regions, the Khartoum government agreed to the transition that the CPA had proposed. However, these developments also made it hard to negotiate a broad-based resolution of all the conflicts, given the Sudanese climate of multiple armed actors and opposition groups, and hardened and acrimonious positions fraught with racism, religious radicalism and government hyper-militarism. Although it primarily involved the SPLM and NCP, the CPA process included various regions within traditional northern Sudan but only as part of the SPLM delegation, not as equals, even though their issues were historically specific and quite different from those of the south.

It is hard to envision a single peace process that could have dealt with all the deep-rooted and diverse problems and regions. This created a dilemma for both mediators and the parties to the conflict. Seeking a comprehensive resolution of all Sudan's woes risked producing an unwieldy and superficial agreement that would exclude some people and some issues, leaving huge problems for the future and almost impossible to implement. But a piecemeal approach, one issue at a time, accommodating South Sudan, the Nuba Mountains,

Southern Blue Nile, Abyei, Darfur, Eastern Sudan and Nubia, and the multiple political rivalries within each of these regions, risked a collapse of the whole process, because the problems of the various regions were not always mutually exclusive. Solving the problems of one or more regions but not the others meant that problems could easily spill over to the remainder. Experiences in many countries affected by war show these are the main reasons why countries often return to war shortly after signing peace accords. Not only do excluded groups become immediate spoilers, but inviting them to the table without genuinely including their demands on the negotiation agenda will lead to only a superficial commitment to the peace agreement. This is undoubtedly what the CPA did to the Nuba Mountains, Southern Blue Nile, Abyei and other parties to Sudan's conflicts, armed or not.[31]

Judging by how the government of Sudan has reacted to the continuing wars in these regions since the country's split, very little has changed in Khartoum's prioritization of military solutions over any kind of mediated settlement, usually delaying dialogue until it is too late for the country's territorial unity. The results of continued war, as documented and reported by the United Nations, Non-Governmental Organizations (NGOs), human rights groups, research centers and individual researchers include the displacement of almost half a million people in Darfur by Khartoum's military activities in 2014 alone, a marked deterioration from the slight improvement for a few years after the split. In South Kordofan and Blue Nile, which became relatively stable after the CPA, war broke out immediately after South Sudan's declaration of independence in July 2011, confirming the skepticism of the leaders of these regions about the utility of the CPA for their regions.

The start of the new war between Khartoum and the "the new south" calls for understanding the background and position of these areas within the CPA. The accord offered these areas only vague protocols that left them with no clear idea of what would happen to them in the future. It is as if these regions were an afterthought in the CPA: Mahmood Mamdani calls these protocols "the *et cetera* of the CPA."[32] These vague provisions did not even come close to addressing the root causes and the grievances that had compelled the various groups of Sudanese to go to war, let alone the issues of justice and accountability, reconstruction, repatriation of refugees and political concessions that were the cornerstones of their revolution. The CPA's most significant reference to the status of the Nuba Mountains and Southern Blue Nile was something called "popular consultation"; that after the six-year interim period the people of these two areas would engage in debates, facilitated by their legislators in state parliaments, on the question of whether the CPA and its implementation, as it stood at the time of the consultation, had or had not satisfactorily addressed the grievances that prompted them to join the war on the side of the south.

Another issue in the agreement regarded the status of these areas' fighting forces during the interim period. The manner in which the forces were referred to in the agreement and how they were to fit into the CPA was at best ambiguous and at worst derisive. The forces were lumped together with those of Abyei and other aggrieved areas as "other armed groups," who were required either to join the government armed forces or stay with the SPLA in the south or in their provinces. This called for a "security arrangement," one of the main pillars of the CPA, in which Sudan would establish three armies for the south, the north and a "joint integrated unit" that would form the foundation of a national army, should southerners vote against separation and the country remain united. Abyei was offered its own referendum, to be held concurrently with the southern referendum, on the question of whether to remain part of Sudan or rejoin the South. But this arrangement did not provide for a separate status for the armies of Nuba Mountains and Southern Blue Nile; it was assumed they must already be part of the SPLA. The armies remained with the SPLA during the interim period, as Division 9 in Nuba and Division 10 in Blue Nile, and even though they were stationed in the geographical north, they were commanded, paid, equipped and trained under orders from Juba, South Sudan's capital. The cursory arrangement offered to the Nuba Mountains and Southern Blue Nile could only have caused problems, and it did.

When the time came, only South Sudan was able to forge ahead on schedule with its referendum, in January 2011, due to the effort and pressure from the international community. South Sudan voted in favor of separation, etching another step toward independence, which ultimately took place six months later.[33] Significantly, the other "popular consultation" exercises, and the Abyei referendum, were not fully carried out in 2011, as the CPA had stipulated. The Abyei referendum was thwarted by disputes between Khartoum and Juba over the legitimacy of each side's claim to Abyei. There was also an intense dispute, centered on who should vote in the referendum, between the Dinka, who reside in Abyei and claim ancestral ownership, and Arab nomads, the Missirriya, who use the territory for grazing every dry season. More to the point, the dispute focused on whether the Missirriya had a right to vote, a suggestion vehemently opposed both by the Dinka and the government in Juba.

The result was that the vote was postponed. The conflict between Khartoum and Juba over Abyei has raged ever since. The postponement continued until 2013, when the Dinka population of Abyei held a unilateral referendum without Khartoum's approval. The outcome was in favor of joining South Sudan, but no one outside South Sudan recognized these results and thus Abyei remains, four years since the split, a hotly disputed territory and a serious threat to bilateral relations, economic relations and peace. We will return to the issue of Abyei later.

The CPA provision on popular consultation exercises for the Nuba Mountains and Blue Nile was never carried out, despite massive efforts by NGOs, the UN, media and civil society in the north, south and those areas. These groups had prepared for the consultations, and training had been offered to the state officials who would execute the process. Their efforts were handicapped by a number of obstacles, most notably the opaque nature of the process: no one really knew what the consultations were about, how decisions would be recorded and what it would mean if the people declared the CPA unsatisfactory.

The CPA negotiators had almost deliberately left such issues vague; Lual Deng describes these loopholes in the CPA as "creative ambiguity." The process was also hindered by the fact that the parliaments of the two states were NCP-dominated because of the massive rigging of the 2010 general elections. The NCP members of the two state legislative assemblies, although they were citizens of the states, were far too loyal to the NCP to oversee a process that could both indict the ruling party for marginalization and cause the citizens of the two states to demand more and better political reforms. Instead, the legislators frustrated the process and threw obstacles in its way. Eventually, it became clear that Khartoum was gradually backtracking and did not want the popular consultations to proceed, preferring to drag its feet until the break-up, so that without the south it could bully the two areas as soon as the world looked away.

When South Sudan's independence was declared in July 2011, this automatically raised questions of what would become of the new country's allies in the Nuba Mountains and Southern Blue Nile. The SPLA forces (Division 9 in Kordofan and Division 10 in Blue Nile) had been declared "other armed groups" by the government of the Sudan and were expected to join the Sudan Armed Forces, but without a clear mechanism for their absorption into that army. The agreement short-changed them, leaving them in a situation in which they either had to join the Sudan Armed Forces (SAF) with no power to negotiate the terms of their absorption, or forcibly re-assert themselves militarily. Essentially, the CPA gave the governments of the two Sudans the right to decide the fates of the "other armed groups," which left little in the peace deal to be desired by the people and leaders of these areas.

On the side of the Republic of Sudan, the unresolved status of the two areas meant that Khartoum was likely to attempt to kill the demands for reform over which the people of the two areas had gone to war. There was more to fear for the fate of the SPLA forces in Nuba, as Khartoum was likely either to try to absorb them into its defense force or demand their disbandment. The Nuba SPLA, however, had not simply been a sideshow during the north-south war; for them, this was an indigenous war to fix what they believed to be wrong with the Sudanese state. The Nuba SPLA numbered no fewer than 20,000 soldiers and enjoyed the popular support of the Nuba people. Any attempt to squeeze them out of what they perceived as rightly theirs was bound to return the country to war. Sure enough, when Khartoum demanded that the fighters who hailed from these areas, and who had been part of the South-based SPLA, either moved to the new republic in the south or disarmed, the Republic of Sudan was plunged into a new civil war a few weeks before South Sudan's independence. This is the war that has continued, with grave consequences for the people of the "two areas."

The politico-military leaders of the "two areas" – Abdel Aziz Adam al-Hilu in Nuba and Malik Agar Ayir in Southern Blue Nile – together with Yasir Arman from the north, were adamant in their objections to Khartoum's proposal for them either to disband, be absorbed into the SAF or move to the south. Although these leaders were quickly declared enemies of state, to be arrested, they rapidly took control of the situation and renamed their forces the Sudan People's Liberation Army North (SPLA-N) and their political wing the Sudan People's Liberation Movement North (SPLM-N). They have continued to fight the government of Sudan, and despite many attempts at reconciliation and various peace deals, Khartoum has continued in its intransigence. When presidential assistant Nafie Ali Nafie, the most senior civilian hardliner in the regime, signed a framework agreement with the SPLM-N in Addis Ababa on June 28, 2011, he was over-ruled by the SAF Command and President Omer Hassan al-Bashir. Subsequent efforts for peace, including the most recent attempt by the African Union (AU) on February 18, 2014 in Addis Ababa, Ethiopia, have been to no avail.[34]

After the country's split in 2011, the AU engaged the former president of South Africa, Thabo Mbeki, to mediate this phase of conflict. However, his many peace proposals have so far all been frustrated by Khartoum's apparent unwillingness to compromise and reach a deal with the opposition from the two areas. The SPLM-N has continuously offered to negotiate but Khartoum has only issued threats to militarily defeat them. Mbeki's African Union High-level Implementation Panel (AUHIP) was tireless in trying to mediate the Sudanese conflicts but ultimately admitted defeat on March 2, 2014, saying that it could not see how to bridge the gap that exists between Khartoum and SPLM-N, and returning the case to the African Union Security Council.[35]

Meanwhile, hundreds of thousands of Nuba, the Ingessina people of Blue Nile and Darfuris, seeking escape from the fighting and aerial bombardments, which many say target civilians, have been forced from their farms and villages to shelter in caves and IDP centers or take refuge in South Sudan and Ethiopia. Those who remained in their homes are braced for ever-more intense government attacks every dry season, when the SAF are able to drive tanks and other war vehicles on roads that are impassable during the rainy season. Genocidal actions reminiscent of the 1990s have been unleashed; the survival of the Nuba people hangs in the balance depending on the ability of Nuba SPLA to defend them, the intervention of the international community, changes in government in Khartoum and another peace deal.

Despite many new approaches, by numerous countries and organizations, to re-start the intermittent mediation efforts, conflict in these regions continues to be driven by the hardened positions of government representatives and opposition forces. Peace processes continue to be pursued, sometimes reaching promising levels of compromise, only to collapse. Negotiations about Darfur have continued in Qatar since 2011, although handicapped by the fact that many of the main Darfuri rebel movements refuse to participate, and African Union-sponsored talks between Khartoum and the SPLM continue in Addis Ababa, Ethiopia. There were separate peace talks between one faction of the SLA and the JEM and the government, and between the government and SPLM-N, both in Addis Ababa, while the other Darfuri groups remained in the Qatari process.

The rebel movements see this fractured approach to negotiation as a delaying tactic by Khartoum, a way to deny the opposition forces a unified position. The Darfuri rebel groups, the JEM and a faction of the Sudan Liberation Movement/Army, and the SPLM-N from the "two areas," have responded to Khartoum's divisive schemes by forming an alliance, the Sudan Revolutionary Front (SRF), both to plead for a single negotiating platform and to join hands in the battlefield should war become the only option. But Khartoum remains relentless in its pursuit of parallel negotiations and the world community seems to have succumbed and granted Khartoum its wish for multiple peace platforms. That happened despite the argument of rebel movements, Sudan analysts and other observers of Sudan that a comprehensive dialogue aimed at tackling the country's many intractable problems and reimagining a new basis for governing the country, including a good understanding of the root causes of the wars and the restructuring of the state, wealth-sharing, equitable development projects in all areas of the country, the system of government and development services, was the only way to a sustainable peace. The piecemeal approach that Sudan has pursued since the Darfur war began in 2003 has resulted in failed peace agreements and further fueled the conflict by causing frustration among the fighters and reinforcing Khartoum's continued commitment to a military solution.

The importance of reimagining the basis of governing Sudan was underscored by the dynamics of conflict and the similarity of the root causes of the wars in Darfur, Kordofan and Blue Nile. All Sudan's wars are often triggered and fanned by a social and political disease referred to by the people of the regions as *tahamish* or "marginalization." This is a term loaded with meaning and known to every Sudanese with even the smallest interest in discourse about the nature of the state. It means exclusion from the distribution of goods and services, lack of adequate representation in government and the failure of the state to provide protection and human security. It also means inequity under the law, as some citizens seem to benefit from state protection and justice while others face discrimination. The term has become so popular that it is sometimes used to refer to the socio-economic hierarchy, including the racial and religious meanings that accompany class differentiators.

Police harassment of people from some regions, denial of due process, long detentions without trial and lack of legal representation are but a few grievances offered by non-Arab citizens as evidence of marginalization. *Tahamish* suggests that wars are a manifestation of a crisis of governance, of a social system that privileges certain categories of people, such as "the Arabs," and diminishes others, such as the non-Arabs or "blacks." This has prompted the leaders in marginalized areas to call for a more comprehensive approach that explains the dynamics that fuel the war and that accounts for the ethnic, racial and religious sentiments that widely prevail, as the only approach that could provide a way forward for the country. However the viability of such an approach, as the north-south case attests, remains uncertain.

In 2014, the AU Peace and Security Council finally agreed to press for a merger of the peace talks between the government and the Darfuri rebel movements and SPLM-N, to reflect the merger of these groups into the SRF. Both processes took place, haltingly, in Addis Ababa, Ethiopia; Thabo Mbeki mediated both for many years. The efforts were still under way at the time of writing, more than a decade since some started in 2005. The chances that these renewed processes will produce a comprehensive peace accord are anyone's guess, but the history of peace deals in Sudan does not provide hopeful evidence. The 2006 Darfur Peace Agreement, which was signed by only the faction of the SLA led by Mini Arko Minawi, collapsed in 2010, when Minawi abandoned it from frustration with the NCP's unwillingness to implement it, and he returned to war. Likewise, the 2011 Doha Document on Peace in Darfur (DDPD), which was signed in the Qatari capital by a coalition of smaller Darfuri rebel movements, hangs by a thin thread; the government holds on to its implementation as the solution, while the prominent Darfuri rebels have stayed out of it. Similarly, the July 2011 agreement signed by SPLM-N in Addis Ababa, Ethiopia, was summarily rejected by the president and NCP military diehards within a few days.

With this history in mind, the Mbeki mediation team has tried to change the order of negotiations followed in agreements to prioritize the cessation of hostilities in the conflict areas, followed by a national dialogue. It was hoped this would pave the way for a constitutional review and reform process and a schedule for free elections. But Sudan is a country where one stands a better chance of success if predicting future war than if believing in the possibility of peace, negotiated or otherwise.

At the time of writing (May 2016), it is obvious from the statements made at the opening of negotiation sessions between Khartoum's representatives and SRF delegates that Khartoum is sticking to the Darfur peace process, saying that it simply needs cessation of hostilities to pave the way for real dialogue. But the stronger and most popular Darfur rebel movements have long rejected this route. The rebel side puts the blame for war squarely on the doorstep of the ruling NCP and President Omar Hassan al-Bashir, invoking al-Bashir's ICC indictment for genocide and war crimes in Darfur. Such exchanges, and such starkly diverging views, do not bode well for the future of peace. Negotiations between SPLM-N and the government are blocked by the growing calls for autonomy for Blue Nile and South Kordofan, which President al-Bashir has dismissed. Khartoum's desire is to keep the negotiations for each issue separate; the "divide and rule" policy that had characterized the north-south war for decades. Both negotiations were only likely to produce fruit if they were merged into a comprehensive national peace project, as a unified negotiation process would be the best foundation for a national dialogue involving the government, the rebel movements, civil society and the political parties. This was the daunting task that the mediators faced; to persuade the warring parties to stop fighting and then start a conversation about how to save Sudan from continued ruin, and how to govern it.

However, whatever chance the negotiated settlement stood in April 2015, it was quickly eviscerated by the general elections, which were boycotted by many political parties, allowing President al-Bashir to win with an overwhelming majority and giving him another five-year term in office to continue his incumbency (since 1989) as Sudan's longest-serving head of state.

SOUTH SUDAN AFTER THE CPA

Unlike Sudan, which is older and probably more resilient, at its secession South Sudan faced many threats and its viability stood in the balance. The burden of fifty years of war and violence combined with the weakness of its governance structures to obstruct its move towards stability, development and social cohesion. The obstacles to the prosperity widely anticipated and attached to independence were largely identified and fairly well known to analysts and policy researchers, but the willingness or ability of its leadership to accept the diagnoses and possible remedies offered and debated by a variety of South Sudanese and foreigners was not readily evident.

Most of the fears that the country might fail, or that it would be too weak to respond to the expectations of its citizens in the wake of the comprehensive peace agreement, were utterly ignored or dismissed offhand. It was suggested that the end of the war, and the country's independence, widely celebrated as a panacea for the old Sudan's tortured political history, would most likely come with multiple burdens that would weigh down the new country and possibly return it to war, either civil war, or war against the rump state, the Republic of Sudan. Independence (or separation, depending on how one looks at it) was a euphoric moment for the people of South Sudan, almost unequalled by any other political transformation in its history. But the happiness of freedom all the more heightened citizens' expectations and the risks of disappointment.

The gravity of the situation in South Sudan from the post-CPA interim period to independence was unmistakable. The country was probably the world's most war-torn since World War II. It had to cope with what the UN and international aid agencies described as "scary statistics" about poor health, education, living standards, safety and many other burdens that the war had left on the shoulders of its people, while ethnic relations were at the most acrimonious level ever recorded in the country's past. Poverty, expectations, substantial revenues from oil production and the monopoly of power by a single liberation movement, the SPLM, combined to worry analysts and observers, who saw in South Sudan a possible repetition of the disastrous African liberation movements that wrecked their countries through claims of entitlement to the rewards of liberation. Examples of liberator's grip on power and resources abounded, especially in the East and in the Horn of Africa, from Uganda to Ethiopia to Rwanda.

Oil was seen as a vital resource to fund programs that could deal with the weight of war problems, but at the same time as a curse that could cause the country to implode. "Resource curse," "the Dutch disease," and the experiences of corrupt oil-rich countries such as Nigeria, Angola and Equatorial Guinea, were invoked in an attempt to alert the leaders of South Sudan and urge them to think very carefully about the kind of country they were cutting out, and how it could all go very badly wrong, if caution was not exercised.[36]

All the challenges that stood in South Sudan's path to prosperity, stability and peace, were obvious to anyone who paid attention at the start of the CPA and through to independence. Many solutions were suggested by well-wishers, including an open letter to President Salva Kiir Mayardit written by a group of American activists which had campaigned for South Sudan's independence for many years,[37] and an article in *The Economist* that called South Sudan a "pre-failed"[38] country even before independence, with the Fund for Peace ranking the country as one of the world's most fragile states. However these, and numerous other attempts, failed to alert the country's leadership to the looming crises.[39] On the eve of the referendum, Daniel Howden, of *The Independent*, wrote:

> There is little doubt that the result will be an overwhelming vote in favor of splitting Africa's largest country in two. What is less clear is what kind of country is being delivered. South Sudan's moment of choice is happening amid a popular atmosphere of impossible expectation and its legion of doubters believe the globe's first "pre-failed state" is being ushered into existence.[40]

The leaders, or the "rulers," as one citizen who seemed disappointed in the political class quipped, dismissed these descriptions and the suggested solutions, saying that the talk of state failure was the business of doomsayers who wished the young country ill. At other times, this dismissive attitude was born of denial, pride and possibly a simple disconnection between the country's rulers and the pain being experienced daily by ordinary citizens. It was also born of a defensive attitude toward the critique aimed at the government led by the SPLM, the opposition movement that championed South Sudan's liberation cause, now turned ruling party. Like many African liberation movements, the SPLM had adopted the attitude that it knew exactly what was in the best interest of its people because it had "liberated" the country, and it did not accept the criticism that it was losing direction with regard to its programs for nation-building, state-building, democracy, equity, security and the welfare of its citizens.

In the years leading up to the referendum, independence and for a year or so into South Sudan's existence as a sovereign state, a disturbing disparity between hope and reality was already glaringly manifest. The SPLM's signature programs of the liberation war, of "taking the towns to the villages," "peace through development," "empowering the people so that they can empower the state," or "a classroom for every martyr's child," were all but forgotten. When challenged by opposition parties, human rights organizations or civil society activists about the insecurity that was engulfing the country, mostly clearly emanating from the struggle over resources, the corruption that was rapidly turning the young country into an ugly class-divided society, the behavior of the nation's security forces, the huge and unsustainably expensive public sector, nepotism, exclusion based on ethnicity, land-grabbing, constitutional problems, a weak justice system, and the withholding of funding for national reconciliation, social cohesion programs and nation-building projects, the country's rulers were often arrogantly dismissive or outraged.[41]

Sometimes the rulers recognized the truth of the criticisms but did not feed them into policy design, or claimed that the country was newly born and, like a newborn baby, needed assistance before it could walk on its own, a characterization many South Sudanese ordinary citizens found insulting. One angry critic wrote:

> Some of our leaders probably think it is a good excuse to liken the country to a baby, but I find it odd and simplistic that they would ignore the long history of civil service, the level of education among so many people in the cabinet and the fact that its new status as an independent country does not mean the country did not exist before … It is the independence that is new, but the land and the people are not.

By the middle of 2013, as the country edged into its third year of independence, it was evident that nearly everything was going wrong. Poor management of expectations and risks, mounting disappointment and the level of desperation experienced all around the country were bound to result in an explosion that risked bringing the whole country down.[42] Although the South Sudanese had expressed disappointment in the way their young state was run since it became independent in 2011, they were even more appalled in 2013 by increasing government failures, fiscal misdeeds, unclear government policies, uncertainty about what the future held in terms of security, development, livelihoods, basic freedoms, the constitution, reconciliation, the census, elections and the balance of power. They were especially concerned that the legislative assembly was increasingly seen as at the mercy of the president, instead of upholding its constitutional mandate to oversee the actions of the executive. Many people I interviewed described the country's National Legislative Assembly in varied and negative terms, as a "rubber stamp parliament," an "appendage to the executive," "full of bench warmers," or made up of "people who eat on our behalf." One social media commentator suggested that South Sudan legislature should "borrow ears" from their counterparts in the neighboring countries. Another one wrote that "our lawmakers admire America but are unwilling to see that the US is great because of the wisdom in its balance of powers." The euphoria of independence, the expectations of dividends and prospects for a different and more hopeful future, met their match in skepticism and cynicism born of negative memories of war-time interactions between the "liberator" and the "liberated."[43]

Leadership tussles within the SPLM almost stifled the organization and the fate of the ruling party became increasingly uncertain. When the president suddenly dissolved the structures of the SPLM in November 2013, against the existing regulations of the ruling party, he almost paralyzed it. The noose seemed to be tightening ever more strongly around the neck of the nation and no one seemed certain about what might come next. The constitutional review process, which aimed to turn the 2011 transitional constitution into a permanent one, had wasted an entire year without producing a program of action or a work plan, let alone the review itself. With this delay of the review of the constitution came a delay in everything else, from the conduct of elections to the registration of political parties and reform of the system of government; everything that relied on the availability of a constitution as a guide and rallying point for nation-building. Without a permanent constitution, there was growing uncertainty about the general elections that had been scheduled for 2015, which increased citizens' unease about the future of the country, and whether or not the country would show signs of a move towards democracy.

With oil the sole source of revenue for the young state, the impact of the government's 2012 decision to shut down oil production, due to wrangling between South Sudan and Sudan over shipping fees through Sudan's oil facilities, began to bite most painfully in 2014. The austerity measures instituted in the wake of the oil shutdown rendered the country unable to pay for the basic needs of its population, including the salaries of the armed forces and the civil servants, which at this time constituted more than 80% of national expenditure. When it was revealed that the country had continued to borrow at very high interest rates, with short repayment schedules, during the austerity period, shock waves rippled across the country, intensifying disappointment and raising questions about whether the government could legitimately mortgage the future of the country. The announcement that South Sudan had accumulated a huge debt, of 4.5 billion South Sudan Pounds (US$ 1.5 billion at the time), in the two years since the oil shutdown was a huge bombshell. The South Sudanese heard about this debt quite late in the day and there was no clarity as to who had approved the borrowing, and whether the nation's legislature had known about it. There was no transparency about what projects had been funded with that borrowed money, and the public did not know what channels were used to transmit these loans to

South Sudan. Nothing could be more worrying than this about the immediate future of the country.

After agreements were reached between Khartoum and Juba, including a schedule of fees to be paid to Khartoum for the passage of oil through its territory and facilities to the Red Sea, and eight other related outstanding post-separation issues, oil production resumed and revenues began to flow again. However, the government found itself doing very little other than servicing loans that had been acquired in circumstances at least highly opaque, if not entirely fraudulent.[44] How could a government that had declared an austerity program continue to spend at the same rate, without anyone bothering to ask the legislature for approval? How could a government that, in the wake of the 2012 oil shutdown, declared it had sufficient reserves to cover two years' expenditure find itself in such unfathomable debt?

In South Sudan's towns, it is customary for unemployed or marginally employed young people, mainly men, to sit together under trees or in the corridors of shops to discuss politics and drink tea, often sold by women. These questions were the subject of animated discussions among South Sudanese in those teashops, in government offices, on university campuses and elsewhere. Discussions filled cyberspace with questions of where the country was heading, the fate of the many communities increasingly engulfed by insecurity, food deficits, youth unemployment and how long the people's patience would hold out.

Had the government of South Sudan not been given enough benefit of the doubt? Had the people of South Sudan not been strategically patient enough about the promises of independence, saying that "our country is new and we must give it time?"[45] What about President Kiir's 100 days of projects, which he had promised in his independence day speech? Were any of the projects implemented and supervised? Why hadn't the president or the parliament asked for such reports about the programs progress? Few other countries allow, as South Sudan does, spending agencies to receive appropriated budgets but not require them to make periodic accounting reports, was another objection.

When the parliament proposed currency devaluation in November 2013, to unify the exchange rate between the black market and the official rate and so root out the out-of-control cronyism and black marketeering in currency exchange, many people applauded. Unfortunately, the law makers forgot to ensure their own instructions were heeded. When the Central Bank, realizing the importance of such a move, went ahead with it, parliament backtracked and forced the bank to retract, to the dismay of all. Were underhanded politics going on in these institutions, where corruption over-rode good policies? Such questions were often raised when citizens met to talk, but were not pursued collectively, or at least not concertedly enough to challenge the government to provide explanations. The country's leadership presumably thought that everything was well, because its citizens had not formally and publicly presented their grievances. But citizens could not because they did not have an adequate platform for joint positions on any number of shared problems. Civil society was not yet vibrant enough to rally collective citizen action on these issues. Political parties were too weak, too fearful and too desperate for alliances with the ruling party to question the government.

Questions about visible failures, mistakes and the threats of state collapse eventually became more than a matter of institutional weakness, mediocre staff performance, greed or human errors. The real issue was that on top of the inevitable human frailties and the get-rich-quick attitude the South Sudanese had adopted, the central government and state authorities violated every constitutional provision on governance. The president fired elected officials in the name of national security, forced law-makers to accept his choice for Speaker of Parliament, allowed ministers and administrators to raid public coffers with impunity and, above all, in November 2013, used his executive powers as president, not only as chairman of the party, to dissolve the structures of the ruling SPLM and to cow his critics.

The SPLM Secretary for External Affairs – incorrectly – invoked party constitutional provisions as the basis for the president's action. Although party officials referenced the 2008 party constitution, Chapter X (25) sections (d), (e), (f) and (g) as the provisions on which the president based his decision, these articles list the powers of the chairman, but do not mention anything about the chairman's powers to dissolve party structures. The president and his advisors had deliberately reneged from the regulations agreed by the party membership and from the national constitution, but faced no consequences.

State governors had also referenced unverified constitutional powers to justify a total abuse of office. In northern Bahr el Ghazal state, Governor Paul Malong Awan often threatened elected members of the state legislature with dismissal or jailing if they did not go along with his policies. In 2013, Lakes state was thrown into total mayhem after the president fired the elected governor, Chol Tong Mayai. The caretaker governor, Matur Chut Dhuol, seemed to take the view that he could fight the increasing inter-sect violence among the Agar Dinka by ignoring procedure and issuing decrees to use violence against the citizens, whether they were suspected of involvement in the tribal blood feuds or were critical of the governor.[46] The governor also threatened the state lawmakers and swore in state cabinets without consulting the legislature.[47]

At local government level, the third layer of the decentralized system of government in the country, it was increasingly clear that a rampant disregard for the constitution had caused state and county officials to be more interested in answering to the president than to the people who had elected them into office, rendering the whole country almost entirely ungovernable.

By July 2013, after the country's second anniversary of independence, it was evident that the majority of the people were increasingly weighed down by a mix of problematic governance practices, inflation of 50% and rising, sky-rocketing food prices, economic inequality, waning pride in the nation and ethnic warfare. Public criticism of injustice and inequalities born of corruption and mismanagement were either ignored or treated as unwarranted and hasty criticism of a fledgling state that was trying to manage unrealistic expectations. Political leaders and public officials responded to people's complaints by referring to the challenges that faced the country from its long history of liberation wars, which had left a big gap between the demands of post-war rehabilitation and the resources available to meet these needs. None of the leaders was willing to take responsibility for this situation, despite the obvious leadership failures.

There was some truth in the response that there was a big gap between the massive rehabilitation needs and resources, though it was only part of the problem. Many post-war societies had faced similar common challenges, and the young state of South Sudan was not immune from them. The lack of accrual of peace dividends could not be blamed entirely on government officials but rested partly on the realities of its history. South Sudan began life as one of the world's most war-destroyed countries, with some of the worse quality of life indicators in the world. It had high infant and maternal mortality rates, low literacy rates, rampant insecurity born of the long war and poor or non-existent infrastructure. Any expectations that the country could tackle all of this in short order were unrealistic. But the growing culture of corruption, the shameless theft and misuse of public resources by government officials, the eye-watering divide between the new, small group of wealthy people (whose sources of wealth were dubious) and the bulk of the population who still lived quite precariously, if not entirely desperately, meant South Sudan did not have a good start in life.[48] But this was not sufficiently explained to the public

The attempts to explain the situation were neither articulated nor communicated widely as part of the state-citizen relationship. The potential of this potent mixture for South Sudan was never explored by its rulers. To the keen observer of these dynamics, the longer this situation continued the more likely it was that the political structures that underpinned the country's relative stability were being questioned by its citizens, and potentially eroded as more and more people became more and more desperate. To the analyst, it looked more and more likely that there would be an explosion. But it was not clear what form this explosion would take if it happened; would it be a North African "Arab Spring"-style mass protest? Or perhaps more regional rebellions, rising violent crime, xenophobia against East African migrant workers, military revolts or a *coup d'état*?

A popular uprising of people from across the nation and over sectarian fault lines would have challenged the state and its rulers without further fracturing the fabric of the nation, which had already suffered immeasurably from the liberation war. But it did not happen; instead, the burden of post-war realities expressed themselves differently, taking the country back to war in December 2013, in ways that magnified the sectarian and ethnic tendencies in violent conflict. I shall return to this conflict in later chapters.

What so long prevented the explosion was the lack of political organization among the public, weakness of civil society organizations, the absence of opportunities for collective citizen action against the state and its rulers, the remoteness of the majority of citizens, who lived in rural areas, and the ethnic divisions that allowed ordinary citizens to support leaders on the basis that they were from a given area, not because of any vision they might have for the country. People also feared government reprisals, as the SPLM/A had practiced a culture of violent silencing of dissent throughout the liberation war.

Their fear might also be related to the populism of the SPLM, at least the populism that its leaders think it has, since the party has never had a chance to test its popularity in a democratic process. The SPLM, due to its historic role as the party that championed the independence of the country, had come to see itself, and to be seen as, synonymous with the country. SPLM was South Sudan and South Sudan was SPLM, and the result was its leadership became complacent, taking the support of the people for granted. The 2010 general election that brought President Salva Kiir Mayardit to power was held in a united Sudan and seen as a bridge to the referendum on unity or separation stipulated in the CPA and scheduled for January 2011. It was not a real democratic exercise, and taking that exercise as evidence of popularity was deliberate naïvety on the part of the SPLM and the government it set up.

This appearance of popularity allowed the SPLM leadership to assume that all they had to do was to strive for positions within the party, and that once they held a party position, they were assured high level government positions, whether or not the party membership wanted them in the executive. Individuals vied for public office, for example when the party's deputy chairman and vice president, Riek Machar Teny, developed an interest in running for the country's presidency in the next elections and decided that aiming for the party chairmanship would be a guaranteed ticket to the top job. During the 2010 mid-term elections, the SPLM organized what appeared to be primary elections, such that the membership of the party could choose the candidates to contest all elected levels of government with the other parties, but the political bureau, the party's highest executive organ, disregarded the results of certain primaries and chose its own candidates, completely ignoring the decisions made by the party's voters.[49] This became one of the most important root causes of the conflict that started in December 2013, which pitted the government of Salva Kiir Mayardit against a rebellion led by Riek Machar Teny.

When the conflict started in Juba in December 2013, its violence quickly fed the desperation, anger and frustration that had been building up among the members of the public. But unfortunately, unlike the old pre-separation Sudan, where such political and economic tensions often translated into popular political action, there was clear subversion of the people's genuine concerns and grievances by the political class, all to very different ends. This subversion has made the political contest over power deadly, and the conflict extremely difficult to resolve, because the citizens of South Sudan have been robbed of their ability to organize across ethnic lines to collectively challenge their "leaders." Many South Sudanese simply supported contenders because they reasoned that the survival of their ethnic group was tied to the political survival of the leaders. I have devoted a significant part of this book to an attempt to chronicle how decisions have been made to support this or that leader, how to survive in times of war, how to relate to the state and where to give one's loyalty.

Although the political crisis that engulfed South Sudan from late 2013 to 2016 was a struggle for power among the political élite, it was made all the more spectacularly destructive and deadly because of the deep ethnic divides that the political rivalry had incited. This ethnic dimension, more than any other issue in the recent past, was the factor that drew international attention, shook the confidence of the South Sudanese in the viability of their young state and led to South Sudan's classification in 2014 as the most fragile country in the world, the position that Somalia had held for six years in a row.

The outbreak of the conflict was understandably shocking but not by any means surprising. The instability had been in the making since the 2005 CPA, and was partly rooted within the CPA itself. The many security challenges that the country had faced since 2005 were signs of the complex web of the history of violence, the configuration of social landscape and the weakness of the idea of state responsibility for the welfare of the citizen. The country was bound to experience crises that threatened its very existence. The history of South Sudan, rooted in protracted and taxing liberation struggles, was inevitably likely to reveal itself in such a ghastly form as this conflict has shown, simply because of the way liberation wars are conducted, how they end and what they leave behind. There is a strong link between this new conflict and the legacy and complex history of the previous liberation wars.

In this book, I shall try to document the reasons why the end of the prolonged north-south conflicts and the break-up of the country in the name of peace have created more wars, or near constant threats of war, between and within the two countries. I shall focus more particularly on chronicling the South Sudanese's everyday experiences of war and how the people of the world's newest country have dealt with these experiences since 1983, when the people of the southern portion of the old Sudan started what they termed the "liberation" war for the creation of a "new Sudan" that eventually split the country into two.

I shall also try to make sense of the more recent conflict that started in December 2013, a conflict sparked by struggles for power among former liberation leaders and by the split within the SPLA, the liberation movement turned independent nation's defense force. The new conflict is rooted in the legacies of the previous wars, as the many social, economic, political and security consequences of protracted liberation efforts remained unresolved, weighing down the new state after independence. I shall review the reactions of the South Sudanese to the new conflict, and analyze the various dynamics that followed the end of the north-south war (1983–2005) before South Sudan separated from Sudan, how these dynamics are connected to why the country exploded into this new deadly conflict a mere two and half years after independence, and how the struggle for power in the capital Juba took a ghastly ethnic turn, almost unprecedented in the history of the country.

In trying to make sense of this new conflict, I shall comment on personalities, the kind of men and women who ran the country, some of whom were involved in leading the 2013 rebellion against the elected government, with an eye to unpacking the concept of "leadership" in the South Sudanese context, probing some of the root causes of the conflict and describing the reactions of the citizens and the global community to this tragic moment in the short history of this new country.

I argue that the renewed conflict within South Sudan, coming at a moment when everyone expected the euphoria of independence, and the long history of collective resistance to northern Sudan, to help the country sail to stability was extremely shocking but not entirely surprising. Anyone who paid attention could have seen it coming, although there was uncertainty of which form it would take. The unprecedented level and scale of violence that accompanied the return to war was shocking but the political trajectories, problems of insecurity and problems of governance, corruption and deficit in development programs in the post-independence era made the outbreak of a renewed war almost inevitable. It was not surprising because, despite the political transitions beginning with the CPA, the referendum on South Sudan's political future and its eventual independence on July 9, 2011, which had raised expectations and promised security, peace, stability and prosperity, there was quite overwhelming evidence that all was not well in the country. Despite the celebration of the CPA, it was clear the country had not stopped being at war and that the expected peace dividends were proving extremely difficult to accrue, all to the great disappointment of the people. An Australian newspaper reporter, Tim Costello, succinctly described this disconnection:

> Three years ago there was dancing on the streets of South Sudan as a new nation was born with hopes and dreams for a free and independent future. There was cheering for days after the long battle for secession from the north – even in Melbourne I was able to join in celebrations with South Sudanese living in Australia. Finally there was to be a future of democracy and peace, with plans for rapid development and construction of infrastructure funded by newly found oilfields. More than one million South Sudanese, including many who had been living in Australia, returned to their homeland full of hope and expectation. But the joyous innocence of new nationhood would be short-lived, with pre-existing political tensions quickly spilling out, the latest and worst of the conflict erupting last December. The violence, with no end in sight, has pulled the world's youngest country apart at the seams ... This was not the future South Sudanese imagined as they danced and hooted and slapped each other on the back three years ago. Peace, security and optimism have become shattered dreams.[50]

Despite peace agreements and political arrangements; despite the calm and thriving businesses in Juba and other major towns, there was no peace and security at various levels of society. Cattle rustling, regional rebellions, ethnic feuds, militia activity, urban crime and lack of justice for crimes committed in the course of the liberation efforts remained extremely challenging to address. The judicial system, the police service and the entire security sector remained unresponsive or unable to respond to citizens' pleas for protection and recompense. The warning signs that this background could cause trouble for the country were visible everywhere, and in this book I will try to assess whether these signs were invisible to the leaders or whether they were deliberately ignored, and why. The wars of liberation might have ended with the independence of the country, government structures might be in place and the South Sudanese might be able to say that they are a sovereign people, but violence had not stopped, and seven out of the country's ten states continued to be wrecked by communal violence, militia activity and regional rebellions.

With violence engulfing much of the country, with many communities reflecting on the value of the CPA and the meaning of independence based on their everyday experiences, with death, destruction, lack of justice and abuse that had taken place during the war and beyond, these political developments might well have become meaningless. In fact, there was no official recognition of the abuses, let alone any meaningful talk of a plan to assist war-affected communities to come to terms with the heavy price they had paid for independence, a price that had been paid in life, limb and the destruction of property, and weighed down the whole country.

A combination of the legacy of previous wars, continued communal violence, the inability or the failure of the new country to provide security and stability, and the lack of anticipated peace dividends kept the people of South Sudan in a state of perpetual insecurity and made the new conflict almost inevitable. Access to justice, for example, was one key peace dividend that people had expected, but when they could not get it, due to a complex web of reasons that I will try to untangle, it is easy to see how violence was fanned between the 2005 CPA and the outbreak of new violence in 2013.

The material for this book comes largely from ethnographic research conducted over several years in various locations throughout South Sudan and among the diaspora. It comes from interviews, surveys, published academic and policy research, journalism and reports from local research centers, the UN, NGOs, state security agencies and government departments. The book approaches the challenge of violence in four ways. The first is to chronicle everyday experiences with war in the two Sudans and how the split, a process that was seen as an avenue to stability, has further entrenched violence in both countries. The second explores the unique ways in which the people of the world's newest country have coped with these experiences since 1983, when the southern portion of the old Sudan started the liberation war that eventually split Africa's largest country into two. In explaining the South Sudanese experience of violence, I will devote a significant part of the book to the conflict that started in December 2013, reviewing the reactions of the South Sudanese to this new conflict, analyzing the various dynamics that followed the end of the north-south war, and pointing out how the new conflict is rooted in the legacies of the liberation wars that delivered the independence of South Sudan but left unresolved the many social, economic, political and security consequences of protracted liberation efforts. These were some of the most difficult challenges the country experienced after independence and they explain, at least for the most part, why the country returned to conflict so soon after this most celebrated political transition. Countries that have experienced long wars are always likely to return to war soon after a negotiated settlement, as many other African conflicts have shown.[51]

The third approach for the book is to describe the way rural people affected by violence live through that violence, destruction of assets and livelihoods, breakdown of social institutions, and militarization of society. It describes their experiences, starting with the recent outbreak of conflict between the government of

President Salva Kiir Mayardit and forces loyal to the former vice president, Riek Machar Teny, who led a rebellion in the Upper Nile region between December 2013 and April 2016.

The causes and the dynamics of the north-south wars have been much analyzed and well documented and I will therefore only refer to them in passing.[52] My main focus is the dynamics and impact of violence within Sudan and South Sudan, with a view to uncovering the myriad factors that fanned the violence and the communities' attempts to come to terms with the ethnic conflicts or try to resolve them. So many of the people interviewed for this project spoke of fundamental differences from how ethnic wars were once fought; the emergence of a modern ethnic warfare that disregards established norms.

What changed in social structures, cultural norms, and the perceived moral universe? Why was such extreme violence, nearly unknown in living memory, meted out against tribal opponents? Many South Sudanese contend that for actions such as rape and destruction of assets to become part of modern ethnic wars, something in the social order must be broken. This new war ethos has shocked everyone by its gruesome nature, including sexual violence against women and children, a brutality almost unparalleled in living memory. Rape of women was heard in the course of the north-south war, as the soldiers from the SAF stationed in southern garrison towns used it as a weapon, but it was never a part of local ethnic rivalries. Why did it become part of war practices within South Sudan after it became independent from Sudan?

This book examines local opinions about what aspects of the social fabric must have changed to permit such vicious violence. Is there any evidence that this type of violence did not previously exist in South Sudan, or is it a perception based on faded memory? Or has the brutality shocked people into thinking that it had never happened before? History can be a tricky endeavor if it is pieced together from people's memories alone.

The history of conflict in South Sudan can be approached from a perspective of three streams: the north-south liberation war that unified most South Sudanese, the conflict between well-defined warring factions within South Sudan, and perhaps a newer and more insidious stream, violence within communities and by individuals. The first two streams are well-documented, due to their political visibility; when militaries confront one another there can be an alarming death toll among ordinary people who are not party to the war. The last stream has become war in its own right, able to continue unabated because it occurs within, and under the cover of bigger wars, and its victims are often less politically visible. These are the wars that continue long after peace agreements have been signed and relative calm has returned. Violence within communities, and its continuation even after the peace agreement and the establishment of South Sudan as an independent state, is both a legacy of the main war and the pressures of independence and expectations that accompanied it. South Sudan's separation, locally viewed as the biggest political transformation since Sudan's independence from Britain in 1956, was a moment on which so many hopes for a better life were pinned.

My fourth aim is to provide an account of the current political, economic and socio-cultural climate in order to explore the future of Sudan's two new states. This account focuses mainly on South Sudan in relation to its historical connections with what used to be "the north." I shall appraise the policies, programs and implementation efforts that the government of South Sudan has tried to pursue to combat localized ethnic conflicts and regional rebellions, reconcile warring communities, establish a security sector, disarm informal militias and protect citizens against rampant violence. Programs of community security and security promotion initiatives such as Disarmament, Demobilization and Reintegration (DDR), Security Sector Reform (SSR) and Small Arms and Light Weapons control (SALW) are common phrases among government officials in charge of ensuring the transition from war to peace. What they actually mean to the citizens affected by internal conflicts is important when assessing whether such security initiatives will bring peace to rural communities or whether new conflict has created circumstances that require a total overhaul of security.

Both government and citizens view everyday security as the single most important peace dividend. But for a variety of reasons, security has proved one of the most elusive of independence promises. Security policies must involve both the state and the communities that live with violence. If these policies are to be meaningful, respected and contribute to the reduction of local violence, a review of the social order, rural livelihoods, youth engagement, communities' self-protection and the structure of the state security forces must be carefully studied and widely discussed with all stakeholders. I shall attempt to elaborate on such concepts in ways that are both helpful to South Sudan authorities in their quest for post-independence stability and to the donor countries and regional powers in their effort to support a new, successful emerging state, and contribute toward regional peace and stability in East, Central and the Horn of Africa, a region that has seen its share of conflicts.

This book will emphasize the changing nature of local conflict within South Sudan. The people I have interviewed since 2005 have identified three types of conflict as the most likely to disrupt their livelihoods, endanger their physical security and jeopardize the survival of their new nation. First are the ethnic conflicts that have plagued the region over the years, keeping more than half of the country's population under the constant threat of insecurity. Historically, at least between 1991 and 1998, these conflicts occurred over indigenous resources such as cattle and grazing land. Local people were familiar with such conflicts and had negotiated and successfully reconciled them, with minimal involvement of the state or any third party. However, they had the potential to be politicized and escalated by the élite.

The second type is conflicts triggered by feelings of exclusion from national resource distribution and contest over political space. These began as competition among key political figures, but now ethnic loyalties have become the basis for competition for public office. This type of conflict is most feared in terms of its threat to unravel the new republic, or at least render it so unstable as to be ungovernable. It is also the type that has negatively affected the level of infrastructural development in towns and cities.

A good example is the conflict of 1982–3, when the then president of Sudan, Ja'afer Muhammad Nimeiri, threw out the Addis Ababa Agreement that had ended the first round of war (1955–72). He dismantled the autonomous status that the agreement had granted the south, and re-divided the region into three weaker polities: Equatoria, Upper Nile and Bahr el Ghazal. This division was instigated by the people of the Equatoria region, who complained that the government had been dominated by the Dinka and the Nuer. The Equatorians demanded that all non-Equatorians leave Juba, the capital and heartland of Equatoria, and return to their homelands, a call supported by leading Equatoria leaders such as Joseph Lagu and James Tumbura.

To the regret of many of the leaders who had supported it, the "re-division" of the south[53] became one of the major causes that triggered the onset of the second round of the north-south war, because it was a political decision that affected many important issues in the relationship between north and south. It related to the autonomous status of the south, the identity of the country – Arab or African – the distribution of national resources and the Khartoum policies of divide and rule. After the CPA and the establishment of the new government of South Sudan, tensions rose again between the Equatorians and the rest of the South Sudanese in Juba. These tensions came from people's perceptions that practices of land allocation and competition for public office, similar to those of the 1980s, were returning. There were also daily encounters between soldiers, who were mainly Nuer and Dinka, and the civilian population of Equatoria. These encounters involved abuse of the basic rights of civilians and discriminatory practices by law enforcement agents. Regardless of whether the claims of exclusion made by Equatorians were based on facts or perceptions, the people's unhappiness became a thorn in the side of the central government in Juba and one more cause of instability, especially since no appropriate corrective policies were put in place.

The third type of conflict connects the first two. This involves rivalries among the political élite over political office, often taking advantage of the fragility of ethnic relations to ethnicize their quest for office and sometimes making political aspiration a matter of survival for their entire ethnic nation. The December 2013 conflict between the government of President Salva Kiir Mayardit and the rebel movement lead by former Vice President Riek Machar Teny was the most recent manifestation of this type of conflict, involving the manipulation of ethnic identity for political gains.

This conflict began in the capital, Juba, on that fateful December day and rapidly spread to engulf a third of the country within three weeks. It has been explained as emanating from a power struggle between the top leaders within the ruling SPLM.

This book attempts to make sense of the sequence of events from the moment of a squabble within one unit of the army to the massacre of a large number of Nuer people in Juba. How could a simple fracture so quickly grow into a massive rebellion and all-out civil war? What factors fanned this escalation? How did the leading personalities in the crisis justify the massive death toll that resulted? Why did it prove so easy to draw such a large number of young fighters into a conflict they barely understood? What tools did the leaders use to ensure popular support for their war efforts?

Several explanations for the roots of this conflict have been thrown up and pursued by all sides, including the government's claim that there was an attempted *coup d'état* led by Riek Machar, a split in the presidential guard unit of the SPLA, or unhappiness among some elements in the SPLA who were reintegrated in the army but marginalized within the structures of the institutions. Others suggest that the policy of amnesties and absorptions of militias, long pursued by the president as a way to buy peace and stability in the country, created an army that did not reflect the country's diversity; the army had essentially become majority Nuer. The Nuer is just one of around 60 ethnic groups in the country but made up more than 60% of the force. This resulted in two issues: first, some Nuer leaders saw an advantage in this majority and wanted to use it to take power by force; second, so many senior officers who had been leaders in the absorbed militia were given high rank in the process of integration, making them higher in rank than the officers they had fought against. This angered many officers from other ethnic groups, and these grudges became central to how the officers behaved toward one another and against civilians during the conflict.

The question remains about how a conflict triggered by a disagreement between the leaders of the ruling SPLM led to a split within the SPLA, the nation's defense force, and resulted in a war rather than a civic contest of power. How could disagreements within a single army division, the presidential guards known as the Tiger Battalion, extend to an army-wide revolt? How did the struggle for power among political leaders escalate to a level where some soldiers and police decided to target civilians on an ethnic basis? To this day, both South Sudanese and foreigners alike find it difficult to explain this development, and the links between the struggle for power and ethnic targeting.

In this book, I shall argue that the plunge into a new war had deep roots in the history that gave birth to the country. Its spark may be pinpointed on a specific moment or event, but its rapid spread is testament both to the rebel leaders' planning and the multiplicity of pre-existing factors that fueled the conflict, including the burden that liberation wars left on the shoulders and conscience of the young state. The Juba incident found fertile ground in which to grow into a civil war with an ethnic hue.

Despite the fantastic hopes attached to the 2005 peace agreement that ended the north-south prolonged war, many rural communities in South Sudan have continued to suffer from local ethnic violence, militia attacks and cattle raiding. Between 2005 and 2011, when South Sudan was still a sub-nation, the security deficits of its government were often blamed on the north; rightly so, for a number of intertwined reasons. As in many African wars, Sudan's civil wars were always multi-layered, and the 2005 peace agreement, remarkable as it was in ending Africa's longest-running and most deadly war, did not solve the many-layered conflicts that operated under the shadow of the main war.

These low-level wars manifested themselves as ethnic feuds, militias vying for recognition as credible political entities, mini-rebellions against the state, cattle-rustling, criminal violence and the inter-familial violence that accompanies the militarization of society. These issues were not only unresolved by the CPA but aggravated by the claims of exclusion that many of the armed elements had begun to express. The new war, regardless of what triggered it, was rooted in many unresolved grievances and fanned by a combination of other, less obvious, factors.

This book is divided into eight chapters. The first three chapters deal with the December 2013 outbreak of conflict. They describe the main events in the period following the CPA, and how they caused increased violence, especially for rural populations in Jonglei, Upper Nile, Unity, Lakes, Warrap and Eastern Equatoria states. I shall reflect how, despite the peace agreements, the continued violence in these states may be part of the explanation as to why South Sudan returned to war so soon after independence. They deal with the legacy of the liberation wars between the south and the north of pre-split Sudan. These chapters approach conflict and the impact of the multi-layered nature of conflict in Sudan and South Sudan from the perspective of human security. They consider the challenges facing the state in its responsibility to protect its citizens, enforce the rule of law, address the humanitarian consequences of violence and development deficits such as food security, as manifested in poor service provision, high levels of malnutrition and the poor state of infrastructure throughout the country, with a view to outlining the prospects for future welfare of the citizens.

The next three chapters deal with the experiences of the long and taxing liberation wars. The following chapter deals with the litany of peace agreements that have been attempted, signed, violated and failed; the final concludes the book and offers some recommendations on how South Sudan might approach its stabilization and ethnic cohesion projects.

In short, this book is about the social and political history of South Sudan, a study in political violence, war and ethnic relations, peace negotiations, post-independence statecraft and nation-building.

1

THE TWO SUDANS AND THE DEFEAT
OF THE CPA REFORM PROJECT

Although the break-up of Africa's largest country was applauded as a relatively clear solution to the prolonged north-south conflict, the split threw up more problems than it resolved. The primary objectives of the CPA were to end violence and rescue the country from the threat of further disintegration after the weight of many decades of misrule by the small clique of central river Arabs was lifted. Yet, in these two missions, it spectacularly failed. Sudan's split was only able to change the dynamic from a north-south civil war to two other, equally deadly, forms. The first problem was a protracted brinkmanship that threatened to catapult the countries into an inter-state war, or at least put the governments into positions where they could fight each other by means other than direct military confrontation. The second problem was a localized sub-culture of violence within the two countries.

In terms of political and economic reforms, the CPA was envisioned as marking the beginning of an era in which diversity was celebrated and governments were willing to share the resources of the country on the basis of citizenship. In short, a totally re-imagined country where race, religion, ethnicity and regional affiliation, although important identity markers for people and communities, were subsumed under constitutional rights. Unfortunately, the war continued in other forms and by other names including the arming of non-state actors to carry on the conflict by proxy, especially along the new, long, international border.

The domestication of violence was most evident in Khartoum's counter-insurgency activities seen in Darfur, Blue Nile, the Nuba Mountains and Abyei; the "new south." Khartoum also proceeded to declare economic war on South Sudan, as punishment for separation. Since the South Sudanese had decided to leave the union with Sudan, the northern reaction seemed to be, then they will have to live with the positive or negative consequences of that decision. Khartoum abruptly introduced a new currency and refused to redeem the Sudanese pounds (worth about US$ 1 billion) in widespread circulation in South Sudan. It also shut down an age-old cross-border trade that had been conducted for generations, even through the depths of the civil war. From the late 1980s to 2002, northern traders negotiated with the military commanders of the SPLA for permission to cross the border and open shops in market towns south of the border. The SPLA and the local population needed the supplies and the northern traders needed markets and cash. The two sides were content to bury their grudges for temporary mutual benefits. After the break-up, Khartoum banned trade with South Sudan and threatened to kill Sudanese traders found trying to smuggle goods into South Sudan. The NCP authorities' aim was to strangle the new republic, but they hurt themselves in the process.

There was also intense negotiation on the CPA arrangements on the sharing of oil revenues. Most of the oil was produced in South Sudan, but Sudan had taken ownership of the oil processing facilities, the pipeline to Port Sudan and the marine terminal where the oil was loaded on to ships for export. Sudan was in a better position, as most of the local oil workers and technicians were Sudanese. Khartoum was willing to sacrifice these workers by withdrawing them from South Sudan's oil fields to spite the government of the new state. The authorities in Juba, capital of South Sudan, pleaded for Khartoum to agree to a phased program to replace the oil workers, to no avail.

It became clear that the CPA had given birth to fraternal twins: two countries that were starkly dissimilar and that did not recognize each other as equals. There was stiff sibling competition right from the birth of South Sudan. The leaders' egos, national pride, misreading of the two countries' political pulses, memories of war-related destruction and the built-up history of mistrust all stood in the way of the re-imagination of the relationship between the two countries. It was also implied in the CPA that the border communities could become a link at the local level, if not at a macro-level, such that the historic social relations could become a basis for reconciliation.[1] The CPA proposed that a new socio-historical foundation be laid, one that acknowledged the power of social relations over state laws, and offered the Sudanese on both sides of the divide the chance to continue social intercourse, with the understanding that such inter-ethnic historic relations could become the essence of a "New Sudan," if that were their desire.

The idea was that the split was a political project and that historic social relations formed over many decades, despite conflict, could become connecting threads between the two sides. For example, there were the cattle-keeping people who occupied the borderlands and the seasonal movements of the Baggara, for trade and to feed their livestock. Population mobility, whether voluntary or forced, is by far the most significant factor in the formation of states and societies; the border people, and their need for seasonal migration, were a far more important factor in the relationship between the two states than regulations and border controls.

Border populations on both sides reasoned that what they needed, in view of the reality of the split, was to imagine and work for a border where both countries could simply keep track of who crossed, and for what reason, instead of insisting on the impossible task of blocking the flow of people, livestock and goods, something no country in African history has ever successfully managed. The separation of South Sudan, it was assumed, could build a new basis for a modicum of coexistence, where discord lay between the governments and the élites who ran them, not between the ordinary people, whose concerns were more mundane. The border area, in recent history and the language of ethnic relations, became known as the "*tamazuj*" or transitional zone, where "to move is to live," as a Baggara trader said.

Another example of the new relationship was the question of nationality and citizenship. Unfortunately, the first order of NCP business following the separation was to declare the South Sudanese living in Sudan to be foreigners. They were threatened with expulsion from the north within four months if they failed to register, or to demonstrate their adherence to Sudan's legal requirements.

Chapter 2 describes the consequences of Sudan's break-up, how the people on both sides reacted to this monumental political dispensation, how the two new states experienced and dealt with the reactions of their citizens, why the Khartoum government had such mixed reactions to, and how the independence of South Sudan, the promises it offered and the failure of the state to honor these promises seemed to pose existential threats to the new state. There was, on the one hand, a sense of relief at being rid of the fifty-year burden of the southern wars, even though the separation meant a great loss to northern Sudan, at least in terms of resources. But on the other hand there was a sense of anger and bitterness toward the South Sudanese, at least among the political forces outside government, for leaving the union and taking with them the natural resources and the unique status of Sudan as Africa's largest country.

This chapter also examines how citizens' unfulfilled expectations and unmet promises, and their hopes and prospects for human security, civil liberties, justice, service provision and future prosperity, became some of the drivers of conflict and instability, that threatened the viability of the state in both countries, most especially in South Sudan. In other words, when expectations remained unmet and the euphoria of the peace agreement, the referendum and even independence itself began to run out of steam, disappointments turned into anger directed at the state and the élite that ran it.

Once the CPA was signed and the split became ever more evident, many observers highlighted warning signs that showed how these expectations, if not managed intelligently, would quickly threaten the stability of the two countries. But the warnings were ignored for far too long, until the threats of new wars between and within the two countries became tangible realities, that triggered retrospective reflections and criticism fed by hindsight. By the time it became clear that the CPA was not the universal remedy it had been made to appear to the leaderships of both countries and their international allies (and in the process propped up the ruling élite), the ability of the two countries to cater for the needs of their citizens was irrevocably compromised, and the ruling élite entrenched, unwilling or unable to respond effectively and meaningfully to the many demands triggered by the peace accord.

In the case of South Sudan, this chapter attempts to document what these reflections say about the connection between the new wars and the old liberation wars, and how the peace agreements that ended the north-south wars elevated the stakes, instead of resolving the sources of conflict that had driven the wars. Rather than turning to a program that would massage away the burden of conflicts to build an open democratic society, the contest over the state had just become more valuable due to the proposed distribution of power and wealth-sharing. It is unclear whether lessons from the CPA-related rivalries could be learned by the current search for lasting settlement of the ongoing new conflict in South Sudan.

With regard to Sudan, the chapter aims to explain why the continued political turmoil, the protests and the violent reactions from the state have remained a feature of politics and state-sponsored violence has continued unabated. Furthermore, why has the destruction of civilian lives and livelihoods in Darfur, Nuba Mountains and Southern Blue Nile by Sudan's military and its proxies escalated since the break-up of the country, and why have the attempts to resolve these conflicts through a negotiated settlement have become increasingly less promising?[2] Obstacles were many but, as one informant said, "independence is not the solution to all our problems, but let us try to search for our own solutions as a free people." In describing these lives, this book is based on a combination of interviews with a cross-section of South Sudanese society, personal histories, journalism about the conflicts, online discussions among the South Sudanese diaspora, and debates among students, researchers, and academics about the future of South Sudan. While it is important to point out the problems facing the two Sudans, my goal in this book is to describe the lives of South Sudanese as they have lived their unique history, and their aspirations to forge South Sudan into a better country than a united Sudan was able to be.

The rest of this chapter will describe the two interlinked "burdens" that the two Sudans have confronted since the split and will most likely continue to face well into the future. The first set of challenges is a number of complicated post-CPA north-south unresolved issues that have been, and will continue to be, negotiated and settled. Some of these issues threaten to create perpetual instability into the future, if not an all-out war between the new countries. These include wealth-sharing, particularly oil resources, border demarcation, the fate of contested border areas, security arrangements for border control and the future of former South Sudan's military allies from the "new south." To this can be added Sudan's staggering external debt, which stood at $US36 billion at the time of the CPA, international treaties and the question of citizenship for Sudanese who hail from one side but found themselves on the other at the time of separation.[3]

The second set of challenges is that South Sudan was confronted by its own development needs, ethnic competition for public office, rebellions and ethnic wars. The weakening SPLM, the liberation movement turned ruling party, increasingly seemed to have lost its vision for the country. The emphasis here is on the shifting relations between Sudan and South Sudan and the changing nature of conflict within each country. Two types of possible conflict have been at the top of the list of fears that the population has expressed since 2005. The first is tribal conflicts, which plagued the old Sudan and kept more than half of South Sudan's population under the constant threat of insecurity. The other is the ongoing civil war that broke out within two years of independence, triggered by contest among the élite over political power and fueled by feelings of ethnic-based exclusion from the distribution of state goods and services.

In Sudan, the days leading up to the referendum, and the subsequent separation of the south, saw the ruling NCP leaders act as if South Sudan's breakaway was their chance to tighten their grip on power within the rump state, to the exclusion of the rest of the political forces. It was as if they no longer needed to sustain dialogue and compromise with the remaining armed opposition groups in Darfur, Blue Nile and the Nuba Mountains, the many political parties in the country and with the discontented citizenry.

The new wars intensified in the country's "new south," beginning soon after the south officially broke away on July 9, 2011. The continuation of war in Sudan is entirely unsurprising, as Khartoum's preference for a military option followed a pattern that successive Sudanese governments had always maintained. What was surprising, however, was the NCP's willingness to risk losing the small amount of international good will that it had gained through the CPA. Sudan, still under international trade sanctions, had discussed making joint efforts with the leaders of the breakaway state to persuade the West to lift these sanctions, but this was not to be. Khartoum was not ready to change its ways *vis-à-vis* the war with the peripheral regions.

SOUTH SUDAN AND THE BURDEN OF INDEPENDENCE

When South Sudan finally gained "independence" on July 9, 2011, after long and deadly liberation wars against the government of Sudan, the fever of celebrations that seized the entire country masked the problems towards which the new state was heading.[4] In a colorful celebration, every sector of society and foreign dignitaries (including a delegation from northern Sudan) converged in Juba. The event marked the grandest ceremony ever put together by the government. But the gathering was held in a climate of tension, made more tense by the presence of Omar al-Bashir, the president of the rump state. Reports and accusations of war crimes in Sudan's multiple wars hung over al-Bashir, and the memories of atrocities his government had inflicted on the south remained vivid in the minds of many South Sudanese present at the ceremony. Nor were worries of possible further conflicts on the border lost on the minds of South Sudan's leaders.

For South Sudan, the celebrations were as much a moment of triumph and happiness as an expression of mourning for the lives of close to three million people who had perished in the liberation struggle, both directly from war and from other related causes such as famine and disease. The participation in the parades of a large number of war veterans, disabled soldiers and units representing all sections of South Sudan's armed forces, including women-only units, was testament to the history of the struggle. Their presence was intended to symbolize the price that was paid to make the day possible. The celebrations seemed to send a message reflecting some of what the citizens expected from the government regarding the rewards for everyone's contribution to the effort for independence.

The perceived government neglect of the wounded veterans, and the suffering they experienced during the six-year period since CPA ended the war, were particularly lamented as an area in which the government had disappointed public aspirations for post-war services. Their participation on independence day was seen as their due recognition of their role. Many people said that they hoped that the government would translate this recognition into services in the post-independence period. In fact, as the speeches, including that of the newly inaugurated president, Salva Kiir Mayardit, indicated, this was not just a celebration of the past and present. The jubilation was as much about the good things every citizen expected the future to bring, now that freedom was achieved, and "now that the country's leadership is going to be entirely made up of our own people," as one person remarked.[5] This was a clear juxtaposition of expected peace dividends against the fears that the troubled history left behind, including about relations with the north. South Sudan was a country in which the past remained a burden on the present and future.

Many people who participated in the independence ceremonies, in the referendum that preceded it and in the liberation war before that, spoke of their own reasons for their participation in these historic moments. Some of the most common reasons for such excitement about independence, about the "final walk"[6] in the long journey, were "because future generations of our people will live in peace," or "because we will use our own natural resources more efficiently in order for our country to become a prosperous nation," and "so our children will live better lives than we did." Many hopes and aspirations hung on that day. But a few skeptics had other thoughts.

One commentator who watched the march of the wounded veterans saw that the display at "freedom square" did not represent how veterans were treated in the rest of the country. In other places, many languish in poverty, some still live with bullets in their bodies and others are unable to afford crutches to walk on or to replace the prosthetic limbs they had received in the 1990s at the war hospital run by the International Committee of the Red Cross (ICRC) in northern Kenya. Another added:

> If they cannot even take care of their own comrades who lost limbs on the frontlines, the orphans whose fathers paid the ultimate price so that a day like this may come, or the widows of their own fallen heroes, why should we expect them to care for the rest?

Soon after that most celebrated moment in South Sudan's history, the new country immediately started to seek its place in the global community of nations and its relationship to other countries in Africa. Despite many fears that that South Sudan might set an unhealthy precedent on a volatile continent and open the flood-gates to other African countries with similar colonial histories, the country was declared Africa's fifty-fourth and newest nation and the 193rd member of the United Nations (UN). In South Sudan, the euphoria over the country's "freedom," and its warm reception by the world's other nations were seen as testament to the achievement of a long-overdue objective.

But the birth of South Sudan was accompanied by myriad complications, great trepidation and deep fears that it might not prove viable, at least not immediately. Later, some observers remarked that it was a stillbirth, and that the country had little of the quality of leadership needed to effectively guide and steer such a country to success. It was feared that a number of outstanding and thorny issues with its new northern neighbor, the Republic of Sudan, would lead to a relapse into the devastating wars that had caused the split. There was an apprehension that the split would leave Sudan in a dire economic situation, a dark reality that could also drag down South Sudan, given the two were so historically, socially and geographically intertwined. Problems in one could have serious implications in the other, and in this sense South Sudan's independence might not be the solution to the Greater Sudan's woes it was hoped, but neither was the forced unity that had driven South Sudan to war in the first place. The compromise agreement was as much beset by trouble as it was a solution to an intractable history of violence.

One of the significant post-independence developments was the involvement of the UN, in response to heightened tensions ahead of South Sudan's independence. As Independence Day approached, tensions between the two sides erupted into conflict. Troops from the north occupied the highly contested region of Abyei in May 2011. It was greatly feared that Abyei, more than any other contested border region, might become the trigger for a renewed north-south war. The fear of renewed war was so great that it warranted Abyei's own peace mission; the UN Security Council voted unanimously to send a 4200-strong Ethiopian peacekeeping force to the disputed territory of Sudan–South Sudan. This gave greater Sudan the unprecedented mark of having three separate UN missions in a single country, in Darfur, South Sudan and Abyei.

The resolution established a new UN peacekeeping force, called the United Nations Interim Security Force for Abyei (UNISFA). The resolution came a week after northern and southern leaders signed a deal in Addis Ababa, Ethiopia, to demilitarize Abyei and let Ethiopian troops monitor the peace. It was made in accordance with an agreement between South and North Sudan endorsed by the African Union (AU) and the Inter-Governmental Authority on Development (IGAD) and facilitated by Thabo Mbeki, chief of the AUHIP. For its part, Ethiopia announced that it would deploy its troops to the disputed region immediately.

Both Sudanese parties saw Ethiopia as a credible partner and its potential to resolve the Abyei crisis was recognized by both sides and the international community. But within Abyei, the ability of UNISFA to keep the peace was not particularly evident. The Messiriyya Arabs of Kordofan were able to penetrate and attack Dinka villages numerous times right under the noses of the peace-keeping force. The paramount chief of the Ngok Dinka, Kuol Deng Kuol (widely known by his nickname, Kuol Adol), was killed by the Messiriyya in the presence of UNISFA forces during a joint mission of dialogue between the two sides. A host of similar, and similarly heinous acts, continued throughout this period.

The tensions between Khartoum and Juba, and between the Ngok Dinka and Messiriyya Arabs, historically specific and local as they might have been, were simply the bigger troubles between the two countries in microcosm. There were issues of how the 1,200 mile-long border would be demarcated, protected and used as a trading artery. Both sides were urged to maintain "soft borders," in the interest of the border people whose livelihoods depended on mobility and good management of inter-ethnic and inter-border relations.

South Sudan came into existence encumbered by threats of instability, general insecurity and its citizens' sky-high expectations.

The new republic was also burdened by the uncertainties that shrouded the nature of future relations with the rump state, the Republic of Sudan. The two countries needed to seek a peaceful resolution to the crisis on the north-south border, including the regions of Abyei, South Kordofan and Blue Nile.[7] They needed to quickly resolve other outstanding issues that threatened a return to the north-south war, including wealth-sharing, the citizenship status of people caught on either side of the border and the demarcation of the border, the second longest in Africa.

Furthermore, wars were raging within each country; in Darfur, Blue Nile and Kordofan in Sudan and in Jonglei, Unity, Lakes and Upper Nile in South Sudan. All these conflicts had continued impacts on human security and development programs in both countries. There were global efforts to assist the two countries to focus on their shared interests and keep at bay the problems posed by war. The international community also supported the countries to reflect on their own internal issues. If both countries were to quell the turmoil and civil wars within their borders, South Sudan needed to face the problems of security for all its people, including protection against militia violence, ethnic warfare and the accountability of its security forces, while the Republic of Sudan needed to find an acceptable resolution to local demands for democratic governance, civil liberties and a comprehensive political transformation.

Throughout the turmoil of separation, however, hopes remained that the "two Sudans" would eventually recognize their mutual interests and work through their outstanding issues, transforming the historical connections between their people from acrimony to enterprise, commercial exchanges and the establishment of neighborly relations. Politicians on both sides were quick to increase these hopes, publicly stating that it was in the interest of both countries to maintain cordial relations, given that the stability and economic prosperity of one would be undoubtedly beneficial for the other.

Despite the occasional antagonistic rhetoric, this expression of mutual interests was a thinly veiled recognition by both sides of the value of shared history, whose intertwined social relations and economic interdependency cannot be brushed away by the simple act of political separation. Unfortunately, judging by the massive protests of September 2013 in Khartoum against the regime, particularly against the lifting of fuel subsidies, and by complaints throughout South Sudan, people in both countries seemed to think that recognition of such hopes was diminishing by the day and that initially positive public statements were likely to be quickly contradicted as soon as it suited the politicians.[8]

These premonitions were quickly vindicated when the time came for the implementation of the many post-CPA and post-separation deals; it was ominous that they were not enacted. Bilateral relations remained rocky, affected by an exchange of accusations about the meddling of one in the internal affairs of the other. However, it was really the internal challenges in each country that drew each into suspicion about the other and blurred the line separating the internal problems from the bilateral ones. Sudan was already fighting wars in Darfur, South Kordofan, Southern Blue Nile and, in a bid to demonstrate its strength and force the South's hand in the negotiations over other border issues, threatened a return to war with South Sudan by occupying Abyei in May of 2011, just weeks before independence. Yet Khartoum has continued to blame South Sudan for continued insurgency within Sudan.

South Sudan faced the threat of civil wars in Upper Nile region and in Western Equatoria, and increasing insecurity caused by resource competition, ethnic-based conflicts and several rebellions of disgruntled army officers. Just weeks into independence, for instance, a massive cattle raid in Jonglei State, in which the Murle attacked the Lou Nuer, led to the killing of almost 600 Nuer, the abduction of 200 children, the burning of entire villages, the theft of more than 30,000 head of cattle, and the wounding of scores of people. The tragedy that most of the victims were children and women suggested a shift in war ethos, which I shall discuss later.[9]

Both countries also faced unresolved post-separation issues of wealth-sharing, debts, division of national assets and questions of nationality and citizenship for citizens of one country living in the other.[10] In a sign of a rockier road ahead, Sudan unleashed an economic war on South Sudan, blocking trade links, introducing a new currency and refusing to redeem old currency that was circulating in South Sudan. This cost South Sudan huge amounts of money, around a billion dollars, which the new state did not have and could not spare, in view of the need to build its infrastructure from scratch and provide basic services to a population that had lived under desperate war conditions for close to a quarter of a century.

The euphoria of independence in South Sudan, therefore, quickly began to be mixed with a sense of worry both over relations with Sudan and with internal challenges. The festive atmosphere of independence day, and several days after, was soon replaced by questions over several daunting scenarios: would the north-south war re-ignite over outstanding separation issues? Would the Republic of Sudan cooperate with South Sudan or would Khartoum do everything in its power to destabilize the South, if only to spite the southerners for choosing to opt out of the union? Would the government of South Sudan live up to its citizens' expectations of adequate basic services as an independence reward, or would there be widespread disappointment? Would the equal sharing of oil revenues under the CPA cease, and would the North create obstacles that would force the South to relinquish some of the profits? Would South Sudan invest in other economic sectors, or would it be afflicted by the resource curse that has led many other African countries to autocracy, corruption and demise?

So many questions were asked and debated but no easy answers were to be heard. Independence in and of itself was reward enough; at least it seemed like that at the beginning. Immediate challenges were to be expected but it was anticipated they would eventually smooth out as the country matured.[11]

The questions were about issues central to the very notion of state and nation building. South Sudan recognized it had a long journey ahead in its attempts to answer them. Finding answers preoccupied the country after independence, until the search for answers was brought to an abrupt and grinding halt in 2013, when the country plunged into civil war. This war was in part due to failure to quickly answer the questions, and in part to the history of the struggle that weighed the whole country down. In exploring these questions, the people of South Sudan were watching one another: what they would do, what their government would do, how the global community would react and who would judge the outcome.

However, the question that most occupied the minds of many South Sudanese at the time, and which also concerned international supporters, was whether the élite of South Sudan would build a stable new state and a cohesive nation, in which citizens shared the desire for a coexistence between the ethnic nationalities, and where a broad-based government and inclusive development programs were in place. This was also the question whose answer would have shaped the ability of South Sudan to answer all its questions. In the affirmative, as post-independence euphoria seemed to suggest, South Sudan stood a good chance of success. In the negative, as so many South Sudanese feared, the country would not have the right foundation on which to build. Sadly, the latter view was confirmed by the outbreak of the tragic civil war.

As well as the impediments posed by the north, South Sudan inherited a poor, dilapidated or non-existent infrastructure, a volatile and uncertain regional and international political climate, a limited capacity for governance, weak state institutions, massive diversion of resources by public officials, financial crises and violent ethnic divisions. These conditions were not the stuff of a viable state. The leadership was aware of the facts but it did not act, as it was either directly involved in the making of such negative circumstances or allowed them to flourish.

Taken collectively, these realities suggested that the new state would, in practice, be an artificial state for quite some time. A state that did not make itself felt in the lives of its citizens, except in negative ways. It meant that for the short term, South Sudan's unity and strength would be driven more by the euphoria of independence, by the political pronouncements of its leadership and by the collective lived history of an extremely violent conflict with the north than by any natural affinities between its population groups or the country's practical abilities as a nation-state.

South Sudan is ethnically diverse, with more than sixty cultural and linguistic groups; there is a stronger sense of citizenship towards an ethnic group than to the nation-state. These groups' idea of citizenship in the nation is only as strong as the optimist nationalists wished it to be. At the moment of independence, South Sudan was only slightly more than a "mere geographical expression," to borrow the words of the Austrian statesman Metternich regarding the unification of Italy in the late nineteenth century.[12] State-building and nation-building are a dual project, and highly important requirements for viability. As it struggled to become independent, South Sudan needed to wage an internal struggle to find the most inclusive national identity as much as it needed to build state institutions and deliver services.

At independence, the main glue that bound South Sudan's multiple nationalities together was the shared history of their struggle for freedom and collective opposition to the north. The more recent phase of this struggle, long and hard, under the leadership of the SPLM from 1983–2011, transcended ethnic boundaries with its emphasis on the unity of purpose during the war. This binding accelerated the concept of, and conviction about, separate nationhood *vis-à-vis* the north, most especially in the period leading up to the 2011 referendum, and as the dream of independence increasingly became a reality.

Despite violent discords within the SPLA, the military arm of the SPLM, and the creation of ethnic militias that fought bitter wars against it, the undeniable fact is that southerners remained focused on the need for unity of purpose in the fight against the north. In implementing the CPA, the SPLM leadership under Salva Kiir Mayardit embarked on reconciling the various fighting forces. One of the most prominent was the South Sudan Defense Forces (SSDF), led at the time by Paulino Matiep Nhial, a Nuer from Western Upper Nile. Matiep was the most staunch and steadfast opponent to the SPLA under John Garang. But when he agreed to join hands with Salva Kiir to work for a successful referendum, he did not waver. He committed himself to the cause and saw it through before he died on August 12, 2012.

However, unity remained undefined. At independence, despite its philosophical unity, South Sudan had only a hazy notion of its collective national identity. Given its history of political rivalries along ethnic lines, there were strong predictions about possible disintegration.[13] Most major think tanks, from the United States, Europe and within Africa, wrote extensively about why these issues meant South Sudan faced a huge challenge to remain united and have a sense of collective identity.[14]

Major publications, from the *New York Times* to *The Economist*, predicted everything from a mayhem of ethnic squabbles, to post-independence all-out civil wars, to starting life as a "pre-failed state."[15] The *Poverty Matters* report described South Sudan as "the world's biggest development challenge,"[16] listing everything from education, health, food security, to violence and insecurity, as matters the new country would need to prioritize. This was not news to any South Sudanese who paid attention between 2005 and 2011. The oppressive behavior of the SPLA during the bush war, and the quick decline of that "nationalism" soon after its leaders took the helm of power in 2005, painted future failure as a scenario in the minds of many citizens. This report, and other similar ones, demonstrated the inability of the state to immediately provide the highly expected peace dividends and the fruits of independence. It was almost a guide to how to manage expectations. It further showed the potential for violence and insecurity that was likely to accompany the mechanics of separation and disrupt progress.

All these publications showed that the viability of South Sudan was still a matter of speculation. In 2009, for example, the UN produced a list of what it called "scary statistics" showing some of the world's worse human development indicators, which showed what the new state inherited.[17] There was also a presumption that the allocation of state resources and services would cause an increase of ethnic squabbles in the south, with a significant potential to unravel national unity among the people of the new country, especially if the dominant political party, the SPLM, did not democratize in its own ranks and leave some political space to other parties.

Subsequent reports warned against the absence of a broad-based system of government, both in reference to political parties and ethnic representation in government. Accusations that South Sudan's biggest ethnic nations, the Jieng (Dinka) and Naath (Nuer), would capture the state, exert their dominance or exclude the other groups from state benefits and persecute them were flying around even before independence, and have intensified since. These might have been perceptions, but they revealed the prevalence of the politics of ethnic-based rivalries for public office. Ethnic politics have plagued many African countries, to the detriment of their progress, and was fresh in the new state. In a 2011 publication from the United States Institute of Peace, I remarked that "Such rivalry, if not managed in the most tolerable and inclusive manner possible, could easily thwart South Sudan's much anticipated nation-building project."[18] Nation-building was the political, social and economic phenomenon that would test the capacity of the SPLM to govern and unify the country to the limits, together with the ability of South Sudan's political class to look beyond tribe and to put the country ahead of the ethnicized quest for political office.[19]

In response to these predictions, the South Sudanese political leadership, while acknowledging the challenges of building a nation from scratch, discounted talk of failure and the collapse of South Sudan. It assured the people it would tackle their expectations, deliver long-denied state goods and services, deal with corruption and insecurity, and establish a stable and unified country.[20] But however strong its conviction about its ability to cater to its people, South Sudan was bound to have an arduous journey to nation-hood; something my interviewees all agreed on. Its development projects needed to be based on a strong foundation of security and stability, something in disastrously short supply in the new state at independence.

Did the South Sudanese need a new "north," an external factor that they could cohere against? Or did they have enough histori-cal connections to feed the new fervor for national belonging, no matter their ethnic, political and class differences? Their road has been littered with difficulties, some from within and others from outside. Nothing revealed the mixed reactions to independence more strongly than the answers to these questions. "We are very happy about our new state, about our independence and our free-dom from oppression, but are we going to build the country we deserve and yearned for?" asked a former freedom fighter who had left the military after concluding that the SPLA had abandoned its fight for the welfare of the South Sudanese.

This is a bleak picture, but I do not intend this book to add to the drumbeats of "Afro-pessimism" that have long written off the ability of African societies to chart their own paths.[21] This is not a dismissal of South Sudan. This new country is uniquely important, with a history that offers an opportunity to study the histories and trajectories of nationhood and statehood in Africa. Its independence has sparked debates about the fate of the Pan-African Movement, the AU, the future of state boundaries in Africa, the expansion of the East African Economic Community and the revision of the "Let's stick together" model of governance by the post-colonial African regional élites.[22]

The "challenges" outlined depict how the world was thinking of South Sudan and underscore the fears that the South Sudanese have expressed regarding their future. But we should note there is huge hope for the future, and many opportunities exist for South Sudan to get on its feet quickly, as soon as the right mix of devel-opments takes shape. When and if the recent peace agreement to end the civil war is implemented, if the economy is stabilized along the lines being discussed with the International Monetary Fund (IMF) at the time of writing, and if security is restored, nothing will stop the people of South Sudan from regaining their footing.

The burden of war on the young state is unmistakable. Between 1991 and 2002 there were two main types of conflict, whose legacy remains a serious challenge to the rise of South Sudan. The first type involves the conflicts that originally occurred over indigenous resources, such as cattle and grazing land, but holding the potential to be politicized by the élite. The second type refers to the protracted north-south civil wars, which by some accounts date back to 1955. At present, and since South Sudan is now a separate state, I will use the term "civil war" to describe wars within its borders, between the government and the opponents trying to overthrow it. Whether we are talking about conflicts between different ethnic groups or all-out wars between the state and non-state ethnic-based groups, the world has keenly watched how South Sudan has dealt with conflict. The prognosis has been rather gloomy.

The country's ability to tackle ethnic issues would provide an example to countries in the region that are beleaguered by such conflicts, especially clashes over cattle and grazing, which are common in Ethiopia, Kenya and Uganda. Conflicts in all four countries are exacerbated by their porous borders and by easy access to firearms, which means that insecurity in one country often escalates the level of insecurity in all the others. This pattern of conflict compels countries in the region to work together to address these and other common security concerns. South Sudan will become central to the discussions on regional stability, both because of its economic potential and its situation as a possible spoiler of regional security.

POST-SEPARATION RELATIONS

Throughout the CPA period, the NCP felt threatened. Its hold on power was a prolonged but rather shaky affair, despite the fact that it was the longest-serving government since the end of colonialism, and the most brutal of them all. It was held in contempt by its citizens and vilified by the whole world, except of course those parts of the world living under al-Bashir like-minded leaders.

The NCP's future was uncertain. It seemed it had decided to fight with everything it had to survive, whether against internal insurgencies, the international community that had indicted its leaders for war crimes or against any aggression from its new southern neighbor. The political future of the NCP under al-Bashir was also threatened by economic vulnerability, as a majority share of the country's most profitable resource – oil – was lost to the independent South Sudan. The NCP fought to ensure that revenues continued to flow to it from the South Sudanese oil fields, imposing hefty fees on South Sudan to pay for the passage of its oil through Sudanese facilities and its marine terminal at Port Sudan on the Red Sea. As part of the CPA, cash payments were negotiated and agreed with Juba, to offset the loss of revenue should the south decide to secede. The SPLM had played tough since 2005, but had occasionally drawn back, in a climate of mutual assurances arranged with the NCP so the two parties could remain in power in the two countries.

There was both a culture of mutual threats and a tit-for-tat relationship, which began in the CPA negotiation phase, when the SPLM's John Garang, and the NCP's Ali Osman Taha recognized the need for agreement on straightforward and easy issues but left ambiguous everything that was either tough to compromise on, or uncertain. The SPLM demanded assurances from the NCP that the southern referendum would happen, and that Khartoum would both accept the result in good faith and be the first to extend recognition if the vote were in favor of secession. The SPLM was expected to ignore the NCP's misdeeds in the north, especially with regard to human rights abuses in the troubled regions of the north. The SPLM proved that it was willing to deal but its single focus on the referendum at times curtailed the negotiations on the future needs for mutual support for each other's internal stability. Some party members appeared to calculate that it might be wiser – for domestic political reasons – to talk in concrete terms about cooperation with the North only after the people of southern Sudan had exercised their right to self-determination. There was also a desire to deal with some issues on what they hoped might be a more equal footing after the referendum. The NCP, on its side, wanted assurances that its hold on power would not be tampered with and that the SPLM would not put its weight behind its former allies from northern Sudan who, on separation, would be required to submit to Khartoum.

This confrontation came to a head in late 2011, a few months after independence, when the implementation of the wealth-sharing portion of the CPA broke down. The CPA had provided a formula for the interim period (2005–2011) with regard to the distribution of oil revenues. Seventy-five percent of Sudan's oil was located in southern Sudan, and was the primary source of government revenue, indeed a major factor in the north-south war. The formula was that the Government of Sudan (GoS) and the newly formed Government of Southern Sudan (GOSS) would share the southern oil equally, while Khartoum took all of the oil in the north. This was one of the major compromises the SPLM made, in a sense to buy the opportunity to conduct the referendum on separation. The fact the South Sudanese were willing to let go of billions of dollars worth of oil, a resource Khartoum had tapped since 1999 when the oil first began to be exported, was testament to how much they wanted the referendum. Political freedom seemed to trump any talk of the economic value, or lack thereof, of separation.

When independence was declared, the South Sudanese, leaders and ordinary citizens alike, seemed convinced that 100% of their oil revenue would revert to their new state, as total control of the country's natural resources was seen to be as much a matter of sovereignty, a right of the people, as an issue of total economic sense. The problem was that to exploit its oil resources South Sudan needed Sudan. The technical staff, the oil facilities and the export terminals were all under Sudan's control; landlocked South Sudan had to pay for these facilities if it wished to continue oil production and export it through Sudan. South Sudan had no options, and attempted to negotiate with Sudan how much it would pay in exchange for oil passage. The negotiations, mediated by the AUHIP, led by Thabo Mbeki, former president of South Africa, frequently broke down. The teams from Khartoum and Juba could not reach a compromise, especially on the fee to be paid to Khartoum for oil passage and the cash payments to Khartoum that the CPA had stipulated as a way to offset the loss of oil and the burden that this left on Sudan's economy. Khartoum used underhand tactics, such as confiscating oil that was already aboard ships and selling it, or cheating the figures for oil production and oil processing.

The result was a very serious impasse. Breaking that standoff was a tremendous challenge for the AU and the other international actors involved in the negotiations. Moreover, the strained relations between the two countries had widened the divide, due to their dispute over border demarcation (especially the status of the disputed region of Abeyi), debt-sharing, the citizenship status of South Sudanese in the north and the alleged use of proxy forces in armed conflicts on both sides of the frontier. Agreement on wealth-sharing independent of these other issues looked increasingly impossible. The Khartoum teams insisted on tightly connecting the negotiations on oil to security on its southern border, to force South Sudan either to compromise on oil or agree to support Khartoum on security.

In response to this, out of frustration, Juba decided to shut down oil production in early 2012, in protest against Sudan's demands. South Sudan calculated that this would force Khartoum to soften at the negotiations, as its economy was still heavily dependent on revenue from southern oil. But Juba was the most dependent of the two on oil, for up to 98% of government revenue, and could not weather the impact of the shut-down. The shut-down went ahead, nevertheless, and the government of South Sudan declared austerity measures that would reduce government expenditure by up to 50%. The authorities announced that there were enough financial reserves to keep the country afloat until the oil came back on tap, especially with the austerity measures in place and public expenditure reduced. However, it was not long before this spelled a near collapse of the country's economy, not just due to the absence of oil revenue or mismanagement of the reserves, but also because the austerity measures were a farce. The government continued to spend at the same rate by borrowing from the Arab Gulf countries and from China, a development that was bound to prove unsustainable. The shut-down was also a crisis because Khartoum tied future deals to ship oil through its facilities to numerous other post-separation issues, especially the question of security on the border and opening of the borders for cross-border trade.

The NCP radicals, such as Nafie Ali Nafie, issued one press statement after another indicating that they would never allow South Sudan to ship its oil through Sudan after this incident. The international donor community, especially the countries that had supported the southern referendum, such as Norway, the USA and UK, all condemned the government of South Sudan for the oil shut-down. The UNSC followed suit, in what became the first test of the new country's ability to manage an international crisis since independence.

South Sudan failed to convincingly explain and justify its actions. The reactions of the South Sudanese citizens were mixed, with the majority applauding the shut-down, but some unsure whether it was a good tactical move. Others were totally opposed, describing it as suicide, given that South Sudan needed the oil to flow more than Sudan, at least in the short term. The termination of revenue, the austerity measures and the already dire economic situation of the post-war country created extremely difficult fiscal circumstances for the people of South Sudan, halting infrastructure projects and the delivery of goods and services. Before independence, the economies of both countries had many similarities, the most obvious which was their dependency on oil, but Sudan's economy stood far ahead of her counterpart's in terms of diversity, which included industry, mining, commercial farming and food production. But oil was the area in which the independence of South Sudan became most negatively influential in how the economy of Sudan fared. Sudan lost 75% of the oil it had depended on for the previous fifteen years, putting South Sudan in control of even bigger oil revenues to depend on and become addicted to.

Even more important than Sudan's loss of the oil from South Sudan was the total focus of the South Sudanese economy on oil, to the extent of almost deliberately squeezing life out of other, potentially more sustainable and accessible, sectors. South Sudan has some of Africa's most arable land and its highest concentration of livestock. Given this, agriculture, livestock development, fisheries, mining and tourism were obvious and easy options. When South Sudan shut down oil production in January 2012 it drove home to the South Sudanese the dangers of depending on a single and finite resource.

Among the economic challenges facing the two countries, each party pegged the solution to addressing inflation and currency fluctuation, the two most ubiquitous consequences of their lack of cooperation. Economists suggested that the two countries tackled the problems of inflation and currency instability, or at least reduce their impact, through economic cooperation and each country's own domestic policies. But how? Economic cooperation facilitates trade, banking and the movement of labor, goods and services. Apart from security cooperation, this is the most crucial aspect of cooperation between any two countries, although one of the most difficult to implement, especially in a climate ripe with mutual suspicion, as it was with Sudan and South Sudan. Its success in this case hinged on a variety of factors, including "soft borders," transportation infrastructure and security. It became a monumental task to ensure the availability of these factors, especially in view of the geographical conditions prevailing along their long border, not to mention the fact that these factors are intertwined and cannot be addressed independently. Reaching a comprehensive deal that solves all the complexities and mutual suspicions has proven extremely daunting. But it is the most crucial if the two countries are to peacefully coexist and be stable.

The best and most obvious action was to return to the negotiating table but South Sudan was negotiating from a weaker position this time around. Sudan had much more "wiggle room" and the capacity to bluff for much longer. It was increasingly evident that South Sudan and Sudan needed to reach a new agreement on wealth-sharing, but through a comprehensive approach that attempted to tackle all the other separation matters. They both needed oil revenue and the politics of brinkmanship, holding out for as long as possible to hurt the other more, were not working. Neither Khartoum nor Juba was more likely to collapse before the other. Mutual destruction was the most apparent outcome, but neither was willing to make a compromise at the AU-mediated post-CPA talks. The pride of the men leading the delegations took precedence over realism and the need to reach an agreement that worked best for the welfare of the countries they represented.

Under international pressure, the governments of the two Sudans eventually signed a deal in Addis Ababa, Ethiopia, in September 2012, on what came to be known as post-referendum outstanding issues. The sharing of the oil wealth was the most important, but there were nine agreements in all, covering border disputes, security at the border, citizenship and the movement of people and goods across the new border.

By the time the nine agreements were signed, the consequences of Sudan's loss of oil from South Sudan, Khartoum's demand for exorbitant passage fees and the decision by South Sudan to shut down its oil production had resulted in dire economic circumstances for both countries. They experienced serious levels of deficit, inflation, currency fluctuation and issues with trade balance. The post-independence negotiation over these and numerous other issues, which culminated in the September 27, 2012 "cooperation agreement," revolved around finding ways to put into effect the CPA's central point of the two countries living in peace and harmony. The negotiating teams from the two countries forced each other into hard corners, until they were convinced about the unavoidability of cooperation while still trying to find room to get the best of each other. Neither country can really be peaceful, stable and prosperous while the other is in crisis, hence the omnipresence of the language of cooperation in all the agreements that have been reached. We will return to the nine agreements below.

In addition to the economic problems related to the separation, the transition also presented many other challenges. One challenge was the position of people who were caught in the middle of the contest over sovereignty and the right of each state to assign or deny citizenship. At the time of secession, many people who presumed they were from one side of the new border found themselves stranded on the other. More South Sudanese were stranded in the Republic of Sudan than vice versa, because more than two million people from South Sudan had been displaced to the north during the north-south war. These Internally Displaced Persons (IDPs) lived in horrific circumstances in camps and makeshift dwellings throughout northern Sudan, waiting and hoping for the end of the war so that they could return home. Many, especially younger people who were born or grew up there, had only known northern Sudan and may have wanted to remain there. But in the country's division at the conclusion of the war, they found themselves in a legal quandary regarding their nationality and citizenship status. They were South Sudanese by virtue of family connection, but were northerners in terms of what they knew about life, language and livelihood. Neither country granted them the opportunity to choose which country they would wish to belong to or allowed them to maintain dual citizenship.

These stranded people were faced with serious problems, logistical and otherwise. How to move across the new borders to the side that they believed to be their home was the most pressing.[23] This large and unfortunate population was used as a pawn by political leaders and their supporters to achieve political gain. The leaders of the successor state tried to demonstrate their capacity to attract their citizens back, while the leaders of the rump state used citizenship as a way to express their frustration with South Sudan's decision to vote for separation. All the post-separation agreements that were crafted to deal with the issue of citizenship, to legitimize the nationality of displaced people and their movement across the new border, were constantly linked to numerous other deals under way between the two countries. The question of nationality and citizenship was tied to border security, to the rebellions that were raging within Sudan's new southern border in Blue Nile and South Kordofan, to the disputes over the demarcation of the new border and to economic problems such as the national debt and the distribution of state assets.[24] Very little was done to address the question of nationality and citizenship as a challenging problem on its own, and as an issue affecting real lives.

When South Sudan declared independence, the Republic of Sudan announced that all South Sudanese would become foreigners in Sudan within nine months. The deadline for all South Sudanese to register with the immigration authorities and thereby regulate their status was set for April 8, 2012. The Republic of

Sudan's reaction, and the way it has since dealt with the status of South Sudanese stranded in the north, was not entirely surprising to observers. The behavior of successive Sudanese governments toward the South Sudanese had been forged by foreign rulers, beginning in the 1820s and taken over by the northern Sudanese elite when the last of the foreign rulers left in 1956. It was also not surprising in view of the wider problem of how states across Africa have treated their citizens selectively in terms of their basic constitutional rights, such as the right to citizenship of a country where a person has strong ties, regardless of birth or ethnic background.

After South Sudan's secession, there were three choices for dealing with the question of nationality. The first, and best option, based on lessons learned from other cases of state secession, was an agreement between the governments of the two states either to implement the pre-existing laws that guaranteed humane treatment of citizens whose nationality had become uncertain, or to introduce new legal acts to clarify that uncertainty over an agreed period of time. The second, less desirable option, was to allow the state to denationalize certain people to accommodate moralizing popular voices whose calls had no basis in local or international law but who wielded local political might. The third, somewhat impractical option, was to allow citizens to choose in which of the two countries they wanted to declare their nationality.

In the Republic of Sudan, the second option seemed to prevail, with the government's declaration that "South Sudanese will automatically become foreigners in Sudan."[25] In South Sudan, it is probably fair to say that the pre-separation authorities of southern Sudan did not carefully reflect on the deeper implications of separation on the lives of citizens living in the north. Amid preparations for South Sudan's independence, a few voices tried to remind the world, and the authorities on both sides, about post-secession violence in India-Pakistan and Ethiopia-Eritrea, but they were

ignored. The many activists who fought for political transformation, whether the creation of a "new Sudan," regime change or
independence, were preoccupied by the sense of national freedom
that would emerge from independence. Comparatively little effort
was spent thinking about the minute details and mechanics of
separating after 192 years of forced unity. Interviews and surveys
conducted in the lead up to the 2011 referendum, and soon after
independence, revealed hope and aspiration that the euphoria of
freedom, not just in abstract nationalist sentiments but also in
terms of everyday livelihoods, would massage away the wartime
suffering, abuse, and discrimination by northern Sudanese. Most
of the South Sudanese I interviewed expressed high hopes that
political independence would be accompanied by greater social
freedoms, better economic conditions and the return of displaced
people and refugees to a more stable and peaceful South Sudan.[26]

The majority of people of both Sudan and South Sudan remain
citizens through their physical presence in the country, by birth
and by self-proclamation, but are not legal citizens in terms of
documentation. Both states recognize all these forms of citizenship as bases for access to nationality certificates, but still resort
to ethnicity/race, religion and language to establish eligibility for
legal status, and thus subject the law to the possibility of abuse.
The Republic of Sudan is a diverse country in every way imagi-
nable, and the fabrication of specific characteristics that a citizen
must hold as the basis for inclusion or exclusion would likely be
the death knell for a peaceful and stable Sudan. Unfortunately,
Sudanese officials, including President Omer Hassan al-Bashir,
made it clear that following South Sudan's independence, Sudan
would be "100% Islamic and Arab," giving the lie to the reality of
the country's religious and ethnic pluralism.[27]

Some of the actions of the Khartoum authorities have raised
fear of a vengeful attitude towards Muslims in South Sudan. Since

independence, the activities of Christian organizations, especially in Khartoum, were closely scrutinized. Christian schools and church compounds were destroyed or confiscated, under the pretext that they were built contrary to zoning rules or on property they did not own. Many church-affiliated institutions, such as orphanages, schools and clinics were forced to close and had their property confiscated, while their foreign staff were accused of proselytizing Christianity in a Muslim land, and deported.[28] One particular incident that was widely reported took place in June 2012, when officials from the Ministry of Planning and Housing sent bulldozers to destroy two church buildings belonging to the St John Episcopal Church in Khartoum. The officials claimed that the worshippers from South Sudan were now foreigners and lacked permits to stay in the country.[29]

In South Sudan, surprisingly and to the credit of the government and people, neither government officials nor ordinary citizens have reciprocated with anti-Muslim rhetoric or action. Government officials publicly pronounced that Muslims would be treated as equal citizens and that people of Sudanese descent would be free to remain in South Sudan. However, the danger still exists that the actions of the Sudanese authorities might trigger retaliation against Sudanese or Muslim people living in South Sudan. If not carefully monitored, individuals within the Department of Immigration and Nationality might apply their own prejudices, due to negative experiences they may have had while living in Sudan before the separation. The central government in South Sudan has received complaints regarding Muslim-owned properties reportedly being confiscated by state governments in towns such as Wau and Malakal.

Nationality and citizenship became a site for contests over sovereignty and national pride. The South Sudanese authorities simply invited all South Sudanese in the north to "come home" without any rapid action either to move them or provide them with documents pertaining to their nationality in the new state.[30] Meanwhile, the Khartoum authorities' declaration that all South Sudanese would become foreigners was made without a clear legal basis for how a South Sudanese person who had not self-identified would be identified and selected for exclusion.[31] Religious, racial and historical animosities replaced the constitutional basis for citizenship. Loud voices from the northern side of the border, such as the newspaper *El-Intibaha* to the Just Peace Forum, and a number of other groups within the ruling Islamic movement of the Republic of Sudan, exerted tremendous pressure on the government to expel anyone who "looked" South Sudanese or supported the independence of South Sudan.

For some northern Sudanese, separation represented the most opportune moment to create a more perfect and homogenous Arab-Islamic state, which they believed had been hindered by the presence of southern Sudanese. They argued that the state of Sudan should focus on people's religious and cultural identity for assigning nationality and citizenship, rather than parentage (*jus sanguinis*), location of birth (*jus soli*) or length of residence, as in many countries.[32] By campaigning to restrict nationality and citizenship to specific identity characteristics (such as ethnicity, skin color, native language or religion), they hoped to exclude South Sudanese, even though the constitution of Sudan did not call for this.[33]

Despite laments and cries about the country's break-up, there were celebrations in Khartoum. People such as Al-Taib Mustafa of the *El-Intibaha* newspaper, who was President al-Bashir's uncle, and Ghazi Salahuddinn Atabani, who had been prominent in the ruling NCP, saw South Sudan's independence as ridding the north of the menace of ethnic and religious pluralism in a country that they wanted the world to see as homogenously Arab and Islamic.[34] Al-Taib Mustafa slaughtered a black bull at a celebratory event marking the end of racial and religious diversity in Sudan. "We can now breathe and develop an Arab and Islamic nation," he remarked.[35] The irony of some within the Sudanese government talking about punishing the South Sudanese, while others celebrated their separation was not lost on observers. The contradiction revealed the turmoil within Sudan, despite talk about the new Republic of Sudan being more cohesive, homogenous and peaceful now that the "south" had seceded.

THE COOPERATION AGREEMENTS

The nine cooperation agreements were signed under pressure from the world community, particularly the UNSC and the AU. They tried to tackle the main issues that the whole CPA hinged on. Generally referred to as "post-CPA outstanding issues," they proved very difficult to implement, especially in the environment of long-standing mistrust between former warring foes. There were many outstanding CPA implementation problems, but the most daunting included wealth-sharing, security of the border areas and the border itself, citizenship and population movements, and the question of who took responsibility for the national debt. The failure to agree on these issues revealed the weaknesses that had been built into the peace agreement that ended the protracted war in 2005.

The cooperation agreements seemed to invoke the national sentiment prevailing at the time of the CPA; that any compromises made would be an acceptable price for stability. The CPA was both applauded and heavily criticized at the same time. Criticized because it did not live up to its name, that was comprehensive neither in inclusivity of all parties nor in addressing all the issues that had caused the conflict in the first place and driven it for almost fifty years. The CPA was applauded, particularly in South Sudan, for having reduced the state violence meted out by Khartoum against the civilian population in the name of counter-insurgency.

Its inherent weaknesses notwithstanding, the CPA produced some desirable results for South Sudan; the referendum and sub-sequent independence. No matter what shortcomings of the CPA, it seemed as if independent statehood was worth all the past and future sacrifices. Similarly, the Addis Ababa-based AU-sponsored negotiations, and the resultant cooperation agreement, could also be understood in the same way. Despite the skepticism of some citizens, the agreements could buy stability, open borders, allow the resumption of trade with Sudan and create time for South Sudan to explore alternative routes to export its oil.

The agreements came about through outside intervention and offers of a helping hand to two governments whose heads were locked in near-irreconcilable differences and the possible return to war. Briefly, the signing of the agreements sent waves of hope within the two Sudans and around the region. It generated a consensus of sorts on the need for opening a new page on which war was not written; a consensus of cooperation, mutual understanding and the need to focus on improving the lives of citizens hard-hit by austerity after South Sudan shut down oil production.

The initial announcement of the agreements happened in a climate of heightened trepidation and fear about the outcome of the negotiations. The public in South Sudan had little idea what to expect; when the announcement came, there was no clear under-standing of what the agreements actually said on a number of issues. The result of this ignorance was all manner of reactions, some about what the agreements contained, and some latching on to single-region issues, especially the border communities. People seemed unwilling to look at the agreements as a whole.

Because of the fear that the agreements might be misread, and cause the public in South Sudan to oppose them, the government and various analysts embarked on a mission to study the agreements more closely, both individually to allow for a clear understanding of what the agreements contained, and collectively to see how weaknesses in some might be compensated for by the strengths in others. The president of South Sudan quickly instructed his senior colleagues to move around the country to explain the content of the agreement to the people, and disseminate the analysis more widely, and parliament rapidly ratified the deal.

Once the agreements were signed, many people thought it was the responsibility of the government and people of South Sudan to uphold their side of the bargain and ensure that they were implemented to the best of their ability. South Sudan needed to regain its international standing, as the shut-down had tarnished the image of the leadership's ability to think clearly. Implementing the agreements also sought to help South Sudan clear itself of the brinkmanship that occurred on the border in April 2012, when the SPLA took control of a border town that South Sudan claimed Sudan had illegally occupied.

South Sudan was almost globally condemned for these incidents, although it partially managed to convince some members of the international community of their necessity. Achieving a full implementation of the Addis Ababa agreements, it was hoped, would help Juba project itself as a more reasonable party in the struggle for settlement. The trick to success was popular domestic support, but this was greatly lacking at the time, especially among the border communities that would be more affected by any concessions that the government made either towards Khartoum or the border people.

The political leadership of South Sudan saw the domestic criticism of the agreements against the context of the frustrations felt by many South Sudanese about the conduct of the negotiations. These included the composition of the negotiating teams, the opacity of the process, lack of consultation with stakeholders and the secrecy that surrounded how the decision-making process was conducted. Major policy decisions, they felt, were being taken without coordination within and between the institutions of government. People in civil society and affected communities did not necessarily feel that they should be represented on negotiating teams or even attend the negotiations, but many asked why they were never consulted, even on issues such as border disputes and resource-sharing, which local communities understood better than anyone.

What did the nine agreements actually say? Some were straightforward, and easily concluded, but some, especially security and oil, were far more nuanced and couched in such qualified language as to be almost incomprehensible. Oil and border security were linked in two main ways, both in terms of the difficulty of their negotiation and their implementation. The contest over the border areas, which created security problems for both countries, was linked to the assumption that contested areas such as Panthou/Heglig and Abyei were oil-rich. For Khartoum, claiming and clinging to these territories was more strongly related to the prospects of wealth beneath them than to any conviction about its historical rights to the areas.

Implementation of an oil agreement hinged on the assurance of security. For Sudan, oil was related to its claims that South Sudan supported the SPLA-N. Without guarantees that such support would cease, Khartoum claimed it could not be expected to honor its obligations to South Sudan. For South Sudan, although it seemed to have a genuine interest in honoring these agreements, if only due to economic pressures, its commitment to an oil agreement was related to Khartoum's withdrawal of its forces from Abyei and other areas that Juba characterized as occupied territories. Because of such conditions, some of which were asserted after the agreement had been written, any agreements had in-built weaknesses as each government discovered other issues on which to peg its commitment to implementing the signed deal.

The nine cooperation agreements can be grouped into three categories:

1. Agreements directly related to economic matters. These included the agreements on:
   A   Framework for Cooperation on Central Banking Issues
   B   Agreement between the Republic of Sudan and the Republic of South Sudan on Certain Economic Matters
   C   Framework Agreement to Facilitate Payment of Post-Service Benefits
   D   Agreement on Trade and Trade Related Issues
   E   Agreement on Oil and Related Economic Matters

2. Agreements directly dealing with security and border issues. These included:
   A   Agreement between South Sudan and Sudan on Border Issues
   B   Agreement on Security Arrangements

3. Agreements on sovereignty, citizenship and population mobility. Some previous agreements related directly to this category, such as the so-called "four freedoms": freedom of movement, property ownership, employment and residence. The Addis Ababa agreements focused on:
   A   Framework Agreement on the Status of Nationals of the Other State and Related Matters

The thread that bound these deals together, the ninth, was the "Cooperation Agreement." In this tense climate, no word was more important than "cooperation"; that both parties had an interest in giving meaning to the old CPA phrase of "two viable states living side by side in peace and harmony with each other."

However, because the agreements were signed under duress, both from international pressure and domestic economic and security challenges, it can confidently be said that the deals were reached begrudgingly. Each side made unwilling concessions, amid fear of a possible backlash. They were damned if they did not sign an agreement that they knew did not give them everything and damned if they insisted on their position to the point of stalemate. The alternative, especially for Khartoum, was to sign a deal that could easily be watered down should issues arise during implementation. It is the nature of all negotiations and agreements between countries to involve give and take, but the history of north-south relations was steeped in an atmosphere of win-lose negotiation. Khartoum was especially active in trying to tip the "win" part to its favor.

On economic issues, it was clear that South Sudan was dealt a raw deal. The clause about liabilities that called for South Sudan to play a role in a global campaign for debt relief on behalf of Sudan made the agreement utterly unworkable. Why should South Sudan bear the responsibility of whether or not its creditors would forgive Sudan's external debt? The fees South Sudan had to pay for the passage of its oil through Sudan, according to the calculations of local economists and other analysts, demonstrated that South Sudan paid far more than the US$36 per barrel (159 liters) that Khartoum demanded before the shut-down, with South Sudan getting a much lower share than it did during the interim.

On security, if the resumption of oil production had pivoted on the security arrangement that Khartoum demanded, there would have clearly been no agreement to implement. On borders, movement and boundaries, if the history of border disputes in the rest of the world was any guide, this was the sort of deal clearly unimplementable by one peace agreement.

At a public event organized to debate and highlight what South Sudanese analysts had teased out of the agreements, a leading economist from the think-tank, The Ebony Center for Strategic Studies, gave his assessment of the numbers contained in the oil agreement. His conclusion was that the agreement gave South Sudan far less of its oil proceeds than it had received before the shut-down of oil production in protest against Khartoum's demand for fees for production, passage and export. His analysis suggested that after everything – processing fees, transportation tariffs, transit fees, and the Transitional Financial Arrangements (TFA) – were considered, the balance came to 55.5% for Sudan and 44.5% for South Sudan over forty-two months, even taking fluctuating oil prices into account.

The economist also pointed out that the deal on oil set Sudan's fee as a fixed amount per barrel, rather than a percentage of revenue. When oil prices plummeted a year later, South Sudan was forced to continue paying the fixed amount, which was far greater than the revenue from a barrel. Sudan walked away with much of South Sudan's oil revenue, and was unwilling to renegotiate the fee on the basis of the new and lower world market oil prices. This led to a political fallout in South Sudan, between the chief negotiator, Pagan Amum Okiech, who was also the secretary general of the ruling SPLM, and the rest of the country, who felt he had failed them by allowing his team to be duped into such a shoddy deal.

Another economist, from the University of Juba, who also works as a consultant for the World Bank, made another observation about Article 5 of the agreement on "mutual forgiveness of claims of non-oil arrears and other assets." He considered this clause lacked sufficient qualification and conditions to make the Republic of South Sudan interested in implementation. At independence, he stated, the Republic of South Sudan owed nothing to the Republic of Sudan. On the contrary, Sudan owed much to South Sudan, as Khartoum had refused to redeem about 1.8 billion of its own currency, the Sudanese Pound, when South Sudan introduced its own currency at independence; a clear liability for the new state. Khartoum was also adamant about keeping all state assets, including the oil facilities that had been built during the war using South Sudan's oil, while insisting that South Sudan either took a share of the international debts or assisted in the campaign for debt relief. "Mutual forgiveness," a concept that normally means that the two negotiating parties recognize their obligations to each other, meant South Sudan had to forgive billions of dollars in favor of Khartoum, while the latter forgave nothing.

The agreement came to appear as an agreement in preparation for future agreement, one in which the parties "agree now to agree later," and defer the difficult issues for the decision of the next group of officials or even the next generation. Some issues agreed upon appear bizarre and will forever remain a thorn in the side of the relationship between the two states. On the question of external debts, both parties were required to campaign to persuade external creditors to offer comprehensive relief of the external debt then held by the Republic of Sudan. The clause said that in the event of failure to secure debt forgiveness, the parties had to return to the drawing board. The question of the TFAs refers to the US$3.028 billion required to be paid by South Sudan to the Republic of Sudan to fill one-third of the financial gap left behind by South Sudan's independence. This is unheard of in the history of secession; that the poorer, the more war-ravaged and the least developed of the two countries should be forced to pay the party that was entirely responsible for the extraction of resources, economic marginalization, destruction and oppression.

These were the issues that exasperated so many sectors of South Sudan's population, as the government endeavored to implement the deal despite the people's misgivings, while Khartoum continued to make new conditions, in the face of what the South Sudanese considered to be too many concessions.

THE COOPERATION AGREEMENTS AND CONTINUED MILITARY RAIDS

Within a few weeks of the signing of the agreements, the people of South Sudan were reminded not only about Khartoum's penchant for signing agreements it does not intent to stick by, but also of their horrific wartime experiences. At one time, Sudan's air force randomly and indiscriminately dropped bombs from high-altitude Russian-made Antonovs on to villages and civilian facilities. On Tuesday, November 20, 2012, the terrifying Antonovs returned with their well-known terror. They dropped bombs over northern Bahr el Ghazal State, specifically in the Gok Machar, Kiir Adem and Kiirkou Payams districts of Aweil North County. Seven people were killed before the raids stopped, and 900 families were displaced from their homes. Shocking pictures of destruction and death were published in the media.

The questions asked throughout South Sudan about the raids were obvious, but the answers eluded everyone. They were elusive not because they were difficult to find, but because little was understood about why Khartoum would engage in such behavior just when efforts were being made to give meaning to the creation of peace and harmony between the two countries. People were puzzled by why the air bombardments should happen in the midst of efforts to honor the pact, particularly at the moment of the September 27 Addis Ababa agreement.

In a practice that was familiar, Sudan's army denied that Khartoum was involved in the bombing of South Sudan. All

Khartoum would say, as it had often done in similar situations, was that it was engaging the SPLA-N, a Sudanese opposition army that fought as part of southern Sudan's opposition forces during the north-south civil war (and which Khartoum accuses Juba of continuing to sponsor). This left hanging the question of whether the bombing was truly linked to the hunt for the rebels in the border area, or was part of Khartoum's effort to dishonor the agreement it had begrudgingly signed.

Before the bombing, Khartoum had made public pronouncements linking the implementation of the Addis Ababa accord, especially the resumption of oil production, to border security. As South Sudan prepared to resume oil production, as per the agreement, Sudan's government made new demands, the most important of which linked the resumption to the issue of SPLA-N. Khartoum demanded Juba sever its connection to this opposition group before it would allow the oil to pass through its territory and facilities. Khartoum went further, to demand that the Juba government should disarm the SPLA-N that was fighting the government in Khartoum before it would allow its southern neighbor to restart oil exports.

Was this new demand an excuse to backtrack from the compromises that Khartoum thought it had made under duress and now decided it did not want to honor? Was Khartoum truly convinced that Juba should assist in disarming the SPLA-N, or was it simply asking for the impossible so that it could continue to blame Juba for its own domestic political challenges? Was it a way for the NCP government to deflect attention from itself? Or was the bombing more related to the border aspects of the Addis Ababa agreements?

The agreement included a deal on border security, contested areas and the establishment of a 16 km-wide demilitarized buffer zone along the largely unmarked 1,995 km-long border. The bombed area was an important subject of the border negotiations;

territory inhabited by the Malwal section of the Dinka, north of the Kiir River. A piece of this territory, referred to as "Mile 14" of the proposed buffer zone, was included in the Addis Ababa deal. Its inclusion in the demilitarized zones badly robbed the Dinka and was the subject of demonstrations and protests in Juba and in other towns. These protests suggest that many South Sudanese feared that the designation of this territory honored Khartoum's claim to the area. Was Khartoum responding to the protests to test how far the South Sudanese were willing to go in defense of areas they deemed theirs? Or was it a provocation to draw South Sudan into a confrontation that might force Juba to make further compromises on oil and other economic matters?

Whatever the right question and answer, attacks on unarmed civilians and on their property was something many South Sudanese hoped would cease with the end of the north-south war, and especially after independence. When the Khartoum authorities signed the CPA, when they agreed to the conduct of South Sudan's referendum, and when they became the first country to recognize the independence of South Sudan, many South Sudanese remained skeptical about Khartoum's genuine commitment to peace and coexistence. But with the raids, more people had altogether lost what little confidence they had in Khartoum's words about peace. This was a serious development, with implications for overall security of the borders. There was much public commentary on the heinous nature of the attacks and what South Sudan's response should be. It was important that the South Sudanese and their government exercised restraint in response to this provocation: "Swallowing one's pride in the face of such aggression, in order to prevent escalation, can be considered a form of bravery," as one analyst argued in an interview.

The biggest question of all was how the world community would react to the bombing. This was not the first time Khartoum had acted aggressively while talking the language of peace. Not long before, they had invaded Abyei and emptied it of its population, right under the nose of the UN peace-keeping mission and in flagrant contravention of the CPA. Little was done to hold Khartoum accountable. The South Sudan government conceded, willing to absorb any amount of aggression to maintain the peace achieved up to that point. There were vivid recollections of a similar bombing in Unity State in April 2012, which was never condemned by the international community, at least not to the same extent as the condemnation of South Sudan in the aftermath of its retaliatory occupation of Panthou/Heglig.

If the African Union Peace and Security Council was prepared to sit back and watch the citizens of South Sudan being killed while the AU was mediating between the two countries, how was South Sudan expected to trust AU neutrality? What did the UNSC say about the bombing during its session the day afterwards? If history were anything to go by, no one in South Sudan expected any action to be taken against Khartoum. The NCP was emboldened by the silence of the world community and continued to conduct its campaign of destruction. The only party that was concerned about its violation of international law and the killing of innocent citizens in northern Bahr el Ghazal state was South Sudan itself, its government and citizens. What could the authorities in Aweil and Juba do? How could the military authorities on the ground in northern Bahr el Ghazal, the people of South Sudan and the government in Juba react to this aggression? Unrestrained reactions could have broken the hopes for peace between the two countries.

The dilemma that confronted South Sudan was real. To respond to Khartoum's provocation in a like manner could have unraveled the hard-won peace and independence. The extent to which South Sudan could react militarily was questionable, as the country did not possess war planes and could only respond using ground troops, as it had in Panthou in April 2012. But suppressing their anger, calmly attending to the victims and watching what further actions Khartoum engaged in could paint the Juba government as failing to protect its citizens against foreign aggression. However, this attitude of calm was more valuable in the long run, as the South Sudanese appeared more interested in stability and good neighborly behavior.

This chapter has described the difficulties that confronted the two territories of Sudan following the split of the country, the challenges of: overcoming the high levels of mistrust built up over many decades of acrimony between the north and south of the old Sudan; sticking to the terms of the CPA that ended the war; and the win-lose negotiation attitude of the two governments over the implementation of the CPA, especially over oil revenue sharing, border security, citizenship and nationality issues, border demarcation and the settlement of disputes in contested border areas. Having failed to reach agreement, or to adhere to what has been signed, the two Sudans have remained under the perpetual threat of a return to war. The result is that the aim of the CPA, to create two viable states living in harmony with one another and stable within their borders, has spectacularly not been achieved, with devastating consequences for human security, development and delivery of services, a shrinking political space and a total disappointment to the people of Sudan on both sides of the border, who hung their entire aspirations on the end to war and on separation. Neither the territorial unity of the two countries, political stability, nor economic prosperity, the very essence of the political settlement entailed in the CPA, accrued.

It was important for the government of South Sudan to forge ahead with the implementation of its part of the agreement, as its genuine efforts to implement left Khartoum exposed as the only party not sticking to the agreed principles. Rather, Khartoum bent and dishonored agreements, as demonstrated by its military aggression against South Sudan soon after the agreements were signed. It may also be important for future South Sudanese negotiating teams to bear in mind that wider consultations with stakeholders across the country should precede the development of negotiating positions, to give the citizens a sense of engagement with their leaders on matters that concern them. Such consultations may ensure popular support for any deals. As for the current agreement, much remains to be explained to the various communities that are affected by it, to help the citizens come to terms with the idea that any agreement is ultimately going to have costs, as well as produce benefits.

2

INDEPENDENT SOUTH SUDAN AND THE BURDEN OF LIBERATION HISTORY

The ground upon which South Sudan landed at the time of independence was already cracking underneath[1]

At independence, South Sudan had garnered a reputation of being born weak, burdened by a history of war and violence, having a fragile security system, a shattered infrastructure, the world's worst life indexes and a fractured social system. Independent statehood was encumbered by the citizens' high expectations that the new state meant the beginning of a new era of material progress, provision of basic goods and services, democracy and good governance, improved livelihoods and increased opportunities for employment, especially among the country's vibrant young people (73% of the country's population was below the age of thirty at the 2008 census and household survey).

Was it not the conviction that the people of South Sudan were denied these rights that had provoked the north-south war and the drive for independence? Citizens' expectations also included the supremacy of the rule of law, and respect for basic rights, especially the right to state protection. This expectation was heightened by the country's collapsing security system, by the violence that had engulfed many communities, the lack of justice and the actions of public officials, especially security agents, who violated citizens' basic rights with impunity.

The new country emerged into a neoliberal world order, a world in which civil society, freedom of speech and other basic civil rights, and the concept of citizenship as a basis for access to these rights were words that most politically aware citizens knew well. They used that language to press the state and point out its obligations. The citizens articulated their expectations in so many ways, and demanded them on so many popular platforms. The discussion was made all the more intense and widespread by social media and communication technologies that afforded ordinary citizens the opportunity both to engage with each other across the country's vast geography and ethnic divides, and with the government.

The most sought-after expectation was an end to violence, and the provision of security and an improved state capacity to protect life and property. The ravages of violence over the previous two decades were unmissable, and it was therefore unsurprising that security would top the list of expected "peace dividends." The absence of these services in South Sudan was always blamed on the Khartoum government; rightly, given the concentration of power and resources in the hands of the riverain Arabised tribes of Central Sudan and the concentration of services in Khartoum. In the united Sudan, violence was largely either directly sponsored by the state, particularly through its formal security agencies and its sponsored militias, or the state had failed in its duty of providing equal protection to all citizens. The Sudanese state used race, religion and ethnicity to pit communities against one another, and armed groups more supportive of the ruling class to fight, enslave, loot property, and massacre the groups that were peripheral from the seat of power.[2]

Not only did independence fail to meet these expectations, it actually led to increased violence. The new and increasing violence was born of the history that underpinned it, and of the increased value of the new state; value which had to be contested and fought for. Increased communal feuds over resources, the actions of security personnel, rising urban crime and mounting pressure from militias formed by former SPLA officers made unhappy by the political developments of the post-CPA era, all made insecurity more rampant. Other armed groups, who were anti-SPLA during the liberation war and were either excluded from the political settlement of Sudan's prolonged second civil war, or were included on terms that did not satisfy them, were propelled by the desire to seize aspects of the state power.

There was also pressure from regional rebellions stoked by feelings of exclusion from the post-war distribution of power and resources within South Sudan. One example of this competition for state power was the violence unleashed by Sudan's "mid-term elections" in 2010. The elections were part of the CPA's effort to maintain the unity of Sudan and have the north and south share power and resources equitably. However, the SPLM dominated, and rigged, the processes of nomination and voting for key positions within the south, especially the gubernatorial contests. This contest sent George Athor, a decorated liberation fighter, into rebellion in Jonglei State, when the SPLM connived to give the vote to Kuol Manyang Juk, another high-ranking war veteran. The same happened in northern Bahr el Ghazal, when Dau Aturjong ran against Paul Malong Awan, both former field commanders of the SPLA. The vote was rigged in favor of Malong, sending Dau into rebellion and seeking alliances with Khartoum.[3] A bitter feud continued and when the 2013 civil war broke out, Aturjong joined Riek Machar, to the dismay of people from his region.

These factors continued to fuel violence. The end of the north-south war, and the new autonomy of South Sudan, meant very little to the communities directly affected by violence. The cumulative effect, together with a host of other disappointments related to service provision and corruption, was the outbreak of violent political confrontation in 2013. A plunge into a civil war was the obvious trajectory for a country with a history like South Sudan's, and the young state went back to war a mere two years after independence.[4]

As with many African wars, Sudan's civil wars were extremely complex and multi-layered in terms of regional, ethnic, political, religious and racial fault lines. The divides between contending and cooperating groups were blurred, with the huge north-south war often overshadowing the smaller wars beneath. As early as the start of the north-south war in the early 1980s, the South Sudanese disagreed, fought and broke their political and military groups into feuding and deadly opponents.

The biggest, and most damaging, of these splits was the rise of Anya-nya II, the creation of Paulino Matip's South Sudan Defense Forces (SSDF) and the 1991 breakaway of Riek Machar and Lam Akol from the SPLA. The wars they spurred between ethnic groups multiplied factionalization, which continued through to the CPA period and beyond. The CPA, remarkable as it was in ending one of the continent's most violent and destructive conflicts, did not resolve the multiple layers of war. These lower level wars manifested themselves as ethnic feuds, militias (especially in the lead up to the peace agreement) vying for recognition as credible political entities. There were mini-rebellions against the state, cattle rustling and the criminal violence that had accompanied the militarization of society over the previous three decades.

The impact of these small wars on South Sudan was so deep that any agreement that reconciled the top layers simply left the ground beneath bubbling with explosive potential. The liberation wars, the government's counter-insurgency tactics and the intense politico-military confrontations within South Sudan during the north-south war are all directly related to the post-independence conflict that broke out in 2013. Not only were these issues left unresolved by the CPA, but were aggravated by the claims of exclusion that many armed elements began to express.

In this chapter, I will elaborate on the issues and the frustrations built up during the earlier wars, and how they remained drivers of new violence. The paradox of the continuation of violence during a supposed peace, and the outbreak of a new civil war within South Sudan, can be explained in terms of these many unresolved grievances. Other factors came later, but most were still rooted in the history of the protracted conflicts of the recent past.

THE BURDEN OF THE LIBERATION WARS

Since 2005, when South Sudan was still a sub-nation of a united Sudan, the government of South Sudan had pledged to address its crises. However, in my interviews for this project, many South Sudanese people and communities expressed their disappointment in the outcomes, complaining that little of the promised peace and independence dividend, especially in the area of security, has materialized.

With the government unable to protect its citizens, due to challenges it faced in its efforts to establish an efficient security sector, build a security infrastructure, and institute and ensure respect for the rule of law, and the manifold political considerations that post-war countries have to carefully weigh in the design of their security policies, the promise of peace started to dwindle almost as soon as the agreement was written. During the interim period from 2005 and 2011, the many episodes of insecurity and deadly violence continued to be blamed on the government of Sudan. It was alleged that it was continuing to meddle in South Sudan's affairs either to thwart the efforts being made for the referendum, or to ensure a weak independent South Sudan, should the referendum succeed in creating two states.

Many South Sudanese suggested that Khartoum's meddling increased the fervor for separation, as people seemed convinced that independence would be a panacea for their problems. But independence did not bring significant changes to the worsening insecurity and the country's other problems. The level of violence had greatly intensified by the time independence was declared; militia activity, armed tribal youth and SPLA rebellions caused total mayhem in the affected regions of the country. The security apparatus was too weak to rein in the spoilers of expected peace and stability. A weak judiciary, the absence of justice, a lack of reconciliation and the peace-building program were assured drivers of conflict.

The government was confronted with a serious dilemma. The first obvious plan of action was to use the police to provide everyday security. But the police force was ill-trained and ill-equipped, and its translation from liberation rebel movement to law-enforcement was insufficiently complete; consequently, it was often defeated and destroyed by the tribal militias which could outgun the government. Then the government opted to use the army to break up ethnic feuds, or try to prevent them from happening. But this risked a remilitarization of society; using an army to maintain everyday security frequently results in excessive use of force, creating further risk of confrontation between the government and citizens, and causing the citizens to mistrust the state as the ultimate and constitutional protector of basic rights with its monopoly of the use of force. The government eventually decided that the SPLA, the nation's national army, would not be involved in breaking up tribal conflicts, and that it would only carry out civilian disarmament when the time for such an action was most opportune.

Unfortunately, the civilian disarmament program, itself designed to promote security, also resulted in serious security problems. When South Sudan became independent, security was one of the citizens' most urgently expected peace dividends, and the one most unequivocally expressed, especially in communities living in the parts of the country that had been most affected by the liberation wars. Security of lives and livelihoods, the ability of ordinary citizens to move without fear and the ability of the state to provide it, were not only expected as direct outcomes of peace with Sudan, or within South Sudan and of independence itself, but were desires expressed in the clearest terms at all levels of society. However, they were stopped in their tracks by the widespread availability of firearms. Lack of security was the main reason that drove ordinary civilians to acquire guns, so it was only natural that part of the government's security development was civilian disarmament.

The government saw the unregistered and unlicensed possession of guns by civilians as a major threat to the idea of a state monopoly of the use of force. During the liberation war, many civilians had armed themselves, as protection against the Sudanese state and its militias. Although the SPLA was at first able to regulate and control the use of guns by people outside its forces, their use gradually spread beyond control. This became a serious liability, as civilians lacked the discipline necessary for safe and stable use of firearms, and their widespread possession was seen as a disaster that must be urgently tackled. Massive programs of civilian disarmament were conducted, but ethnic divides, and fear that other groups might be better armed, meant people either acquired more guns or ignored and evaded government disarmament programs. The disarmament programs have largely been rated as failures or limited successes. The process was both heavy-handed, which prevented people from coming forward with their guns, and was not carried out simultaneously among competing groups, so that no one could take advantage of another.

The programs were also questionable even in their philosophical origin, assuming that guns are the only problem driving violence. The biggest fallacy was the assumption that the removal of guns alone would solve the security problems, which ignored the obvious fact that security is not about guns, but about why people feel they need them. If the drivers of violence are not tackled, security guarantees put in place, justice allowed to prevail and the citizens assured that the state has the monopoly of the legitimate use of force, guns can always be acquired and reacquired. Far from being a sub-culture, the continued use of firearms, and their spread among the civilian population, are rooted in lack of justice, absence of state protection, suspicion, ethnic feuds and ease of acquisition. South Sudan falls within a region of Africa that is overflowing with small arms and light weapons.

Disarmament programs can only work if the army has the capacity, willingness and resources to effect simultaneous disarmament of communities at war with each other. Attempting to disarm one community at a time meant that some communities kept their guns while others were left without the ability for self-defense. In the Nuer-Dinka conflicts on the borders between Warrap, Lakes and Unity states (the "tri-state border area"), and the strife among communities in each of these states, as well as within Jonglei state, disarming one community meant its members were slaughtered before the disarmament force reached the opposing side.[5] In November 2011, a mere four months into independence, the SPLA was deployed in Gogrial East county of Warrap state to disarm the Dinka cattle guards (known as Titweng or Gelweng). The area was attacked within two days by the Nuer from Mayom County of Unity state who had heard their traditional tribal enemies had been disarmed. The SPLA force that had carried out the disarmament stood and watched as Apuk Dinka were slaughtered, abducted and their cattle looted, mainly because they had turned in their guns and could not defend themselves. Similar incidents characterize tribal relations among various subsections within the Dinka of Warrap and Lakes states, within the Nuer of Upper Nile, between Nuer and Murlei and Murlei and Dinka, in Jonglei state, and among the many cattle-herding communities in Eastern Equatoria state.

POLITICAL VIOLENCE AND THE DEVELOPMENT OF A SUB-CULTURE OF GUNS

When sociologists started to use the phrase "a sub-culture of violence" in the 1970s, they were describing the rise and intensity of urban violence in American mega-cities such as Chicago and New York. It was a phenomenon that accompanied the decline of industry, loss of jobs and increased poverty, especially in areas inhabited by minority groups such as blacks and Latinos. Many people were quick to blame the violence on easy access to guns. While the 1970s urban USA is starkly different from the context in which violence is occurring in South Sudan, the parallels are unmistakable with regard to the drivers of violence; the deprivation of a large swathe of the population and their suspicion about deliberate institutional exclusion. While better control of weapons is one of the key areas of security reforms, weapons alone do not kill; they kill because human beings use them. It is therefore important for all actors in security, be they government law enforcement agencies, the UN, or security analysts, to think carefully about the drivers of violence and the reasons why people feel the need to acquire guns.

In the context of South Sudan, in addition to the evil of guns, it is also important to examine the shifts in the traditional war ethos and beliefs that once governed warfare within and among ethnic groups. These shifts have forced too many people to reach for firearms. The starting point was the Sudanese government's use of counter-insurgency tactics; recruiting, training and arming young people from South Sudan, and deploying them to fight against the SPLA and their own people, in a war by proxy. The immediate consequence of this tactic was to cause serious damage to ethnic relations, and in turn those wrecked relations were more easily settled by the gun.

As the SPLA and the militias opposed to it continued their rivalry throughout the 1990s, some of the weapons acquired by the SPLA from supportive countries found their way into the hands of civilians, with deadly consequences. Guns brought a level of viciousness and destruction unknown to ethnic groups used to fighting with clubs and spears. The anonymous nature of killing by firearms, as opposed to face to face confrontations using spears, clubs and other rudimentary weapons, meant the traditional ethos was utterly abandoned.

Sharon Hutchinson has clearly mapped this in her writing about the SPLA, its war philosophy and its impact on Nuer war culture. Traditional conflict, using rudimentary weapons, was possibly easier to reconcile, due to the proximity of killer and killed, and the ease of identification of the killer. Confrontations with traditional weapons allowed the users to display their skills as fighters, while the ritual ceremonies that accompanied slaying spiritually cleaned the slayer and the payment of blood compensation reconciled the parties. Conflicts involving automatic assault rifles result in killings that cannot be traced and hence are extremely difficult to reconcile.

War through firearms is characterized by distance between the fighters, anonymous killing and the ignoring of traditional rituals and settlement. When firearms are used, especially in a battle of group against group, talk of accountability is irrelevant. The only possible recourse is either collective punishment or mediated reconciliation, in which all agree to recognize the damage they have brought on themselves and try to move forward.

The next step in the development of the subculture of guns was the SPLA's encouragement of civilians to acquire weapons to protect themselves against government-sponsored militias during the north-south war, especially against the Popular Defense Force (PDF), the tribal militias that the government of Sudan had recruited, trained and deployed from among the Baggara on the northern side of the border in Darfur, and Kordofan. This tactic wreaked havoc in northern parts of Bahr el Ghazal and the Upper Nile regions, and the civilians in these regions sought to arm themselves.

The third step was the growing trend in cattle-rustling, which became rampant in seven out of the ten states of the country, leading many young men to acquire arms both to protect their livestock and retrieve stolen beasts. The fourth driver was the splits that occurred within the SPLA, beginning in 1991 when Riek Machar broke away and tried to form his own wing. Other deadly confrontations resulted from the split, some of which complicated the ethnic tint of these conflicts. This quickly took on an ethnic color; Machar, a Nuer, was supported by other Nuer, while the leader of the SPLA, John Garang, was supported by his Dinka ethnic group, to the detriment of the communities that opposed the SPLA. The results, the infamous Bor massacre, in which more than two thousand Dinka were slaughtered by Riek's forces, and one of the worst-ever episodes of famine, have entered the history of ethnic relations in Jonglei and Upper Nile.

A further moment of violence in Bahr el Ghazal came when Kerubino Kuanyin Bol, a founding father of the SPLA, disagreed with Garang. Bol started an anti-SPLA war in his home area of Tuic and Gogrial, in what became Warrap state. He reasoned that if his war against Garang went through the Dinka villages of Bahr el Ghazal, and if he stood a chance of reaching his rival, he had to fight. Between 1996 and 1998 Bol burnt villages, and his forces looted and killed, contributing to one of the worse famines the region had seen in its recorded history. To this day, no Dinka from Bahr el Ghazal who was alive then can claim neither to have not heard of this episode nor been affected by it.

The last step was the CPA, which encouraged all the armed groups to join the SPLA, the national defense force in-the-making, but many sold their weapons for cash or cows; would-be cattle rustlers were the first to buy. This fed into the failed disarmament programs, when weapons collected from civilians, then sold by the soldiery, found their way back into the hands of civilians. The impact of guns was not confined to ethnic feuds. The rising urban crime rate, which reached disastrous levels by 2016, was also connected. Members of the security forces sold or rented their weapons to the robbers and highway gangs that wreaked havoc along the country's main trading routes and eventually recycled into the civil war of 2013–16.

THE CPA AND THE UNRELENTING VIOLENCE

Rampant, deadly and destructive violence has engulfed rural South Sudan. Many communities say that the peace agreement ended one kind of war but left unmitigated the sources of insecurity most relevant to them. The everyday insecurity in their lives was not always about that north-south war; ending that war unmasked the suffering from the "mini-wars" hidden beneath the cover of the main war.

These mini-wars ravaged rural communities. The affected communities increasingly saw the national level CPA as aggravating the local security situation in many varied and complex ways. The CPA was viewed as a façade behind which the government of South Sudan could view its obligation to protect its people with complacency. The government took the view that peace should prevail once the north-south war ended, since that war had long fanned the south's local conflicts. But for some communities, their experience of ethnic violence and sectional fighting was so intense that the end of the north-south war and the independence of South Sudan was meaningless to them. These communities intensely questioned the value of independence and the meaning of the liberation war rhetoric on citizenship and the responsibility of the state.

Human security is often measured by improved livelihoods, a reduction in violent deaths, the state assuming its responsibility to protect the safety of its people and their property, and the upholding of basic human rights. It is also measured by the capacity of all actors to prevent the destruction of assets.[6] The phrase human security was meant to shift security from the previous emphasis on the security of the state to security of the person or community. Viewed from this perspective, the peace agreement and the independence of South Sudan did not really change the lives of ordinary people, especially in rural areas. It was a state-centered approach. Khartoum's aerial bombers, which had terrorized the civilian population for years, might have gone, garrison towns were no longer housing hostile northern armies, abduction, slavery and head-on confrontation between the SAF and the SPLA might have reduced or entirely ceased, but none had translated into peace and security in the communities of seven out of ten states. Measured by the frequency of violent confrontations, death tolls, the amount of property destroyed or stolen, and the ability of citizens to go about their daily lives without fear, Jonglei, Upper Nile, Unity and Lakes had particularly high levels of violence, both in terms of ethnic-based resource wars and the political violence associated with competition for public office. Warrap and Eastern Equatoria follow them, in terms of gravity and the spread of violence.

The seventh state that continued to experience violence soon after the CPA was Western Equatoria, but its problems were drastically different. There, the source of violence was the Ugandan rebel movement, the Lord's Resistance Army (LRA), arguably the worst rebel group currently remaining on the African continent, which has terrorized northern Uganda and South Sudan for more than thirty years. It was dislodged from Uganda by the joint efforts of the Uganda Peoples Defense Forces (UPDF) and international support, including military support from the USA. For the past nine years, its members have taken refuge in the border area between Congo, South Sudan and Central African Republic, and there are reports that the LRA has been sporadically funded by the government of the Republic of Sudan. Its attacks in Western Equatoria state, though drastically reduced since 2011, have caused much misery to the Zande people, who are arguably one of most peaceful communities in South Sudan.

One of the hallmarks of South Sudan's experience with gruesome violence are the ethnic conflicts related, but not confined to, cattle raids or competition for grazing resources. In 2008 and 2009, the state of Jonglei was wrecked by wars between Dinka and Nuer, Dinka and Murle, Nuer and Murle, and internecine Nuer conflict. The number of deaths in these conflicts surpassed those of a conflict that has attracted continued global media attention, in Darfur in the west of Sudan, where the Khartoum government continued to conduct a campaign of mass killings. Mini-conflicts also occurred in Upper Nile, Lakes, Unity, and Warrap states, all gruesome and all threatening to the stability of the country. These conflicts too were suspected to have been stoked by Khartoum to undermine the viability of an independent South Sudan.[7]

Just a month after independence, in August 2011, at a time when the people hoped the new state could quickly begin to rein in these conflicts, the 2009 death toll was outmatched in an attack involving the Lou Nuer and Murle communities in Uror County of Jonglei state. The Murle killed 600 people, burnt scores of villages, and looted 25,000 head of Nuer cattle. The whole country was shocked. Then, in December 2011, a 6000-strong Lou Nuer youth attempted a revenge attack on the Murle town of Pibor. Although this attack was thwarted by the United Nations Mission in South Sudan (UNMISS) and South Sudan's military, it both captivated and horrified the world. It simply revealed the recurrent nature of massive violence and the capacity of these competing ethnic communities to conduct massacres if the state did not control them.

These are just the most spectacular examples of the cycle of cattle raiding and violence that have blighted the region since it gained autonomy in 2005, and which continued after independence. These attacks, some coming even before the independence celebrations had finished, were the new republic's worst nightmare. The tribal violence challenged the authority of the government and revealed the threat it posed to national unity. It also demonstrated that independence was only the beginning of the far more daunting struggle of stabilizing the country through a nation-building project. The media, civil society and the international community were quick to point out the double disappointment that ethnic groups were killing one another in the midst of the momentous national celebration of independence while the government seemed unable to prevent it. Worries about the seemingly shaky ground on which the new state stood, which had existed since 2005, were intensified.

The state faced another dilemma. SPLA senior commanders, who felt sidelined from the political transitions and sought greater political or financial rewards for their role in the liberation war, staged military rebellions. These rebellions caused massive insecurity problems for the communities from which these commanders hailed. The government had to decide how to respond: should it pursue military repercussions and assert itself to crush the rebellions and bring the ringleaders to book, as any sovereign state must? Or should it seek reconciliation, using amnesty and money to appease the rebel leaders in the name of national stability?

A military solution risked causing excessive collateral damage among civilians that could push people into the ranks of the rebellion and escalate the situation into an all-out war. But, the big tent approach, buying peace and stability with amnesties and re-absorbing rebels into the national army, risked making it look as though the state was rewarding violent actions by non-state actors. This could encourage future rebellions, if more military leaders saw rebellion as the quickest way to gain recognition and possibly public office. These challenges are one of the legacies of protracted wars. The government of South Sudan had no quick answers to this conundrum.

THE CPA AND THE EXCLUSIONARY PEACE

The main concerns of people who live through prolonged civil wars, their everyday security, government accountability for wartime atrocities, recompense for loss of life and property, and other immediate peace dividends are often sacrificed in the interest of advancing political settlement between the main parties. This has been the main critique of the CPA; that it focused heavily on the main parties to the exclusion of the rest, with the consequence that the excluded groups have attempted to subvert the deal since the main war ended, threatening the viability of the peace deal.[8]

The CPA was brokered by the regional IGAD; it experienced similar dilemmas as it tried to mediate and settle the new conflicts. The extent to which the strength and weaknesses of the CPA were used to guide the new negotiations, and how much post-war visions of reconciliation and social cohesion were built into the final peace deal, were crucial to this new peace process. People I interviewed for this project were of the opinion that the new conflict, tragic as it was, should have been seen as an opportunity to piece the country back together. The parties could have taken advantage of post-CPA lessons about ethnic divides, exclusionary political settlements, security sector reform, the role of the constitution in nation-building, access to justice and a strategic overhaul of national institutions, especially the military. In other words, everything that was wrong with the CPA and that went wrong in the period following it, are the most important factors in the recent near-collapse of South Sudan. These factors include the CPA's exclusion of very important stakeholders from the negotiating table, its focus on the premise of peace between the two Sudanese states at the expense of peace within the states, on state-building at the expense of nation-building, the slow implementation of reconciliation programs, the opacity of its program of accountability for war-time crimes, delays in the development of the constitution and restriction of the constitution-building process to the élite. How instrumental these lessons were in the settlement of the new South Sudanese conflict will be the measure of whether the country will be more viable, or continue to suffer similar outbreaks of violence.

Many criticized the CPA for having very little to show for the "comprehensive" element of its name, either in substance or representation. In terms of substance, it has been argued that the exclusion of justice and accountability for war-time atrocities and other violations meant the CPA merely postponed war, as injustice could not be massaged away through cursory references to justice. In reference to representation, the CPA flagrantly disregarded the multiple layers of conflict, instead focusing its energies on reconciling the top layers, the principal power contenders.

Many of these criticisms were valid. However, claims of the exclusion of some parties from the Sudanese peace process must be placed in the correct context. The peace-brokers confronted a clear dilemma. There was no question that it was the biggest civil war enemies, the SPLM and Khartoum's NCP, that had to be encouraged to sit at the table but the main warring parties would not have agreed to a process that held them responsible for their wartime actions. Insisting on an inclusive process, and including accountability for war crimes in the peace agreement, risked deterring the main warring groups from coming to the negotiating table. A peace process that included everyone, or tried to solve every problem, would have been an extremely difficult agreement to achieve. But in sweeping wartime abuses under the rug, in favor of encouraging the parties to reach a settlement, the mediations achieved a half-baked deal that left the deepest war wounds unrecognized, unhealed and ready to re-erupt.

These two questions, of broad-based peace talks that include the root causes and grievances that sparked the conflict, and a comprehensive process that involves more than just the primary power contenders, have recently garnered the attention of conflict resolution and peace-building analysts.[9] Chandra Sriram and John Young argue vehemently that focusing the negotiations on issues of power-sharing and wealth distribution, as happens in many African peace processes, reduces the peace process to a division of anticipated peace dividends among the primary contenders. This ignores the root causes, patches over the mistakes the warring parties made and fails to create mechanisms for the repair of the social relations wrecked by war. Without instruments to address them, these grievances can intensify in peacetime, due to high expectations raised by the peace deal. And when these expectations are not met, or are delayed, a return to violence or collapse of the accord becomes all too likely.

The experiences of many countries show that these are the main factors why countries often return to war shortly after peace accords have been made. Not only do the excluded groups immediately subvert the accord, but offering a superficial invitation to the table without genuine inclusion of their demands causes a superficial commitment to the peace agreement. This is undoubtedly what the CPA did in the Nuba Mountains, Abyei and Southern Blue Nile, and with other parties to Sudan's wars with regard to truth, justice and reconciliation within South Sudan.[10] But even when these instruments are provided for in the agreement, their implementation is often difficult to enforce, especially if the agreement's international guarantors become complacent, as was the case with the CPA.

Any peace agreement, urgently needed as it may be, will only be meaningful to ordinary citizens insofar as its ability to reduce insecurity, offer compensation for life and property, ensure basic rights and provide a climate of freedom, can offer hope for the future. Having failed in these basic but crucial elements of peace, the Sudan's CPA, although its success was rated highly by mediators and negotiating parties, has been appraised differently by the rural people whose lives and livelihoods have continued to be destroyed by the mini-wars that the resolution of the main war was not able to address.[11] That violence has continued to ravage rural communities, and more recently poor urban centers in South Sudan, threatening the stability of the whole nation.

To summarize, the CPA was heavily criticized on several very valid points, notwithstanding having ended fifty years of violent conflicts between north and south of the old Sudan. Many analysts suggested that the peace deal focused on reconciling the main warring parties, the NCP-led government of Khartoum and the South-based SPLA, to the exclusion of the other armed groups, and that exclusion was perhaps the main reason why violence has not ceased entirely. Others condemned it for only including fighting men and excluding women, young people, political parties, civil society organizations and professional associations. Representatives of population groups did not see exclusion only in terms of physical attendance but also in terms of the agenda of the talks.[12] Comparative literature on peace negotiations suggests that merely inviting a representative of a group to the negotiating table, perhaps someone attending on behalf of a region, does not necessarily make the process inclusive. It was also said that the CPA had no mechanism to force the parties to implement programs of reconciliation and peace-building that could address the factors fueling the insidious cycle of violence. The signing of an élite-focused accord could not address these issues.

The people of the Nuba Mountains, Southern Blue Nile, Abyei and all the marginalized people of the traditional north were allied to the SPLA during the war. Despite trusting the SPLM leadership, they could not expect to have their grievances sufficiently negotiated by the SPLM unless both regional grievances and representatives were present at the meetings. The Nuba supported the concept of the "New Sudan" espoused by the SPLA leader, John Garang; Nuba soldiers fought in southern Sudan, Blue Nile, Darfur and eastern Sudan as an integral part of the SPLA. Nevertheless, their war and that of the people of Blue Nile, was a deeply rooted, indigenously mobilized rebellion, prompted in large part by racism, the suppression of unique indigenous cultures, languages, and religious observances. Above all it arose from their exclusion from development and service provision programs.[13]

Prolonged wars, such as the north-south confrontation, inevitably leave behind many long-lasting and ghastly legacies. For the South Sudanese to expect these legacies to be lifted overnight may have been slightly unrealistic. For anyone to expect independence to bring a sudden halt to military actions by ambitious political figures, across ethnic divides magnified by two decades of Khartoum-supported southerner-against-southerner conflict, was a tall order. It takes highly able leaders to sustain inclusivity in the distribution of the national pie and create an environment in which everyone seeks office only through peaceful means. It takes a serious combination of resources, political will, supremacy of the law and technical skill to build an efficient security sector that can combat deeply rooted violence and protect life and property. It also takes time.

At independence, South Sudan was nowhere near prepared, although six years elapsed between the signing of the CPA and independence in 2011. Independence, a euphoric moment without equal in the political history of South Sudan, came to represent a moment of reflection on what independent statehood meant for people and their communities. That reflection was manifest in their expectations, in the hope that the CPA and independence would mark the end of violence, and offer respite from the pathologies of forced unified statehood endured over the five decades of Sudan's post-colonial political crises. But how long is long enough for a state that has broken away precisely because of such political pathologies to commit itself? How long does it take to set up a concrete timeline, define solid policies for equitable distribution of power and resources, avail itself of tangible resources and build the institutions of security, justice, basic infrastructure and a sense of collective nationhood in its citizens? The problem was that South Sudan hesitated about security sector reform, especially the aspects regarding reduction of its army.

The government knew it needed to downsize its army, but was afraid it might need a big fighting force should the two Sudan's return to war with each other.

During the referendum, banner slogans such as "forced unity is slavery," "our freedom our lives," "separation is dignity," "separation is our human right" and "honor the sacrifice of millions who died," captured the attitude of the South Sudanese toward the transition. But such sentiments can also be a source of disappointment when independence did not live up to the people's aspirations. How long did the government have before the people lost hope in the state and violence escalated as they armed themselves for self-protection? The peace agreement was a positive development in significant ways, significant even in the lives of rural people who, because of the volatile security situation, sometimes appeared not to have tasted the fruits of the lull in the north-south confrontation and independence.

Of course the inability of the state to ensure security, whether in South Sudan or the Republic of Sudan, must be seen in context. Understanding that context, analyzing the causes of insecurity and drivers of violence, providing a description of how the South Sudanese live with violence and reviewing government security policies and programs are vital to inform effective policy-making.

SOUTH SUDAN AND THE LEGACY OF LIBERATION IDEOLOGIES

The second of Sudan's civil wars, the most protracted, and the more deadly, was fought at a time (1983–2005) of major shifts in global and regional politics. At the beginning of the conflict, the south-based opposition, the SPLM, and its military wing the SPLA, were socialist-leaning, if we look at public pronouncements such as the party manifesto and other public statements.[14] This ideological path was both opportunistic and taken from its leaders' conviction that it offered a better tool for analyzing Sudan's intractable political crises. Perhaps SPLM's socialism was more opportunism than true ideological commitment.

In 1983, Ja'afer Nimeiri was in power in Khartoum. Although he was beginning to dismantle his political fortunes through his erratic political actions, he was a strong ally of the USA. Typically for the cold war geopolitics of the era, the USA was hostile to anyone who did not want Nimeiri, whether a south-based legitimate opposition or anyone else.[15] The SPLA had very few options when looking for strong backing from the international community. The Organization of African Unity (OAU) was strongly fixated on pan-African continental unity and vigorously opposed to secessionist tendencies anywhere in Africa. For many African leaders, former colonial boundaries were almost sacrosanct; as far as Africa was concerned, separatist southerners should forget ideas about separate statehood. South Sudan, due to its historic demands for separate statehood, and its previous liberation wars, had long been suspected of planning to do the undesirable and act against the direction of African leaders who wanted to steer towards maintaining the *status quo* and continental unity. The SPLM chose the unionist path, pitching its approach to the Sudanese people as a periphery-center problem, rather than a question of a unified south versus the north. It hinged its war against Nimeiri exclusively on aspirations to refashion the Sudanese political system to make it more secular, recognizing the cultural and other diversities of the country, and forging a national identity on a more inclusive basis.

Although the SPLM was unionist in its philosophy, and there was increasing popular support for this interpretation of "the southern question," its genuine commitment to Sudan's unity remained a matter of interpretation, highly suspect to many South Sudanese. This suspicion arose from the long history of north-south divides, from memories of the Sudanese state's brutality against southerners and from experience of development programs that relegated the south to the margins. The South Sudanese viewed Sudan's unity or break-up from the perspective of victimhood. There was too much mistrust between the people of the two regions to make political coexistence in a unified Sudan anything more than illusory. Relationships were too much marred by previous episodes of state-sponsored violence against southerners, and tainted by Khartoum's racism and religious bigotry, for anyone to be fooled that the south would be willing to sweep everything under the rug in the interest of unity. But if southerners wanted external support, the immediate geostrategic need to be seen as interested in unity was too great to ignore.

While keeping the possibility of separation as a fallback if unity continued to prove too costly, the South Sudanese flocked to the SPLA, going along with the ideas of unity increasingly espoused by SPLM leaders and catching on widely throughout Sudan. But African leaders were unconvinced. Most hesitated to assist the SPLM, they feared the break-up of the country would set an unhealthy precedent for the rest of the continent, opening the flood gates for other would-be separatists. However with John Garang, arguably one of the most lucid of Sudan's political thinkers, at its helm, the SPLM was bound to change Sudan forever. It began to look at the north-south wrangling from a completely different perspective to earlier generations of South Sudanese political movements. Until then, the South Sudanese strongly bent to secession, due to a long history of abuse, slavery, invasion, military atrocities, exclusion from basic services, the location of political power in Khartoum and from major development programs.[16] Now, for the first time, the South Sudanese were compelled to reflect seriously on the political cost and benefits of unity versus separation.

The new premise was that Sudan's political crises should no longer be seen as a north-south affair, but rather as a question of a center dominated by a small group who exploited and excluded the peripheral, majority population. The solution, John Garang argued, was a center–periphery confrontation, in which the marginalized people of the hinterland united against the Khartoum élite to transform the country.[17] (The undertones of a call to a class war were clear in this philosophy.) The SPLM thought Sudan needed genuine and fundamental change in the Khartoum political establishment, the creation of a truly democratic and secular state, citizenship that disregarded ethnicity and religion, the breaking of élite domination and the sharing of power and wealth across the whole country.

John Garang expanded on this idea in a letter to Joseph Lagu, the military commander of the southern forces during the previous phase of the war (1955–1972) and part of the negotiation of the peace accord that ended that phase.[18] Garang described this process as "a socio-political mutation," in which the restructured power of the central government in Khartoum led to the emergence of a "New Sudan."[19] This was not the first time this idea had surfaced, but it was the first time that the mind behind it was mature and had the political space to exercise it.

This philosophy had four consequences directly connected to the continuing violence and the inability of South Sudan to provide human security. The first consequence was that the SPLA attracted the support of socialist countries. The second was Nimeiri's indiscriminate counter-insurgency, continued by subsequent Khartoum-based regimes. The third was splits within the SPLA, and the fourth was the formations of various militias, some under the SPLA and others spontaneously springing from communities seeking self-protection and equitable resource competition.

1. The SPLA's external support

John Garang's new approach to Sudan's problems convinced countries from Ethiopia, to Cuba, to Qaddafi's Libya, and many others
in between, to provide military assistance almost unprecedented in
the history of South Sudan's quest for freedom. The leaders of these
countries had two common goals: the SPLA's commitment to the
unity of Sudan and the removal of Nimeiri from power.

Qaddafi cared nothing for the political aspirations of the people
of southern Sudan, but he wanted to support them to get rid of
Nimeiri. During the two years between the founding of the SPLA
in 1983 and the fall of Nimeiri in 1985, Qaddafi supported the
insurgency with enough military equipment to last the SPLA
many years, affording it more significant victories against the SAF
than any other foreign assistance. But Libya's attitude towards
the south became clear after the fall of Nimeiri in 1985. Qaddafi
terminated his assistance; evidence of his initial interests and
actual intentions.

A long history, through an earlier war, connected the people
of south Sudan to the people of Ethiopia. For Mengistu Haile
Miriam, the chairman of the Workers' Party of Ethiopia, John
Garang's fight to change the dictatorship in Khartoum resonated
well. Mengistu was not only convinced by Garang's new insights
on Sudan's political crises but also ready to host the SPLA, provide training and offer the Sudanese people an opportunity to
restructure the governance of their country. Mengistu recognized
the Marxist explanations beneath Garang's words and beliefs, as
did the Cubans. They agreed to host the training of an officer
corps and the would-be military and revolutionary leaders of a
restructured Sudan, such as Pagan Amum Okiech and others who
rose to great heights of military command and political leadership
in the SPLM.

This support helped the SPLA swell its ranks with massive numbers of new recruits, some young people from all walks of life, many of whom did not understand the nuances of the causes of the war, and some of whom came from areas of Sudan beyond the south. Thanks to their Ethiopian training, Libyan arms and the human capital committed to the war, and despite the dire circumstances in which it fought, the SPLA quickly achieved serious victories and asserted itself as a formidable conventional military force dedicated beyond description to the concept of liberation.

To the satisfaction of Qaddafi and others, Nimeiri was overthrown in a popular uprising for which the SPLA owned some credit. It claimed its pressure on Khartoum had ruined the national economy (the conflicts cost Sudan more than US$1,000,000 a day for many years), increased Sudan's international isolation, turned the public against the autocratic government and caused the military to refrain from supporting Nimeiri to crush the uprising.

In Khartoum, governments fell and new ones took over, but the SPLA continued to fight. No change in government personality resulted in any change in the institutions of oppression that had triggered the war. The SPLA, despite numerous setbacks in the field, continued to pose a threat to the powers in Khartoum. The SPLA's military prowess eventually became one of the strongest drivers behind the peace agreement, as Khartoum became convinced that the war was militarily unwinnable. It is safe to say that the outcome of the war most objected to by many African leaders who had supported the SPLA, the right of the people of South Sudan to self-determination, inadvertently became the only viable option, an incentive for the people of South Sudan to end the war.

The philosophical shift from liberating the whole country from the tyranny of Khartoum to the secession of the south is now a puzzle that analysts will comment on for some time. People all around the world who followed the trajectories of conflict in Sudan were left wondering about the turn of events, especially the pan-Africanists and northern Sudanese who had joined the SPLA in the name of unity.

Its much-deserved international backing emboldened the SPLA in its dealings with the civilian population. It was able to represent itself as the *de facto* government in the areas under its control, using its monopoly on the use of force to conscript and collect taxes for the war effort. But this meant the start of a militarization of society that, while useful for the revolution in the immediate sense (a large number of people held guns) had many long-term negative consequences for the long term (people lacked the discipline needed for good civil-military relations).

The SPLA trained its fighters to see the civilian population as an obstacle to revolution if they were "unenlightened," but an asset if properly "educated" on their "obligation to the cause"; terms heard throughout South Sudan in the late 1980s and 1990s. With this model came a lasting military culture that refused to adapt itself to the new realities of the post-war state and nation-building, and the harassment that accompanies such attitudes. It is now common, for example, to hear civilians, foreign visitors and international aid workers complain about the illegal impromptu roadblocks set up by soldiers to wrest fees from travelers. Citizens might wonder if their national army had a constitutional mandate to involve themselves in what is normally considered police work, but in South Sudan the military continues to reign supreme. Its officers see ethnic violence and rebellious militias as military problems needing military solutions. Although the political leadership prevented the military from involving itself in local wars, military leaders often ignored the fundamental political questions underlying the rebellions. Their actions favor a view that suggests in a national liberation struggle, anyone deviating from its philosophy is unpatriotic, and must be done away with.

Throughout the liberation struggle, and to this day, military leaders have rarely been interested in the obvious socio-economic, cultural, and political perspectives on the causes of ethnic violence and rebellions. Their tendency has been to entirely dismiss the political and economic factors of the ethnic wars, and to downplay them, even as they are seen to pose existential threats to the nation. Some of the internal rebellions that remained active after the CPA were caused by disputes over the results of the 2010 general elections. Angered by SPLM schemes to rob them of their vote, David Yau Yau led a Murle-based rebellion in Jonglei state, George Athor fought the government in Jonglei and Upper Nile, Dau Aturjong and Abdel Bagi Ayi led rebellions in northern Bahr el Ghazal state and Gatluak Gai in Unity state. Martin Kenyi and Alfred Lado Gore in Central Equatoria followed suit after the outbreak of civil war in 2013.[20]

The point of the historical background that directly undermines the ability of the state to stem the tide of ethnic violence is the progressive development of a subculture of expecting external assistance for security reforms. The global community responded to the humanitarian needs of South Sudan, and other areas of greater Sudan, during the many war-related famines; the tendency remains to think that external support, from the UN or other multi-national entities, will help stabilize the new country. This expectation has been evident in the post-independence pleas made to international agencies and other countries, including President Salva Kiir Mayardit's speech to the UN 66th General Assembly meetings in New York. In his speech, he emphasized the poverty of the new country and its need for external support.

Such pleas, made before the country had designed its policies, assessed its budgets, and rallied its people, made the country's leadership seem overly-reliant on outsiders, to the detriment of sovereign decisions. Foreign assistance is certainly needed by every developing country, but if sought for the sake of it, without proper national policies, as South Sudan did, it becomes the least effective way to ensure security and national stability.

2. Khartoum's counter-insurgency

Nimeiri's government, and subsequent governments, embarked on a practice little known in the history of Sudan's multiple wars; a counter-insurgency that recruited militias to fight the south by proxy. The goal was to deny the SPLA a support base among civilians by pitting southerners against one another. This policy marks the second historical moment that allows us to contextualize the current state of affairs regarding violence in South Sudan. The National Islamic Front (NIF), which later transformed itself into the NCP, took counter-insurgency to a new, more oppressive level than even Nimeiri could have envisioned. At the start, there were three types of potential proxies, although other types developed in later years when the system had proved effective.

The first, and most obvious, proxies were groups of South Sudanese who opposed the SPLA on ideological grounds such as the question of separation versus liberation of the country "from the corrupt élites of Khartoum."[21] The most prominent of these groups was Anya-nya II, initially made up of veterans of the previous war, who had been separatists all their lives and bitterly disagreed with Garang on the philosophy of liberating the whole of Sudan.[22] When Garang outwitted them, and ordered killings, the remaining armed groups fell into the embrace of Khartoum, and they were used by the SAF to fight the SPLA, albeit with very little success.

The second proxies were ethnic groups that listened to Khartoum's anti-SPLA war propaganda. Khartoum portrayed the SPLA as a Dinka movement, telling the Mandari from the Juba region, the Dedinga and the Toposa from Eastern Equatoria, and the Fertit from Wau that the SPLA was an occupation, not a liberation army; an army they had to fight if they wished to be free of its abuses. Small groups answered Khartoum's call to arm themselves against the SPLA and the Dinka. This conflict not only wreaked havoc in the lives of the Dinka and Juluo people who lived in Wau, and the non-Equatorians who lived in Juba, but also in the lives of the ethnic groups themselves as the SPLA responded against their communities. The deadly consequences of the reprisals almost proved to these communities that the SPLA was indeed an occupation force, as Khartoum's agents suggested. The situation posed serious questions about nationalism. The SPLA and its supporters claimed to be more nationalist by virtue of their sacrifices for the liberation of the country and portrayed other groups as being in the pay of the enemy. But the lines separating loyalty to the cause of freedom and anger about SPLA abuses were blurred. Some communities and individuals were labeled as traitors and sell-outs, a characterization that either pushed them further into anger against the SPLA, or further into the arms of Khartoum.

The third proxies were the groups of urban vigilantes that the government had identified and recruited in the garrison towns of Juba, Wau and Malakal. Their chief task was to point out possible "fifth columnists," people suspected either of supporting the SPLA or of clandestine activities such as secretly recruiting young people to join the rebel movement. Suspects arrested on such charges faced terrible fates. Indefinite detention, sexual abuse, disappearances and summary executions became the *leitmotif* of a regime desperate for a legitimacy it believed could only be achieved through extreme violence. The hunt for fifth columnists intensified every time the government forces were defeated in battle; every incident in which Khartoum's forces were heavily affected was cause for security agents to take out their anger on suspected young people. The counter-insurgency created deadly rifts between Dinka and non-Dinka communities, especially in Wau, where the military commander of the garrison, General Fadalla Burma Nasir, dubbed the anti-SPLA vigilantes under General Tom al-Nur the "friendly forces."

3. Splits in the SPLA

Chief among the other historical moments that had repercussions on the stability of the new country are the many splits that occurred within the SPLA.

The splits began in 1991 when Riek Machar and Lam Akol, then among the most senior commanders of the movement, staged a coup against John Garang. Their claim was that he had become too autocratic in his leadership style and the way he ran the movement day-to-day. Failing to take over the organization, they broke away, causing deadly confrontations among the southern Sudanese between 1991 and 1998. The confrontations were especially severe between Nuer and Dinka, until reconciliations achieved through the so-called people-to-people peace initiative.

The split made the SPLA weak, and granted major victories to the SAF. The SAF regained areas the SPLA had controlled for many years, and had lost many men in wresting the land from Khartoum's forces.[23] The pain of losing places such as Jokou in Upper Nile, which had been liberated at a tremendous cost to the SPLA, is still lamented, and something for which it was thought Riek Machar and Lam Akol would never be forgiven. However, history is sometimes more lenient in passing judgment; Riek Machar became vice president of South Sudan and Lam Akol became Sudan's foreign affairs minister on the SPLM ticket after the CPA. These concessions were made to buy peace and stability, to the consternation of some citizens who clung to their memories of the 1991 coup.

The longest-lasting impact of the splits were ethnic rifts. Both Riek Machar (a Nuer from Unity state), and John Garang (a Dinka from Jonglei state), reached for the ethnic card to rally their respective communities. Their split, and the confrontations that followed, went from ideology to a completely ethnic character; both sides saw the support of their tribes as the only way to keep fighting and stand a chance of winning. Nuer and Dinka elders later characterized these drawn-out confrontations as the "wars of the educated," because the way they were fought, and the forces that fanned them, were completely different from traditional rural feuds the Dinka and Nuer had always known. This reconfigured the relationship between the two groups and their sub-groups, and led to a massive number of deaths. The consequences of the splits haunt South Sudan to this day, and challenges the creation of national unity.[24]

4. The culture of tribal militias

The fourth issue was the creation of ethnic militias, some formed by the SPLA to act as home guards against northern Baggara Arab cattle-raiders, and some to act against the so-called PDF that Khartoum had adopted as the cheapest counter-insurgency allied militia.[25] These militias mainly acted on the northern borders of southern Sudan. Militias also sprang up in response to any south-based government-supported militias that opposed the SPLA. Khartoum armed client groups, such as the Murle of Jonglei state and the Mandari from near Juba, to keep the south weak. When the leaders' political rivalries spilled into traditional competition for resources, such as grazing rights and access to water for cattle, pastoralist communities formed armed bands of young men to guard against cattle raids. Among the Nuer and Dinka, these militias became known as "cattle guards." The cattle guards became involved in fighting against government militias, cattle raids and supporting the political factions increasingly defined by ethnic loyalties, rather than by the liberation ideologies that triggered the factionalization of the SPLA.

The cumulative impact of these tactics was the wide spread of firearms ownership, wrecked ethnic relations that remain difficult to reconcile and an absence of government in rural areas. The lack of police agents, security forces, justice officials and basic health care, education and infrastructure has left rural people with no mechanisms to respond to injustice. Therefore, they have taken justice into their own hands and gone for revenge, and have done so due to easy access to light assault weapons. Firearms in the hands of young men, the disruption of cordial ethnic historical relations strained by violence and the vacuum created by weak institutions of government are the most ubiquitous engines of violence in South Sudan.

The historical mix of poverty, lack of education and future prospects for young people and a lackluster justice system has created a very explosive climate in South Sudan. Any security sector reform or re-establishment must meticulously sift through this combination if it is to ensure effective protection of life and property. Focusing on a military response, disarming communities or improving the police system, important as they might be, are only a small part of the story, and can in fact aggravate the situation if applied bluntly.

In conclusion, in this chapter I have chronicled the security and military developments in South Sudan during the course of the 1983–2005 civil war, with a view to understanding why the new country experienced increased levels of political violence, despite the promise of stability provided by the end of the north-south war, the formation of an autonomous government in southern Sudan in 2005 and independence in 2011. I have explored the reasons why the South Sudanese could not immediately receive security benefits from the CPA and the end of the civil war, as more and more communities became more and more embroiled in violence. This violence included resource-based ethnic violence, revenge attacks for unresolved incidents, the rebellions of former liberation fighters disgruntled by their exclusion from the peace process and its benefits, the formation of militias to fight the government and illegal actions by the state's security forces. I also explored the many legacies that the wars of liberation have left on the shoulders and conscience of South Sudan, weighing the degree to which the political leadership of the country has understood the reality that the achievement of separation could not alone massage away such burdens.

As human security suffers, and as the state continues to evade demands for restitution for war-time atrocities, the more the South Sudanese will view their citizenship through the lens of memories of their victimization in past wars. When a new conflict erupts, whether an all-out civil war, or an ethnic-based resource conflict, many South Sudanese decide whether or not to join, and which side to join, on the basis of what happened to them in an earlier conflict. As communities search for justice, if historical conflicts are not subjected to dialogue, reconciliation, compensation and accountability, historical wars will always be the primary drivers of future wars.

The history of splits and fragmentation within the liberation movements, the history of confrontation between the SPLA and various ethnic groups dating back to 1983, the many incidents of tribal conflicts, sometimes instigated by Khartoum's counter-insurgency tactics, the use of ethnic politics by politicians wishing to achieve public office, the pitting of ethnic communities against one another, and above all the absence of a credible and committed security sector, are all responsible for the decline of security and the drivers of violent conflict. To them must be added the wide spread of small arms and light weapons in the hands of civilians, the growth of a subculture of violence, changes in war ethos and the erosion of certain aspects of social order, such as the role of community elders and spiritual leaders, who traditionally reined in young people and mediated conflicts before they escalated to disastrous levels.

It remains the state's responsibility to take these histories into account in designing a security apparatus, and in working toward reconciliation. It must acknowledge people's experiences and memorialize them so that they become part of a national history, in which every community sees itself represented. The national history of the war is the history of the communities that suffered through it; it must not be reduced to a history of war heroes, as in the old Sudan. If all citizens are to see themselves reflected in the country's body politic, it is important to recognize and highlight all their experiences, and turn the current sentiment of victimization into a stake in the nation.

3

SUDAN'S WARS:
THE EXPERIENCE OF ONE VILLAGE

Much of the literature that tells the story of South Sudan and Sudan is a story of anguish and misery; of violence, famines, brutal regimes, armies, militias, the spread of firearms, dependence on foreign aid and the evils of oil extraction. Almost all the story is told in a manner that paints the majority of Sudanese living at the peripheries of both countries as hapless victims, with very little agency. Simply put, the two countries' populations, their social systems, the nuances of their cultural practices, their historical and geographic specificities and their relationship with the state are almost all buried in favor of the more sensational war accounts. Despite long-established multi-disciplinary research and literature on the two Sudans, much of it is written from the perspective of how the wars have influenced their dynamics. It is as if nothing but war has happened in the lives of the Sudanese people, and as if the Sudanese do not have anything to say about their experience of war and how they explain the causes, conduct and consequences of war, in ways beyond victimhood.

This is a quite understandable picture, perhaps even a correct one at times. The wars have certainly subjected the people to unimaginable levels of violent suffering, including many indirect consequences of political violence. But told in that manner, the story leaves out the nuances of everyday life that goes on despite fragile political circumstances, the physical and emotional agony that war brings. That story misses how people live with the challenges presented by their relationship with the state, an entity they have not always understood.

This chapter attempts to paint the human face of the South Sudanese struggles during many decades of war, juxtaposed with the many little stories of celebration and triumphs that go on beneath war's ugly face. It will tell the story of the reckoning with the realities of living in two worlds, of an old system ordered and run by a local system of memory, and an external system that imposes itself without warning. I will probe the tragic experiences of living with war and the triumphs of overcoming some of these experiences, subtle and minute as these victories might be. It is important to document local reactions to the north-south second civil war (1983–2005) when it started, how people came to terms with the shifting realities of war, and how they explained their participation in or abstention from the war.

Telling the story this way properly situates the South Sudanese in the middle of the conversation about their war experience and the drivers of violence. The gist of that story, told by ordinary people, describes wartime civil–military relations, how they paid the cost of war and how much they understood the reasons for war as articulated by the educated élite who led the war effort. How was this new round of war used as justification to attract the fighters to the SPLA? What were the reactions and reflections of the South Sudanese when that round of war ended in 2005, triggering massive expectations that the new political dispensation would lift them out of war-related security and economic crises?

The story would also locate the South Sudanese disappointments within the debate about the post-war state failure and how that failure, real or perceived, became part of the new civil war in 2013. Past wars have a direct link to new wars; people participate in or abstain from new conflicts based on the memories of their experience in previous ones. This is what gives meaning to the phrase the "cycle of violence" that is common in the massive literature on African conflicts.

Having been popularly held up as the panacea for the many decades of deprivation by Sudan's central government, the culmination of the liberation effort in the emergence of autonomy for South Sudan and its subsequent independence came with highly unrealistic expectations of what that political transition meant to ordinary people. Most of these expectations were utterly dashed. The failure of the promises of the revolution was most felt in rural areas, where people had done so much to aid the liberation effort. They had shouldered the cost of the war, and suffered with the fighters; they expected that any gains accruing from this struggle would directly trickle down to them and transform their lives for the better.

This chapter will therefore try to situate the new wars, especially the shocking 2013 post-independence civil war in South Sudan, in a historical perspective that incorporates people other than the war hero, the liberator, the political leader and the military generals. The leaders' perspective has often taken center stage in the literature of a wide variety of disciplines; this chapter tries to depart from that approach.

This is a chronicle of personal histories, of individual citizens' reflections on the war of liberation and why they committed themselves to it. It seeks to answer the ubiquitous question of what prompted people from all walks of life to join the liberation efforts from the early 1980s and throughout the war. It also asks why they think that South Sudan's freedom, which they had worked so hard to make possible, did not live up to the aspirations that drew them into the struggle, aspirations pegged to the political transformation of Sudan, to the independence of South Sudan.

To present this perspective, I will focus on a description of one village in South Sudan. I will examine how its people have lived and dealt with the legacy of Sudan's multiple wars and consider if war is the major factor that defines their lives, and to what extent violence is a reality that people must succumb to, or an experience that they cannot allow to prevent them getting on with their daily lives.

This is a description of the social order, historical experience, political standing and the role of the state in a community in a remote area in the north of the country. It will look at how the community experienced the liberation war, how it came to terms with that war's history and its inhabitants' reactions to the eventual peace. My narrative includes how the residents of this village get the news about national events happening far away in towns and cities, and how they communicate with citizens in other parts of the country, with the government and with the state. It shows how the villagers received the news about the CPA, the referendum, independence celebrations, and what expectations they pinned to the momentous transition taking place in their country. While this story is specific to one community, the comments of its inhabitants represent all corners of the country. Thousands of other South Sudanese villages suffered fates like this one; rural populations living in similar circumstances had similar experiences of war, and what they had expected to happen in the wake of the CPA, and what independence meant to them, was no different.

The story covers the period between the start of the liberation effort in 1983 and the start of the new civil war in 2013, a conflict that raised the intensity of the debate about what the country's independence is worth in the eyes of people living far from the corridors of power.

This is the history and experience of a village called Ror Col (pronounced "chol"),[1] in Warrap State. It lies well off the beaten path, and remains untouched by the modern amenities that most Sudanese communities aspire to but have never attained. No road connects Ror Col to a major town; there is no school, no clinic and no police presence. Its inhabitants are not represented at any level of government, because none has enough formal education to be able to engage in the élite-controlled political and social climate and speak for their people.

A few statistics will help us make sense of how villages such as Ror Col exist. Landlocked South Sudan has only one highway: it connects Juba, the capital, to the Ugandan border; only one bloodline for trade. Ror Col is approximately 805 km from Juba. South Sudan also has one of the lowest literacy rates in the world, a pathetic 27%.[2] In other words, this community, like so many in this region, can only talk about things close to their everyday world. Ror Col's people cannot comment on the national affairs of their country, or the effects of the actions of faraway government officials; such things, decisions made by distant officials, have a serious impact on them, but they do not have ways to communicate their concerns to the ruling elite. The inhabitants do not picture themselves in relation to the state, and the state, while aware of the existence of the village through the local government system, does not know about individual citizens, because they are not registered and have no identification cards. Government control comes through kinship networks, not through individual recognition. Even tax collection (chiefly poll tax), customary law and recruitment for labor force and military service, are based on kinship relations.

The structure of governance and administration in South Sudan makes it hard for the villagers of Ror Col to feature in the obligations of the state about their well-being as citizens with equal, and constitutionally protected, rights. Governance rests on two parallel systems: the political entity called South Sudan, and the traditional customary administration used to run small ethnic-based communities. Ror Col is part of a section of South Sudan's biggest ethnic group, the Jieng (Dinka), where the daily administration of justice comes under the duties of a chief. However, although the customary and central systems are linked, according to the constitution, the constitution is vague on how tribal chiefs link to the country's political system, other than to local government. The result is that the chief's authority is subsumed under the state's, but the state is glaringly absent from the life of the village. This leaves the people of Ror Col dependent on an authority figure who has very little to offer, as the country's constitution has inadvertently disarmed the chiefs. For example, customary authorities do not have jurisdiction over certain issues such as criminal law, which is the domain of magistrate judges. The village is part of a political constituency that elects members of the national and federal legislature, but no one in the village has the capacity to meaningfully engage with their representative and to demand services.

The ubiquitous feature of villages like Ror Col is the imaginary existence of the state and the physical absence of government beyond tax collection and the villagers' subjection to the laws of the country. Ror Col pays taxes to local, state and national government, but the villagers are unable to question how their taxes are spent, what rights they have to ask how they are spent, what obligations they have to the state and what the state owes to them. The taxes they pay are so nuanced and vague that they do not look like the price of state protection. Nothing speaks more loudly about these villages than the absence of police, the statutory legal system, educational and health services, the absence of even a semblance of private business or an infrastructure that could facilitate such enterprises. There are few innovative ways for the people to maximize their profits from traditional economic activities, other than migrating to the towns.

Beyond the people's traditional livelihoods of subsistence farming, livestock-keeping, fishing, gathering wild foods and occasional petty trading, there is virtually no room for any other activity. In villages across Africa, economists calculate people spend up to 80% of their time in food production. This demand makes it hard for children to go to school, while for those at school, their parents have no time to ask their teachers why children do not seem to be learning properly.

What is it like to live in a village like Ror Col? What happens when insecurity strikes, when pregnancies become complicated, when a poisonous snake bites, when drought or flooding destroys their crops, when they are attacked by an opposing community, when someone is killed, when the children are not vaccinated? What happens in matters that are the responsibility of the state when the state is nowhere near the people? The only circumstances in which the authority of the state is demonstrated, other than tax collection and military recruitment, is when the county commissioner passes through on their way to somewhere else, security forces move through the area, or a native of the area working in Juba makes a visit home and is escorted by the police.

More than a decade since the conclusion of the north-south conflict, very little has positively changed in Ror Col. Between the time of my field research (2011 and 2012) and the time of writing, local government and community members have engaged in a discussion about extending a mobile phone link to the area, but the service remains elusive. Educational service has also been discussed. The community set up a primary school under a tree; a wounded war veteran living in the village offered to teach the children, but there were no textbooks or any other teaching material. The school was suspended one year after it opened, because the war veteran wore down his prosthetic leg and had to travel to Juba in pursuit of his pension as a wounded liberation hero so he could buy another artificial limb. He never came back. The villagers heard that he was pursuing his entitlements but could not receive them, due to corruption in the army's financial institutions. In fact, his pension had been diverted by finance officials for years, but no one was willing to tell him the truth. The school remained without a teacher, and the liberation hero never got his pension. He is dependent on relatives in the city, with no prospects of being taken care of by the state for which he lost his limbs.

Communities around the world have different priorities, priorities influenced by their economic development and level of exposure to technology. One community's basic need is an unaffordable luxury in another. People around the world protest that they have no phone connection or Internet access. Parents bemoan the lack of schools and colleges for their children. Others complain about the environmental degradation of their territory, and the challenges imposed by coal-powered electricity stations, coal mining or other extractive industries. Others speak of the menace of too many vehicles on their roads. In the face of technological progress, food security, medical services and state responsibility for welfare, the villagers' concerns sound foreign to the ears of people living in Beijing, Canberra or Nairobi. They may even sound basic and mundane to people living in Juba.

The inhabitants of Ror Col have never heard of these things. Electricity, farm machinery, a phone connection or a radio station are not their priorities. They worry about the threat of Guinea worm (a debilitating water-borne parasite acquired by drinking from contaminated ponds or streams); the lack of clean drinking water is a serious public health peril. They worry about bovine health, as cattle are the main pillar of their economy and livelihoods. They worry about lack of food when drought or flooding cause crops to fail; peasant farming is another important pillar of their way of life. They worry about malaria, the leading cause of death in South Sudan, according to the World Health Organization (WHO).

The health of the people in Ror Col is severely affected by its location. Ror Col lies on the edge of the swamps of the river Nile in the north-eastern corner of Western Dinka, in Tonj North County. Like most rural South Sudan, Ror Col lacks health services and has high birth rates and certain social expectations that expose pregnant women to malnutrition.[3] South Sudan suffers extremely high child and maternal mortality. Indeed, South Sudan has perhaps the highest maternal mortality rate in the world, at 2054 maternal deaths per 100,000. Babies are at even greater risk; 25% of children die from common, often preventable, childhood illnesses before they reach their fifth birthday. In the rainy season, people are exposed to the mosquitoes that spread malaria; there are major epidemics for almost six months in the year. Malaria kills large numbers of children and pregnant women throughout South Sudan. Nutrition is often poor in rural areas; the people's immunity to a range of diseases is compromised, and children become anemic. Children who are anemic have a weakened capacity to withstand infection; children who share utensils and sleeping quarters with other children might acquire tuberculosis, and go on to infect others. But they will be undiagnosed for years, perhaps not until the disease reaches fatal levels, by which time it is too late to seek help at a faraway clinic. Hundreds of thousands of the South Sudanese die in this manner every year, uncounted by the state. There are no birth and death registers; babies enter the world and exit from it without ever becoming known to the state that collects their relatives' taxes. But above all, Ror Col constantly worries about security, about the ethnic and sectional warfare that beleaguers rural South Sudan. Peace processes reached by the political élite rarely translate into stability in the lives of everyday people.

However, despite these problems, life in Ror Col is defined by established mechanisms of social control and social obligations. Resources are shared; one's good name in the community is far more important than material possessions; people are ready to come to the aid of those in greater need than themselves; and child-rearing is a communal responsibility. Access to justice, or suppression of aggression, is achieved through reconciliation and compensation for bloodletting. Such "blood wealth" is practiced among many ethnic groups in South Sudan and elsewhere across Africa. If someone is killed, the family of the perpetrator must pay reparations – the "blood price" – to the family of the slain. Compensation might be made in the form of cattle; between twenty and thirty heads, depending on the sex and age of the victim, and whether the killing was deliberate or an accident. This too is being reconfigured by the constitutional requirements that place criminal law, especially homicide, in the jurisdiction of state or county judges, far away from the chiefs. As chiefs are the justice authority nearest to the rural people, and given that they have been stripped of their authority, this new constitutional conundrum has left many people in a legal quandary throughout rural South Sudan.

Kinship networks are considered the pillars on which society stands; every single person is accounted for through kinship lines. These expectations and obligations define who marries into which family, and who shares sacrificial meat with whom. Rituals and rites are enforced through religious beliefs and the threat of loss of face and reputation, a highly valued commodity. It has been suggested that these social norms have been disrupted by war and other external factors, but the inhabitants of Ror Col have not relinquished any of them. They cannot afford to, especially in times of turmoil, when the system that maintains order and welfare is most needed.

The Dinka describe times of political instability as *riak e piny* or *piny aci riak*; "the land has become spoiled." Some have blamed *riak e piny* for every social upheaval; some have used *riak e piny* to justify behavior that contravenes social norms. Social scientists and historians have suggested that the fabric of social order might have been deliberately broken, to allow for certain actions like violence against women and children to occur, and blaming the war for everything. But there is a well-know anecdote about a wise Dinka man who, in response to the suggestion of a link between war and a shift in behavior, retorted that *piny ace riak*. Nothing spoils the land, only human beings are spoiled, meaning that the problem is moral decay and disregard for the norms that govern behavior.

This suggests that communities become more resistant to change when their moral universe is violently assaulted, from the fear that allowing change threatens the fabric of their existence. Political instability, security failures, the reduction of resources and the reconfiguration of social networks might drive the loss of the norms that guard social cohesion, but the reverse may also be true; society can be kept relatively resilient, more capable of survival, by adherence to those practices.

This is the backdrop to my story of life in rural South Sudan amidst violent conflict. A mix of complaints about how war has disrupted the social fabric of society, prompting people to advocate more robust adherence to what they believe are the basic threads of a decent life, and attempts to explain new and unacceptable behaviors such as sexual violence and theft, the natural concomitants of conflict. All over the country, it is unclear where the lines separating old values and new war-induced practices lie, even though this is a daily topic of heated discussion. But within this mix are delicate threads that hold the community together despite their altered social landscape.

When the liberation war started in 1983, its location, deep in the forest and close to the swamps of the Nile, insulated Ror Col from the ravages of Khartoum's counter-insurgency campaigns. It quickly became a hiding place for the various rebel forces that eventually formed the opposition forces of the SPLA. Through the second round of north-south civil war, because of the vast distances opposition armies had to cross on foot, Ror Col became Sudan's place of "Good Hope," the main rest station along the route from Greater Bahr el Ghazal to Upper Nile, en route to Ethiopia. As the SPLA developed between 1983 and 1987, the inhabitants of Ror Col bore the brunt of feeding the droves of South Sudanese youth from the region escaping the Sudanese army's command to join the newly established SPLA.

The village was caught in an unavoidable dilemma. Its inhabitants had to create a variety of tactics to cope with a war they barely understood. On the one hand were the brutal practices of an army they were told had been created in their interest, to liberate them from Arab control. On the other were their meager resources; barely enough for them to survive, let alone feed bands of passing soldiers for years. Households hid many of their possessions so that when soldiers came through, they could plead poverty. Families made sure to coordinate their responses when soldiers asked for food; contradictory statements about where the cattle were could land a household in trouble, and expose property that might be confiscated. These – utterly justified – tactics starkly contradicted the established norms of behavior. Food sharing, generosity, and displaying possessions were a source of pride. Being too quick to admit to being poor was something no one was keen to do. Maintaining social norms under such dire circumstances meant depletion of the household's resources, above all cattle, but to act poor was to dishonor one's family.

On their passage through the region to the war front, the SPLA collected a war tax in the form of food supplies, poultry and small livestock, justifying the tax on the grounds that this was a people's army fighting a cause that would benefit all the South Sudanese. Communities developed a variety of ways to spread the cost of war among as many families as possible, or evade the tax altogether. Through these maneuvers, many social issues revealed themselves, allowing members of these communities to comment on the decline or resilience of their society's moral integrity. Some of the responses to new situations, such as the war tax, were considered to fall within the kind of behaviors that would ruin a reputation. Evading the war tax came to be seen as a cunning but acceptable reaction, whereas failing to feed a victim of famine, remained in the realm of the abhorred. People had to reclassify historically unacceptable social behaviors as permissible. It was a test of how much society could hang on to its norms.

The resources available were quickly categorized into the expendable, such as chickens, grains, nuts and valuables, such as livestock. A household might quickly offer small pieces of food to pre-empt soldiers' demands for more. If the household were asked to feed an entire company of soldiers, perhaps hundreds of men, this could mean the slaughtering of several oxen in a single night. When news came of the approach of a large swarm of soldiers, livestock were often driven far away from the village to prevent families losing a bull, a ram or several goats to the hungry and aggressive crowds. Young women and men were often forced to carry the army supplies on their heads and shoulders for hours on end, until they reached a certain location where another group of civilians relieved them and they could return home. The use of violence or threats to force these food and equipment hauls was not uncommon. Many people experienced brutality at the hands both of new recruits on their way to training, and returning soldiers on their way back from Ethiopia to the war fronts in northern Bahr el Ghazal.

But although horrendous stories of beating and forced labor abounded, an array of humorous stories have resulted from these interactions, indicating the tenuous relationship. One tells of a soldier who found a woman preparing a small meal for her household. The woman offered the soldier some peanuts, hoping that would persuade him not to expect a portion of what she was cooking. The soldier quickly ate the peanuts but then said: "Thanks for rescuing me, I was starving and so weak, but now I am strong enough to wait for what you are preparing." Another tale speaks of a woman who, when asked by a vaccination team, could not say how old her daughter was. People in rural South Sudan rarely know anyone's age, since no one keeps birth registers and the calendar generally only refers to major events an area may have witnessed. The puzzled woman looked around and said: "What a strange thing to ask. How am I supposed to know how many years it has been since she was born? I think the child was born in the year when all the goats were being eaten." (The year all the goats were eaten in Bahr el Ghazal region is generally thought to mean 1986, when the SPLA, newly returned from training in Ethiopia, was deployed there to fight on the Darfur and Kordofan front against the nomadic Arab cattle herders who had wreaked havoc in South Sudan as Khartoum's counter-insurgency proxy armies.)

Stories of generosity, kindness and a sense of obligation and indebtedness among the civilian population and the new recruits and trained soldiers were also numerous. Some of them were moving, revealing the human capacity to look past the immediate circumstances. One story, told to me by a young man who lived in another village in the Jonglei area, through which the recruits had passed, went like this. A young volunteer from northern Bahr el Ghazal, on his way to Ethiopia, arrived in the village extremely hungry. He approached a homestead to ask for food, but knowing that the family would most likely have no food to share, only asked to be allowed to go into the cattle byre, where there might be rodents he could catch. He intended to hunt for a hedgehog, a rodent that no Dinka person would eat under normal circumstances. The family felt contrite that this young man had been driven by hunger to demean himself to the point of eating a hedgehog. The head of that household stopped him from going into the byre and invited him to sit down, instructing his wife to quickly milk one of the cows. The young man was given a nice meal of milk in a gourd. Appreciating the generosity of this family in sharing their meager food, the young man stayed for some time and became close to the children of the household. After a while, when he continued his journey to Bilpam in Ethiopia, the SPLA's training center, he left with a heart full of gratitude. After training, he was deployed in South Sudan. On his way there, he passed by Jonglei to visit the family that had shown him such utmost kindness. He brought gifts of clothing, as it had become extremely difficult for the rural South Sudanese to find clothes. Most people had only rags throughout the 1990s, when international trade was blocked by the war. Through mutual generosity, a true relationship was forged and the children of the family, one of whom told me this story, became the volunteer's brothers and sisters. The soldier later met the ultimate fate on the war front near Juba in 1995. Many say that stories of this kind are the stuff through which South Sudan's independence was made possible.

Ror Col is a Dinka community; members of South Sudan's largest ethnic group. It sits close to the border of Unity state, an area inhabited by the Nuer, another Nilotic group, second to the Dinka in population size, who share many of the resources central to the livelihoods of the two groups. They also share a history of rivalry and confrontation that revolves around cattle and the grazing plains of the Nile tributaries. Despite the history of violence, mutual expansionism and recurrent attempts by one to conquer the other, they have successfully managed their relationship, with varying degrees of regard for their mutual interests. They have confronted each other in deadly conflicts as far back as anyone can remember, but they have also engaged in reconciliation that has served them well, creating stability, property compensation and religious ceremonies believed to cleanse their communities from the perceived supernatural wrath and pollution that results from the taking of human life.

At times of lulls in conflict, cordial relations have been created in a variety of ways. Women have historically been used as a medium for cementing ethnic-relations through inter-ethnic marriage, and chiefs and spiritual leaders have forged political and military alliances and made peace. Traditional chiefs are particularly quick to engage in politically motivated marital alliances, or absorption of people they like. These relations have been called on for protection during war, to trace abducted children, or to return stolen cattle. Dinka families or people have been absorbed into Nuer communities, and vice versa. Both sides commonly remark, although it is sometimes contested, that many of the prominent Nuer traditional leaders are of Dinka origin, either born to Dinka mothers or simply absorbed, due to the Nuer's penchant for, and ability to, protect and absorb anyone they trust as a friend or as guest.

The two communities are also connected by spiritual beliefs and practices. A Dinka couple that cannot conceive a child might seek blessings from a well-known Nuer spear-master or prophet. If luck strikes, and a child is conceived and born, that child may be named according to the instructions of the spear-master, to reflect their struggle to conceive and the ritual that delivered the child; a life-time connection is forged between the families. Such an alliance could develop into a kinship; visits between the two families become very frequent, even across battle lines. The relationship can be invoked in the exchange of favors, property and members seeking refuge.

These time-tested methods of coexistence, mutual benefits and reconciliation have been grossly affected by three decades of war, and the erosion of the traditional war ethos and weapons in favor of more destructive, gun-dominated confrontations. Ordinary people on both sides wonder how this came about and how they can restore the old ways. But the restoration of "traditions" is now only a dream. Both groups' traditional worlds, and their old worldviews, have been so reconfigured by state politics that "very little is left to be called a tradition these days," remarked a Nuer chief whom I interviewed in Nairobi. Another Nuer elder I interviewed in 2010, near Mayom, a town in Western Upper Nile (renamed Unity state by Khartoum), close to the border with Warrap state, described the social change thus:

> Where there was a spear, there is now a gun; where there was word of mouth between the chiefs, there are now letters exchanged by our educated sons to send messages that we in the rural areas cannot read. Telephones are used to circumvent the old channels familiar to us and any coward can use this medium to drum up the rumors into war slogans... Where there was once an elder with revered spiritual capacities living among us to make timely decisions, there is now a *payam* administrator, a county commissioner or a governor who lives far away in the town and we can't reach him so easily and yet his instructions reach us anytime; and where there were mechanisms to deter theft, it is now OK among our educated children to view stealing as a sign of intelligence and savvy dealings ... The world we live in now is a jungle, beyond our

control, a new world system that applauds theft ... something is
broken but we do not know what it is or how to fix it.

At the start of the war, large numbers of recruits for the SPLA
walked through the village of Ror Col, one of the last Dinka villages
on the north-eastern edge of western Dinka before Nuer territory.
Ordinary people did not know that a southern opposition movement was being created to fight the north, and many could not
understand why so many Dinka youth were crossing Nuer territory,
heading east. The young recruits expected, and demanded, that
the villagers shoulder the cost of war, both literally, by helping the
army of volunteers carry their supplies, and practically, by giving
the young would-be liberation fighters enough food to sustain
them on the remainder of their journey through Upper Nile. The
Nuer territory is historically hostile to the Dinka, and the soldiers
knew they might not meet with the same sympathies on the rest
of the journey to Ethiopia. Indeed, hundreds of the young Dinka
volunteers perished on the way, dying of diseases made worse by
malnutrition. Others abandoned their mission, and dispersed in
the direction of Bahr el Ghazal. They did not join the SPLA until
much later, when the first batch of trained soldiers was deployed
in the territory in 1986.

Others, perhaps the majority of those who died in Upper Nile,
were killed by the Nuer, who were suspicious about the motives of
the Bahr el Ghazal youth trekking through their territory. Large
numbers were also killed by the Nuer for reasons of political disagreements between the SPLA and the Anya-nya II opposition
movement. Anya-nya II was a predecessor of the SPLA, composed
of prominent veterans of the previous north-south (1955–1972)
conflict who were unhappy with the Addis Ababa accord that had
ended that round of war. Anya-nya II had been organizing for a few
years to fight for the separation of southern Sudan, but the leaders

of what became the SPLA had a different approach to liberation. Their disagreement became extremely violent; most of the leadership of Anya-nya II was killed, including Akuot Atem, Samuel Gaitut and Abdalla Chuol. Although Anya-nya II was multi-ethnic, this confrontation took on an ethnic angle. Nuer and Dinka were pitted against one another, leading to massacres of Dinka youth that almost destroyed the chance of creating a unified southern movement ready to take on the north. But John Garang and his camp prevailed; the sad and deadly Any-nya II affair was closed and left behind, in the interest of a unified southern front. Closed, but hardly forgotten by the families of the fallen fighters. This time period continues to be occasionally invoked, especially in the competing narratives of who suffered the most, as the South Sudanese continue to trade accusations about the targeting of civilians.

The leaders of the two groups took different approaches to their shared goal of liberation. The SPLA talked of liberating all Sudan from Khartoum's maladministration, and Anya-nya II wanted to liberate the south and set up an independent state. The confusion resulted in the lives of many sons of Ror Col, and thousands of other innocent lives, including prominent and dedicated nationalists among the Anya-nya II leaders, being wasted. For a decade, the women and men of Ror Col asked the political leaders of the south what had happened to the children "taken from us to fight your war," or the children "lured out of our hands with lies that they were being sent to Ethiopia for education ... if they have died, where are they buried?"

Freedom came; but none of the leaders came to answer these questions. No one made themselves available, anywhere in the country, to engage with the citizens. Everything had been done in the name of freedom, and it was every citizen's responsibility to do their bit. But "if we are now free as we are told, is there going to be any recognition for them as fallen heroes worth a mention in the books about the history of this country?" asked a young man from Ror Col. Some of the young men who perished in the mayhem have now been given wives by their families, according to the Dinka practice of ghost marriage, and the community wonders whether their children, posthumously born to fallen liberators, could be given something by the government as recognition for the roles of their fathers in the liberation process. "We need these fatherless children to at least know that their fathers did not die in vain?" said a woman from Ror Col.[4]

Ror Col paid a heavy tax for a war over much of which its inhabitants had no control, and only a vague understanding of its causes. The rifts between the Khartoum government and the south-based opposition were analyzed and articulated by the urban, more formally educated, class of the South Sudanese, but not translated for the rest of the people beyond the popular notion of Arab domination. Even the more philosophically sophisticated SPLM, and its many offshoots, did not wholly succeed in mean-ingfully educating the people about its goals. Ror Col had heard much about Khartoum's intent to Arabicize and Islamicize, and about the atrocities committed by Khartoum's forces in northern areas of southern Sudan. But none of Khartoum's policies and practices had reached them; they had no first-hand experience of the ambitions of the Arab Islamic state. They remembered the ravages of the nineteenth-century slave trade and their coercion into British colonial work projects seventy years ago, especially the only road project, which reached the district headquarters some fifty miles away. These historical moments were kept alive in local memory through stories from the chiefs whose fathers had dealt with the state. That they were party to a polity called Sudan was a hazy concept, let alone the notion of complaining about how the state neglected them. There might be an occasional reference to *hakuma*, or government failure, but this rarely went beyond the need for education, police, a health center or, more importantly, a veterinary service, for their livelihood relied on livestock.

The villagers had neither direct communication with the leadership of the new opposition movement nor the advantage of educated sons who could bring home news of local communities' role in this new liberation struggle. They were just hit by demands to contribute to the war effort. They were asked to give material support that was not based on an organized system that assigned to each according to their capacity. The amount of taxation, and the frequency with which it was collected, bore no relationship to what a family could afford. A poll tax had been in place since the colonial era; this was inherited by the Sudanese authorities and enforced through the chiefs, who administered the system on behalf of administrative officers and on to provincial governors before it reached the national treasury. To pay the poll tax, an adult male had to either to work as a migrant laborer in the towns or sell livestock.

In Ror Col and similar villages, selling livestock was the most common way to settle this obligation. It was always justified as payment for services, though no significant service ever reached them. This time, however, the tax was not collected for the central government, nor justified on the basis of service delivery, but defended as the price of freedom, spreading the cost of the war more widely. As they passed through the village on their way to training camps, the recruits asked politely at first: "beg for it, do not take it by force, but do not let go of it, liberate it from its owner." This particular expression was attributed to John Garang as part of the instructions he gave to the fighting forces as a way to rein in potential violence against civilians. It was a plea from the leader to his subordinates to think of the people as the biggest resource for the war; that every fighter must keep in mind the importance of taxing within reason. But when they were refused, the soldiers helped themselves to whatever they could find, from cows, to goats, sheep, chickens and grain. They were even more aggressive on their way back to the war front after their training in Ethiopia. No one could object to the increasing demands that everyone had to do their part for the greater good of the south's quest for the greater share of Sudan's national pie; all were expected to contribute. The more aggressive the collection became, the more jokes about it. When robbed by an SPLA soldier, a woman might say, "my property was liberated from me," mocking what the concept of liberation had become. Many citizens came to think that the "liberators" did not know what the word actually meant, especially in view of the corruption and the state violence that plagued the country after independence.

The village not only paid in material terms, but also in labor, as able-bodied men and women were recruited to haul food and supplies. They also paid in human life; many of the young con-scripts taken to Ethiopia for training did not come home from the many war fronts of Sudan. Some crossed the country, serving in such disparate places as Equatoria, Southern Blue Nile, Upper Nile and as far west as Darfur. Some survivors did not return home for twenty years, bringing harrowing stories of surviving dangerous river crossings, battling wild animals, eating anything they could find and enduring thirst, hunger, disease and violence. I have met so many survivors, who have spoken to me about what some described as their deferred childhood, the dreams they had to put on hold because John Garang called them to the fight. Some talk of now having no life to speak of, and no future equal to their suffering. Others sing heart-wrenching songs about their journeys, some woven into war songs, and others lamenting what they had fought for.

In the summer of 2005, I met Bol Kuek, a young soldier of about thirty years old, assigned to me by the army commander to accom-pany me on my journey to Ror Col from Pan Acier, another Dinka village, in what is now Gogrial East County of Warrap State. This was some two days' walk, and Bol Kuek had many painful stories to tell about his time as a liberation fighter. This is an excerpt from his story about the early days, when the SPLA was taking shape:

It all started like a joke. I was a boy of no more than eight years of age when we started to hear that the war was starting again. Of course I did not understand the "again" part, you know, because I had no idea about the other war that took place before I was born. Our village is so remote, and once in a while someone would come passing through from the direction of Aliek or Lietnhom [Aliek and Lietnhom are the nearest towns to Ror Col] and would report that the Arabs have burnt this or that town, or the army in Wau have killed students who were protesting about something, or the Arabs were bent on piping our oil to Port Sudan. And then groups of young men started coming through the village, and they were talking about how we should all join up, lest the Arabs catch and kill us. Sometimes the very young ones like me were often put in school and were not allowed to go to the war yet. The seriousness of the matter was woven into local jokes that seemed to have been meant to spur us to join the gathering rebellion, despite our young ages. One such joke asked which young people were brave enough to go and defend their country and which ones were cowards. The girls would not speak to you if you were still hanging around. They would call us "the seeds," the ones who are sparing their lives for the future survival of the race, a grave insult indeed. Of course I joined up and was happy to do so. I was not initiated by *gaar,* scarring on my forehead at this time, though my lower teeth had just been removed [both are ritual practices of initiation into appropriate age sets, including adulthood by scarification]. But we were excited about the prospect of being given guns and we could not wait. It made you feel like a man to imagine holding a gun.

We set out, a large number of us, many boys from different parts of Dinka territory, commanded by a few adults who had escaped with their guns from the police force in Wau or defected from the Sudan army. There were very few people with guns in their bands. But after we had been walking for weeks, hardly eating anything and sometimes being bullied by bigger guys who were already trying to assert dominance over the younger ones, or by some of these ex-soldiers who were already self-promoting to officer ranks, the feeling of manhood had all but dissipated and I wanted to get back home. The violence of some of these "officers" against civilians along the way as they collected food by force turned my stomach, it still does to this day. We were already divided into regiments and command structures before we ever saw the training camp. We had to take permission from our commanding officers to do anything. We were attacked several times by Anya-nya II and so we were scattered and some died. My thoughts of turning around to go home became more concrete in my head, but to go back is just as dangerous as going forward. There were three other guys from my village in the group who had all survived the attacks, and we decided to stick together so we can make it to Bilpam, the famed training camp in Ethiopia. That journey was worse than everything else that I would go through later on, including the battles I have fought in, the sickness, the hunger and the terrible food we have had to eat over the years in training or following our deployment. It was even more painful for the simple fact that it was our brothers, the Nuer, who denied us food and attacked us, when we had been told that all the black people would unite against Nimeiri. Those who died long before they ever saw the enemy, and at the hands of their supposed brethren, what were their lives lost for? And look at me, I did not get any education, my village remains poor as ever, so many of my mates from there died in this war and Ror Col continues to suffer the violence we were supposed to have ended by kicking the Arabs out of the south. The Bul Nuer still raid us for cattle, they get guns from the many armed militias that roam the southern parts of Unity state and my people have no protection from the SPLA, even though a few of us from there serve in the SPLA, but we are all mere soldiers and have no say within the force. We are hoping that the peace agreement that John Garang signed with Bashir will bring something good for my village.

Altogether, Bol Kuek and I shared two full weeks of walking, and many nights of camping, during which time he made me laugh, cry, become angry and hopeful. He told me stories of travel to Ethiopia, military training, deployment in South Sudan, the pain of hunger and the jokes the soldiers told each other in the heat of battle to stave off fear and encourage one another, so that no one lost hope or was overcome by battle scenes, sounds and smells. His description of his experiences also made me feel painfully guilty. I had joined the revolution very early on and then abandoned it. I had had my childhood, the chance to attend school in Egypt, and to become a professor in the USA, while he and all the other fighters protected my freedom and liberated my country. If I ever lose my moral compass and humility, this experience will always restore it.

Bol Kuek remained on active duty and was wounded in 2014 while fighting in Jonglei, in the South Sudanese civil war. The strongest indictment against the political leaders who started the war, or allowed it to escalate, is that soldiers who gave their best in the most difficult conditions should return home wounded, or be killed in a senseless war, defeating the whole purpose of independence.

Around 1986, after years of training in Ethiopia, many of the young men from the greater Bahr el Ghazal region were deployed back there, to serve in the war front against Khartoum's forces. Many returned on foot through Equatoria, Lakes, and up to Bahr el Ghazal. These journeys took years; they had to fight their way through, sometimes against the SAF, and at other times against Khartoum-sponsored South Sudanese hostile to the SPLA. But others came back the way they had left, and were attacked by the Nuer on their way, due to complicated disagreements and wrangling among the SPLA leaders who wanted to liberate all Sudan from tyranny, and some southern leaders, especially in Anya-nya II, who wanted the south to secede. Ror Col was once again a rest stop where the soldiers broke their journey, but the mood of the fighters was even less merciful than the time of their outward trip. The people of Ror Col had to bear the brunt of the unhappy and sometimes convoluted politics of liberation.

The SPLA scored many military victories against the SAF, at times inflicting humiliating defeats. By 1987, they had gained much territory in the south and confined the SAF to a few garrison towns. Much of the countryside was now dubbed as "liberated areas," but the SPLA remained entirely reliant on the civilian population for food, logistics and shelter. Although many supporters suggested that the soldiery should engage in productive activities during the rainy season, when the fighting was often low-key, the SPLA and its political wing, the SPLM, instead chose to remain a serious burden on the people, a decision that had serious consequences.

Unlike other liberation movements such as the Eritrean People's Liberation Front (EPLF), which was known and admired for its self-reliance with regard to food, medical services, acquisition of weapons, and so on, the SPLA was incapable of running the liberated areas in ways that promised the people it could become a credible replacement for the hated Khartoum governments. The SPLA also had a very poor concept of the justice system in the liberated areas. Military commanders were given the right to act as judges, and sometimes deliberately undermined the better-established and time-tested customary law. Chiefs were shunned or fired, in favor of SPLA appointees, creating a disconnection between the people and the traditional authorities long instrumental in justice and social welfare. Civilians were abused, not just by having their food and property confiscated, but also by daily threats, beatings and humiliation. There was little justice; soldiers escaped the consequences of their crimes, including rape and robbery, justified as part of the consequences of war. The behavior of the SPLA was most chaotic in Equatoria between 1984 and 1991, when many atrocities were committed against the civilian population. Although the SPLA had standing orders against sexual assault and confiscation of private property, it remained easy for soldiers who committed such crimes to go unpunished.

Despite rocky civil-military relations, the political and military leadership could always deflect attention away from the conduct of the SPLA forces by emphasizing that their suffering was a price the people had to pay to be free. People who complained about the behavior of SPLA were depicted as less nationalistic and uncommitted to the southern Sudan cause. The movement remained popular, or it at least saw itself as popular, particularly in the face of the increasing intensity of Khartoum's attack on civilian targets. The terror of the high-altitude bombings from Russian-made Antonovs was a strong driver for the SPLA's popularity, especially in Upper Nile, Bahr le Ghazal and along the border with Uganda and parts of Eastern Equatoria, where the attacks were most vicious. The more violent the Sudanese counter-insurgency efforts became, the more the southern Sudanese were willing and determined to focus on the war with the north and not on abuses by the SPLA, especially after June 1989, when the National Islamic Front took power in Khartoum and committed the government to a military solution.

In January 1990, the SPLA became more aggressive and successful beyond the "liberated areas." It shelled Juba, although the leadership decided not to take southern Sudan's biggest town, moved its forces into the Nuba Mountains and into Southern Blue Nile. Compared to its 1985–86 offensive in Equatoria, the conduct of the SPLA was now more orderly. Despite the challenges of the liberation effort, much went well for the southern Sudanese. By the middle of 1991, the SPLA controlled several towns along the Ugandan border, from Nimule to Kaya. It also occupied Yambio in Western Equatoria, and Bor in Jonglei, meaning that it controlled most parts of southern Sudan, other than the major garrison towns such as Juba, Wau, Malakal and Torit. But things began to go wrong; several events combined to create a perfect storm that hit the SPLA and caused a massive setback.

Three of these events were highly devastating. The first was the demise, in May 1991, of the Ethiopian regime known as the Derg, which had been the strongest supporter of South Sudan under Mengistu Hailie Mariam. The Ethiopian government had provided the SPLA with military supplies, training facilities and a safe-haven for soldiers during their eight years of training in Bilpam, Dimma, Bonga and Ponyidu. The strong relationship between the SPLA and the Ethiopian regime became a liability for the southern Sudanese in Ethiopia, as the rebel movements of the Ethiopian People's Revolutionary Democratic Front (EPRDF) and the EPLF combined to defeat the Derg. The southern Sudanese had to flee Ethiopia, as the rebels were hostile to them because of their support for Mengistu. Soon after the change of government in Ethiopia, the SPLA accompanied hundreds of thousands of refugees back into southern Sudan, under attacks by the helicopter gunships of the Sudanese air force.

The second event was the split in the SPLA's leadership of August 1991, a development made all the more devastating by the demise of the Ethiopian government. The split, which had simmered since 1990, deteriorated rapidly after the fall of the Derg. The leaders of the split, Riek and Lam, and many of the senior officers, mainly from Nuer and Shilluk, called for the democratization of the SPLA and a halt to human rights abuses. Although many southern Sudanese thought these claims were legitimate, they opposed them on account of their bad timing, just when the region had made significant progress against Khartoum and was on the verge of victory.

The split was announced in what became known as the "Nasir Declaration." When it failed to overthrow John Garang, the incident led to the third event, the creation of SPLA-Nasir. The struggle for the leadership of the movement frayed into a war with the main SPLA under Garang, dubbed SPLA-Torit. Not only did this hamper the SPLA's capacity to maintain the pace of its victories against Khartoum, it also shook the confidence the southern population had in it, and in its ability to speak collectively. The split, and the military confrontations that ensued, were decried by southerners when the leaders of the warring SPLA factions allowed their competition to draw civilians into the conflict along ethnic lines, leading to vicious massacres of civilians in Bor, and a prolonged conflict between Nuer and Dinka, especially in what became the tri-state border area between Lakes, Warrap and Unity states.[5] This weakness was coupled with increases in Khartoum's indiscriminate attacks on civilians; both tested the resilience of southern Sudan to continue the fight.

This is how Bol Kuek experienced the war of liberation, and how he made sense of the internal dynamics of the SPLA. These events had direct repercussions in his village and other communities, most especially the escalation of the disagreement between the leaders and the drift into ethnic war. Between 1991 and 1998, as the Nuer and Dinka were drawn into confrontation, Ror Col, like all border communities, became a battleground. Bol Kuek was a committed fighter; his conscience and his focus on the purpose of this war against the Sudan's government never wavered. He defended the name of the SPLA but was critical of some of its members' and leaders' actions. He was aware of the dangers of speaking critically, and asked me for assurances that I would keep our conversations anonymous. His narrative, and the comments that he made on a variety of events, are corroborated by other evidence, including interviews with people who have been through similar situations. But his reflections were honest, poignant and moral. He summarized his motives as follows:

> Our individual or communal experiences during the war, the behaviors some of us engaged in, what we have witnessed and we have said to one another, soldier to soldier, civilian to soldier, will never be forgotten and will not be easy to overcome ... it will all stay with us in the most unpleasant manner. Violence, once a part of one's life, is almost always going to be part of one's life. The same goes for a community and most likely for the whole country. People in my village have managed to survive, through sheer resilience (*riel puou*), wit and industriousness in survival skills, but it is tragic that they think the responsibility for their welfare, their health, security, food production and their children's schooling will all be better, now that the peace agreement has been signed. What I know, and going by my experience in the SPLA, is that none of these expectations will materialize and the people will be disappointed. I am disappointed and pained. What do you think will happen when we do not get any of the things that we were promised? Do you think the people in Ror Col and villages like it across southern Sudan will understand the difficulty of running a state, providing basic goods and reining in the widespread insecurity? Do they understand that it might take a very long time before we can receive these services, if ever? I do not think

so. I do not think our leaders will care enough about the remote villages and I do not think the people will wait patiently for that day to come. Instead, I think the disappointments, the incapable and unresponsive public officials, the gigantic challenges facing southern Sudan in the wake of the war, the undisciplined security forces and the horrific memories of the war, will all contribute toward further instability, possibly rebellions. I worry and feel the need to speak up in the hope that some of the leaders might hear the voices of war veterans and act according to the aspirations of the whole population who have done so much so that southern Sudan could assert its will on Khartoum.

In conclusion, when the north-south prolonged conflict ended by the fragile 2005 peace agreement, one of the most immediately expected peace dividends was a sense of security and stability. South Sudan was one of the most war-destroyed places on earth; it had no basic infrastructure, was in desperate need of basic social services and had some of the world's worst human development indicators. An estimated four million people were internally displaced, and three million had died in the previous two decades. Notwithstanding these problems, security for their communities and their property was the issue the South Sudanese expected and hoped the peace agreement would resolve, and do so right away. Improvement in the level of security, and the ability of the state to protect communities, was the measure of the value of the CPA and the commitment of the parties to it. If the South Sudanese were to exhibit pride in the nation, rather than in their regions or tribes, individuals, civil society groups, political parties and foreign NGOs and human rights agencies knew security was the single most expected development and the primary demand of the citizens from their government. The CPA may have ended the war, but it also produced political and military disagreements within the south. These disagreements had a direct impact on Ror Col, and villages like it, and prolonged their suffering. Disgruntled members of the SPLA staged rebellions, supposedly against the leadership in Juba, capital of South Sudan, but they picked the softest targets to make their point, randomly attacking villages and looting their cattle as their way of declaring their unhappiness. Two rebellions relevant to the story of Ror Col were staged by Gatluak Gai and Peter Gadet, both from Western Upper Nile, an area bordering the north-eastern part of Bahr el Ghazal.

If the country is to restore stability, unite the people and become as prosperous as its citizens expect it to; if it is to create good policies, strong political and military leadership and fair civil society, its people need to explore their histories and use them as a starting point for reconciliation, attention to veterans and provision of justice for the communities and individuals who have done so much to make South Sudanese independence possible.

This chapter has used one village's and one person's experience of the war and its impact on the society. Ror Col's and Bol Kuek's stories reveal the underbelly of a prolonged conflict and show how people live with alien realities such as feeding armies and protecting their property without being persecuted. Their stories tell us that war is ugly, something no one would wish for, but since rural people cannot prevent it, they have to find ways to live with it.

4

POLITICAL RIVALRIES, THE NEW WARS AND THE CRUMBLING SOCIAL ORDER

A great deal of policy analysis and academic research over the past decade has tried to understand the political economy of violence, unpack the conflict-politics-social order nexus, and bring the voices of ordinary citizens into the discussions on the new state of South Sudan. Interviews and opinion surveys conducted between 2005 (the CPA) and 2011 (South Sudan's secession) reveal a mix of jubilation and wariness about this momentous political transition. South Sudan's independence came amid questions of whether the historical experiences in the context of liberation, which had long united the old south, would endure in the new South Sudan. Could this young country become a unified political, cultural and social entity? Could it become a nation, not just a geographic political creation?

From the nationalist perspective that saw secession as paramount, such questions were considered absurd and reactionary by the country's leadership. These leaders thought that no challenges of statecraft were too large to prevent the drive to be free. But for many ordinary people, whose aspirations were mundane, independence alone was not enough. The unity of purpose that kept the south together as a political unit was, in a sense, a negative unity, primarily driven by opposition to the north, by what southerners did not want, rather than by who they were. Observers feared old ethnic discords would rear their ugly heads in the absence of the most unifying factor, the war between Sudan and South Sudan. The history of the new country was replete with rivalries – both ethnic and ideological – for power and resources. As these rivalries intensified in early 2013, it appeared inevitable that the contest for power would be very messy, and perhaps detrimental to the viability of South Sudan as a unified state. The result was an outbreak of a vicious conflict that shocked the country and the whole world.

In this chapter, I shall describe the root causes and the historical and cultural context of South Sudan's post-independence civil war. This war, which erupted in December 2013, pitted President Salva Kiir's government against forces loyal to the rebel leader Riek Machar, the former vice president. Riek had been sacked in July 2013, leaving him angered by the loss of his public office and powers, his loss of control over the nation's resources and by what he saw as a loss of vision and direction for the ruling party and consequently for the country. He felt the young state was quickly becoming a failed one, and he blamed the president. While his dismissal might not have been the direct cause of the rebellion, it was undoubtedly one of the major factors that triggered the complex conflict.

This chapter also deals with the dynamics of the new conflict in the three states of Upper Nile, Unity and Jonglei. I shall consider how much of the gruesome violence that occurred in these states was due to anger about the violence in Juba that sparked the civil war, how much emanated from shattered ethnic relations and how much was born of fear and the need for survival among the young fighters, especially the famed White Army of the Lou Nuer, who unhesitatingly flocked to the battlefield on Riek's side. Was the White Army fighting for Riek or did Riek subvert their anger about the Juba incident for his own agenda?

I shall examine the make-up of the fighting forces, the commanding officers of both sides, the ethnic composition and ethnic relations, the political structures of the rebel movement, the position of the civilian population on the war and the war's impact on their lives and livelihoods. In the course of the civil war, which lasted nearly two full years before its negotiated settlement, much violence was meted out against fighters and non-fighters alike, including reports of almost-unprecedented levels of violence against women and girls.[1] The chapter also looks at displacement, human rights abuses, the targeting of civilians, the humanitarian situation and the role of UNMISS. The chapter will also review international responses to the crisis, with an eye to identifying prospects for future reconciliation, peace-building, development, and donor and investor trust in the reliability of South Sudan as a promising member of the community of nations.

I also describe why this round of war broke out, what sparked it, and why it was not prevented, despite its near predictability. Both within South Sudan, and among the international community, there was an awareness that tension had been brewing for some time and the situation was certain to explode. How true is the accusation that the ruling SPLM and the government had mismanaged the building crises in the weeks leading up to the country's implosion on December 15, 2013?[2] How much of this war was directly related to the struggle for power in a ruling party gone awry, and how was it rooted in South Sudan's long liberation struggle? How much it relates to the "leadership crisis" in the country and how much is to do with the failure of government institutions to discharge their duties? How much of the war's spread, from its epicenter in Juba to the whole of the Greater Upper Nile region, a third of the country, is to do with the people's disappointment in the government's ability to provide peace and independence "dividends?" Was the trigger of violence in Juba totally unrelated to the power struggle at the center, and more to how socially and economically marginalized rural young people saw the outbreak of violence as their opportunity to register their dissatisfaction with the way the country was run by the SPLM and its liberation "heroes?" Or perhaps the war was about memories of previous ethnic conflicts? People created survival strategies based on relationships that developed over the years of liberation struggle, a process that left behind fractured ethnic relations and a fragile security situation. This chapter will also attempt to look into what in the social fabric of South Sudanese communities might have broken, allowing heinous and gruesome acts of violence to be committed against defenseless people, as human rights groups have reported. I will particularly look at the experiences of women, gender relationships and sexual violence.

One of the greatest fallacies that humanity seems always to have pursued is the idea that freedom, that elusive and slippery concept, is worth dying for; that men should sacrifice everything in the cause of national freedom, or to protect the freedom they believe they have attained. Like many who have fought for their nation's freedom, the South Sudanese had to justify the sacrificing of huge numbers of people – more than three million – in the course of two independence wars.[3] While there is still debate about whether the wars were about separation or reform within a united Sudan, the concept of freedom was always the centerpiece of the north-south confrontations; a freedom the south was determined to attain but one the north was unwilling to grant or understand. The situation was compounded by southern claims of victimhood; that southern Sudan, indeed all the peripheral regions of the old Sudan, was excluded from its government's obligations for the welfare of the citizen. But whatever the goals of such wars, all were characterized by massive death and destruction, and conducted in the name of freedom, regardless of the form that freedom came in. The wars for freedom in all the Sudan's peripheries were fought to protect the freedom, the welfare, the lives, the civic rights and property of the citizens in these regions, but the price these peripheries had to pay in terms of human lives for these rights has been more immense than can be quantifiably justified. For many South Sudanese, it became increasingly clear over the past sixty years that these rights were worth far more than the risks of losing lives. These lives could be justified with regards to the north-south confrontations. But once the south became an independent state, the question was now whether the civil war within an independent South Sudan could be justified in terms of rights and freedoms.

Southern demands for separation, or other forms of autonomy, were first coherently and concertedly articulated in 1947. But all such demands were thwarted by British colonial authorities throughout the Anglo-Egyptian Condominium rule, and by the northern Sudanese leaders after independence in 1956. This triggered wars, beginning in the 1950s, over autonomy for what was then southern Sudan. Over time, their demands tended toward full separation, as it became ever more evident that the established élite of Sudan was unconvinced about the need for reform, or the accuracy and legitimacy of the southern claims of marginalization. Northern Sudanese intellectuals, and the ruling élite, dubbed the southern grievances *mushkillat al-janub*, "the southern problem."[4] Although the southern determination to either get reform or leave the union was clear, not until after the southern referendum did many people in northern Sudan realize how unified southerners were on this issue.

Since the CPA, and more particularly since South Sudan's independence, mourning the deaths of the millions swallowed by the furnace of the liberation wars has always concluded with the consoling phrase, "at least we liberated our country." But two years into independent statehood, inexplicably, the South Sudanese entered a civil war. This war might also have been in the name of freedom, but it was a more difficult freedom to quantify. Was it the freedom the government wanted to protect against the rebellion that they insisted had violated the constitution, or a freedom the new opposition wanted to wrest from a government they accused of murder and tyranny? Or perhaps it was a freedom the ordinary citizen wished they could have against state security forces. The north and south of the old Sudan were set on a collision course and no side was willing to flinch. Few of the southern leaders ever thought about what an independent south would look like, and what it would need to become a nation-state. In 2016, after two years of meaningless and deadly fighting, the leaders of South Sudan once again began to talk of peace, unity and prosperity. But their talk had a certain nonchalance about the deaths that had happened in the civil war; an air that this conflict will also be resolved, at some point, like all the south-on-south confrontations that have come and gone. The attitudes of the leaders revealed more about the degrees to which they were willing to go in order to achieve their political goals, regardless of what life and property was being destroyed in the process of achieving these ambitions.

How these leaders will justify this new loss of human life is something future generations will have to reflect on. In view of how the losses of the north-south wars were mourned upon independence, how will the South Sudanese conclude their mourning for the victims of a South-on-South post-independence violence? Was it freedom that consumed more than ten thousand lives in the first five months of the post-independence conflict, or was it the ambitions of individual leaders? Was any goal, political or resource, worth all these lives? More pointedly, what kind of freedom were the South Sudanese fighting for during this new conflict, after they had collectively worked so hard and so long to wrest their "freedom" from that most formidable opponent, the government of the Republic of Sudan?

Consider these statements, both made by people angered by what many in South Sudan have described as "senseless war:" "These rebel fighters keep talking about freedom and they never say freedom from what," remarked one resident of Juba. "I do not understand what sovereign freedom these people are talking about when they are only supporting a failed killer government," remarked an anti-government displaced person. This chapter chronicles the start of the conflict, what the rebels said about why they fought and how the government reacted to the rebel claims. I do not attempt to pass judgment about the legitimacy of either side's claims, but simply describe the conduct of this conflict from the perspective of a long history of South Sudan's collective liberation struggle.

When the new war erupted in Juba, a mere two and half years after South Sudan's independence in 2011, its violence, and especially its quick descent into ethnic war, shocked everyone, both those directly caught up in it and those watching from afar. But the sudden outburst of violence came as no surprise to anyone who had paid attention to the political, social, security and economic dynamics that accompanied the end of the long and treacherous liberation war.[5] It was so unsurprising that some even said it was predictable; that there was visible writing on the wall. All that was needed was the trigger. Others observed that independence alone could not massage away the burdensome legacy of the liberation wars, that the world's newest country needed to come to terms with its history before it could expect to grow, and more work than its leaders acknowledged would be needed if South Sudan were to transform itself into a viable nation. The outbreak of war validated these and other predictions made by analysts, diplomats and historians of conflict in Africa.[6] It might even be said that South

Sudan never really stopped being at war, despite the euphoria of the relative calm that followed the end of the war brokered by the CPA.[7]

This civil war was born of a series of crises, and the blinded leadership was unable either to pre-empt or prevent them. There was a crisis of overconfidence in the leadership's ability to match the people's expectations. There was widespread thinking among the political class that the euphoria of independence would reduce the urgency of people's demands for immediate access to goods and services. There was too much confidence in citizens' willingness to prioritize the nation's stability over their everyday survival; too great an expectation that people would be patient in the face of delays to their peace dividends. There was a crisis of the refusal of the ruling élite to read the writing on the wall, or at least engage in debates with their citizens. There was a crisis of leadership, of decision-making, of articulating national policies of stabilization and management of risks and expectations.

Finally, there was the biggest crisis of all; the lack of a strong history of collective civic action against the leadership in South Sudan. Collective citizen action might have spared the country its plunge into war, or at least prevent the war from taking on an ethnic tint and instead pit the citizens against the state. In this case, the leadership would either have had to change its approach to the citizens' grievances or itself be changed. Unlike in Sudan, where massive uprisings had toppled strong dictatorships severally since independence, the South Sudanese had spent much of the previous fifty years struggling against the governments in the north. The activists and political organizers were bogged down by their opposition to the north and had focused on organizing political parties or armed opposition against Khartoum, denying themselves the chance to organize trades unions, student associations and other professional organizations that could be rallied to challenge the state within the new country. What has now come to be known as civil society was not so developed in South Sudan. The development and effectiveness of such activist organizations was made even more difficult by sectarian divides; very few activists have been able to overcome ethnic affiliations and press for national action. So many citizens in the new country had become too pre-occupied with local communal needs to think nationally. Even when there were individual organizers in some communities who thought of macro-level national issues, they were not able to overcome the fear and the skepticism of people from the opposing communities. Opportunities to organize across ethnic lines did not exist.

There have been many well-documented violent conflicts within the south during the north-south war; wars within war, so to speak. The South Sudanese have an interesting view on these "south-on-south" conflicts. There is a strange debate and controversy among the South Sudanese élite, especially those in government, about the nature of ethnic conflict within the south, as viewed through the prism of the protracted north-south civil war. While the South Sudanese acknowledge the gruesome nature of their ethnic conflicts, many people who view themselves as nationalists, especially those who were openly separatists during the liberation struggle, have tried to downplay the magnitude of these conflicts. This attitude waned in the wake of independence, but it has revived with renewed fervor since the new war started in 2013. The phenomenon of local violence cost countless lives and caused massive destruction, yet many leaders were unwilling to admit its magnitude, at least not to the point of making compromises with each other in order to arrest the destruction and loss of life. Very few of these leaders have publicly admitted and discussed the impact of this conflict on the viability of South Sudan, and the image of the country it presented to the eyes of the citizens and the world.

There were two main reasons for this attitude. The first was a response to the doubts expressed by foreign observers and the

Khartoum government's supporters about the ability of southerners to become a nation. It is a question of whether or not a moral equivalent could be drawn. If deadly ethnic conflicts were occurring among the South Sudanese, the southerners' condemnation of the atrocities committed by the Khartoum-based government could be seen as hypocritical. The second was an attempt to deflect attention from the South Sudanese armies' involvement in these conflicts. After the signing of the CPA, the autonomous government of South Sudan saw increasing ethnic conflict as a challenge to its authority, the credibility of its independent statehood, and the ability of its leadership to hold the country together when the north no longer controlled the political affairs of the south.

Downplaying the scale of ethnic-based violence was part of a wider political game among the leading actors in the north-south wrangling over legitimacy; an exercise in image-making. But maintaining such attitudes during the interim period and after independence, when the Juba government needed to woo its citizens into the nation-building project, was an exercise in denial, in labeling an obvious problem as unimportant rather than acknowledging its existence and seriousness. However, the South Sudanese could not deny the facts about ethnic violence. The facts of violence, death and destruction were self-evident, heart-breaking and debatable whether they were a price worth paying in order to be "free" of the Khartoum government's violence and neglect.

Reports about the levels of violence, including televised images of massacres such as the August 2009 attack by the Lou Nuer on Jikany Nuer in Akobo, painted a clear and grim picture. However, at independence, many political actors were trying both to project the ability of the state to protect its citizens and downplay the scale of suffering in order to maintain national dignity. They feared lest the world thought negatively about the government and the country.

What they forgot was that the image that mattered the most was the one their own people held. The views of the former would pass with time; the views of the latter were vital for building a lasting cohesive nation. For the citizens of South Sudan, it was not about whether the Americans, who had supported independence, were vindicated, but more about the citizen receiving the rewards of the long quest for freedom.

The country's leadership wanted to wish away violent ethnic divides and sell the image that South Sudan would not plunge into civil war straight from the war of liberation, as many rural and marginalized citizens feared. Above all, they wanted to give the lie to international predictions that South Sudan was a weak or failed state. This characterization had haunted the government of the old Sudan, and invited criticism from human rights groups and donor countries for many years. Such a label would tarnish the image and lower the standing of the young country among other nations, and give Khartoum reason to gloat that the South Sudanese were not capable of domesticating peace and would have been better off staying under northern control. The nascent state needed all the help it could get to become viable; and therefore, such an image might discourage foreign investment, much needed and highly anticipated in the wake of independence. Northern Sudanese government officials, academics and laypeople had long suggested that an independent South Sudan could not be viable, that southerners could not unite and that they would fight each other to the finish. In 2011, just before independence, the Al-Jazeera English news television station broadcast a documentary entitled *Sudan: Fight for the Heart of the South*, in which prominent Sudanese personalities weighed in on the debate. Their remarks showed exactly the sort of attitude that has led the South Sudanese leaders to be determined to appear capable, and to show that their country can prove itself.[8]

By dismissing the ethnic wars as minimal, the South Sudanese were attempting to insist that there is unity among its various ethnic nationalities beyond the unity pegged to the history of opposition to the north. Sadly, however, these conflicts were real, destructive and deadly, regardless of how their causes were understood. In 2008 and 2009, there were more deaths in Jonglei State than in the more well-known Darfur crisis.[9] The conflicts were rooted in competition over scarce resources, most often grazing rights and cattle theft, and involved both the larger ethnic groups, such as the Nuer and Dinka, and smaller ones such as the Murle. They also involved confrontations between sections of the same "tribe." One of the deadliest incidents was an attack in Akobo County, involving the Lou section of the Nuer against the Jikany section, which shattered the common view that wars in South Sudan are only inter-ethnic and not intra-ethnic. If members of the same ethnic group could butcher each other, as this incident showed, what is ethnic about the rest of the wars? This is not to say that other wars cannot be termed "ethnic," but this incident was an example of why more massive conflicts, such as the episode in Juba that sparked the civil war, were more complicated than they appear, and that explaining it as strictly ethnic is to entirely miss the point.

For more than thirty years, since the beginning of the second round of fighting between southern Sudan and the north-dominated government of Sudan, descriptions of South Sudan have commonly included phrases such as "war-ravaged," "the poorest place on earth," "the worst humanitarian crisis," "Africa's longest-running war," "run by warlords," "south-on-south massacres," "the biggest development challenge," and more. This fascination with gloomy descriptions contrasts with statements designed to project a positive image of the country: "war-affected but resilient people," "cost of war" and "the price of freedom." As the opposition armies in southern Sudan, the non-state actors, claimed the high moral ground of liberation, they used such language to describe and criticize the actions of the state, the government in Khartoum, asserting the point that unlike rebel armies, the state has an obligation to not engage in acts of gruesome violence, such as were seen in southern Sudan in the 1990s. International activists, human rights groups and the South Sudanese alike used this language to portray the government in Khartoum in an unflattering light. But the South Sudanese leaders have now found themselves being described in the same terms they once used to describe Khartoum. Clamping down on the press, actions of national security agents, arrests and detention without trial and above all corruption in state institutions, are now happening within an independent South Sudan and are being decried as a total contradiction to the message of liberation. How did that happen? What went wrong with the supposedly nationalist and liberationalist language they used to attract the citizenry into the liberation effort?

THE 2013 OUTBREAK OF CONFLICT: WHAT CAUSED THIS CRISIS?

The crisis that began in Juba on a fateful December day and which, within three weeks, erupted across a third of the country, has been explained in numerous ways. It has been described as emanating from a power struggle among the leaders of the SPLM. It has been depicted as sparked by people's disappointment in the leader of their country, who had failed to honor the promises they made during the war and at independence. There was the government's claim that there was an attempted *coup d'état*. Some said it was due to a split in the presidential guard unit of the SPLA. Others claimed it was triggered by unhappiness among elements in the SPLA that did not agree with the policy of amnesties and absorptions of militias which the president had pursued in the name of peace for many years, the "big tent approach" to peace and unity. But the crisis had many deep roots in the history that gave birth to the country. The incident that sparked it might be pinpointed to a specific moment in the weeks or months leading up to the eruption but its rapid spread was undoubtedly fueled by a host of pre-existing problems.

Politicians, former military generals and officers quickly took sides after the outbreak of war. Some rapidly metamorphosed into analysts and critics, chipping in to the debate about what caused the conflict and how it should be resolved. Peter Adwok Nyaba, former minister of higher education, who was sacked along with Vice President Riek when President Kiir replaced his entire cab-inet in July 2013, has offered his version of the "root causes" of the Juba incident. He believes the fighting in Juba was caused by the president chasing his own shadow. The president had become suspicious of his critics, and decided to disarm the Nuer within his presidential guard, the Tiger Battalion, whom he suspected would give Riek Machar a support base should he move for the presidency. The Nuer officers resisted, according to Adwok, and the affair got out of hand.

This explanation is entirely implausible. All the SPLM heavy-weights, including Riek Machar Teny, the deputy chairman and vice president until the wholesale sacking, had criticized the president's "dictatorial tendencies." They had recently seen their party positions dissolved by the chairman, who claimed they had mismanaged the party. Some were among those accused of being involved in an attempted coup, which they were quick to deny. Though it is hard to speak about evidence of a coup, or lack thereof, it was entirely plausible that a plot by a number of politicians to take over the government existed. President Salva Kiir faced growing opposition from a cross-section of politicians who had lost power, but he had previously seemed to respect and tolerate such opposition as a constitutional right, and never hindered it in any way. There was no reason for the president to suddenly falsely accuse his critics of plotting a coup, not least because the politicians were in the midst of the congress of the National Liberation Council, the ruling party's highest organ and the legislative body of the SPLM. Nor is it logical that these groups should suddenly opt for a coup when they could use an accepted political platform in a civil competition for the reins of power.

The squabbles within the ruling party should be explored as part of the genesis of the crisis, especially the reaction of Kiir's government to the calls for reforms made by the party officials, many of them members of the party's political bureau, whom he had fired from both the party leadership and the government. The officials held a press conference on December 6, 2013, at which they accused the President of running the party in ways that violated the party constitution. These party officials had demanded that President Kiir, the chairman of the party, convene a meeting of the political bureau to sort out the differences between the chairman and the membership, and organize the agenda for the meeting of the National Liberation Council, the party's legislative body. But instead of responding to this legitimate constitutional right of the party officials, the president instructed his new deputy, Vice President James Wani Igga, to issue a very crude response, in which he dismissed their claims outright and accused them of being "disgruntled" by their loss of power. This did not sit well with these party officials, as they felt that the president and his aides had insulted them instead of taking their complaints seriously and inviting them to talk.

When the crisis began, the president did not help the situation or the image of his government. He wore his military fatigues when he delivered his statement in the wake of the revolt, thus signaling his readiness for military confrontation. It is fair to say that the demand for reforms within the party, and the president's frustration with these demands, were clear factors in the crisis. Both sides mismanaged this issue and by their actions buried the country in a chaotic war that was to last some years, a war whose point no one could succinctly explain. All parties to it described it as a "senseless war," but none seemed ready to compromise to end it and all parties engaged in terrible acts of atrocity against the civilians.

HOW POLITICAL DISAGREEMENT TURNED VIOLENT

Investigations show that there were two streams of thinking in the quickly forming opposition, and multiple aspirants to the leadership. The first stream involved Pagan Amum Okiech, the sacked Secretary General of the SPLM, Rebecca Nyandeng de Mabior, widow of the SPLA/M former co-founding leader John Garang de Mabior, Deng Alor Kuol, former minister of cabinet affairs who had been sacked on charges of theft, and others. All seemed to be committed to a civil political battle to replace the president, whether through a deal within the party or through a general election in 2015. The interim constitution of South Sudan had provided for elections in 2015 and all the aspirant politicians had pinned their hopes of office in the next round on that date. They saw that their removal from both party positions and the executive was going to diminish their chances of rising during the next elections. The second stream involved the former Vice President Riek Machar Teny, Taban Deng Gai, former elected governor of Unity state who was fired by the president in May 2013, leaving him extremely angry about the unconstitutional presidential decree that removed him, and a number of senior military officers commanding divisions in Bor, Jonglei state, Bentiu, Unity state, Malakal and Upper Nile state.

While Taban Deng Gai was a recent recruit, Riek Machar Teny had for quite some time been planning to depose the president, first through the planned 2015 elections, but also by force should the civic approach fail, and was ready to move if his political alliances with the other group did not bear fruit. Both groups participated in the alliance without really revealing what they had in mind. They were joined by a common goal, the removal of President Salva Kiir Mayar, but their varying approaches, and competing leadership aspirations, meant they were bound to fail.

The South Sudanese, interviews have shown, concluded that whatever the approach of the two camps was, both had agreed to follow the legal route, pushing for the replacement of Salva Kiir at the party level so that he could not run for the presidency in the 2015 national elections. The failure of this route led Riek Machar to war, as a fallback position. Whether or not he was always prepared to go to war, or whether this was a momentary decision in the final hours is unclear, and perhaps immaterial. In the hours before the revolt, the opposition was still together, boycotting the last day of the proceedings of the SPLM's National Liberation Council. When political action to civically depose the president looked unlikely, Riek Machar Teny made his move to pursue armed struggle, without telling the others; all along he had been unsure if the rest would support him to become their leader.

At the start of this conflict, perhaps the trigger point of it, one of the Tiger Battalion's officers, a member of the uprising, lined up officers of Dinka origin and executed them himself, sparking the outbreak of violence inside one of the military barracks in Juba. On the evening of December 15, fighting broke out inside the main military command center, locally known as *al-Qayada*, located south-west of Juba. By 11pm, all hell had broken loose; the residents of Juba heard nothing but guns and artillery for the rest of that night, all through Monday and well into Tuesday. Not until about 3:30pm on Tuesday 17 December did the government forces finally neutralize the revolt within Juba city limits.

Riek Machar Teny slipped out of town about 6am on Monday morning, December 16, 2016. There was speculation that he had taken refuge in the USA Embassy, the United Kingdom High Commission or the UNMISS camp. By evening, word trickled back to Juba that he had trekked north, together with Taban Deng Gai, the sacked Unity state governor, and Alfred Lado Gore, former minister of the environment. They planned to join the military in Jonglei, who were ready to echo the actions of their Juba-based leadership. Almost overnight, Riek Machar Teny went from denying knowledge of or involvement in any coup, to being the leader of the rebellion; quite an about-turn if he had indeed been unaware of a planned coup.

Local analysts and journalists have reflected on these events, trying to tease out the signs of how the intense competition for political power within the ruling SPLM unfolded and what it produced. How did these events so rapidly translate into an all-out war? It is now clear they were bound to spark violence, as they opened the wounds of three decades of liberation wars, during which the south Sudanese had repeatedly turned their guns on one another in competition for leadership of the liberation movement. The moments of violence during the liberation period, though often extremely destructive to ethnic relations, were patched up in the interest of keeping everyone's eyes on the common goal. They were covered up or brushed aside, but never sufficiently resolved; far too many communities were left waiting for justice. Many incidents, starting from the Anya-nya *débacle*, to the SPLA's action against the Gajaak Nuer, Toposa, and Mandari, to the arrests and deaths of prominent people, stand as examples. In other words, what happened in Juba in December 2013 was only a trigger point for what had been long in the making.

Perhaps the incident most detrimental to the southern cause was the 1991 split in the SPLA, when Riek Machar Teny and Lam Akol Ajawin, then senior deputies of the SPLA's Commander-in-Chief John Garang de Mabior, attempted to depose him, sparking a massacre in Jonglei state. This revolt, occurring in the midst of successful campaign against the Khartoum government, was a massive setback for the SPLA, and led to a prolonged and destructive conflict between Riek and the SPLA that drew in the ethnic kin of the leaders. Machar ordered massacres of the Dinka of Jonglei state, which caused a protracted, seven-year long Dinka-Nuer conflict. In the end, despite the reunification of the SPLA, no one was held accountable either for this incident, or for many others similar to it. Nor was any form of recompense offered to the affected citizens. It set the precedent for the kind of politics in which the political ambition of the individual, or small groups of individuals, translates into efforts to gain power by force. The risks of a repeat of 1991, and many other related ugly incidents, were written all over the political culture in the country. With all those memories at the forefront of everyone's mind, there was no reining in this particular conflict. Everyone used their own memory of past wars to make decisions about how to respond to this new violent incident.

When the mayhem started, many were reminded of their history. Some people, especially soldiers who had escaped or survived some of these incidents, used their memories as their moral compass. Many soldiers fought with few commanding officers to direct them, or prevent them from excessive violence. Others were caught off guard by the fighting and simply ran into the fight randomly, without command, which led to the excesses that were later reported as state-sponsored killings. The revolt, and its subsequent clashes, killed hundreds of soldiers and civilians, partly due to avenging of past actions, as some of the soldiers read the situation as being yet another of Riek Machar Teny's ethnic-based struggles for power.

Another aspect of the liberation wars – the failure of the post-war development programs to bring the citizens their expected dividends – was related to this confusion. Poverty and dashed aspirations were directly linked, as were the security situation, the isolation of communities and poor infrastructure that denied people the opportunity to go to market or easily travel across ethnic lines. The South Sudanese did not know each other's assumptions about their long histories of competition and rivalries over resources and power. The negative stereotypes harbored by ethnic groups created a barrier to social intercourse, cross-ethnic marriages and sharing of space. When small disagreements happened between separated communities, stereotypes became the only reference on which they could base their reactions to the conflict.

The Dinka-Nuer killings and counter-killings exposed and affirmed the fragility of the new state. It also uncovered serious ethnic challenges to social cohesion and national unity, two circumstances vital for the stability of a new country. It exposed the delicacy of the democratic processes, showing that when democracy fails to open their path to office, some politicians are ready to turn to violence and appeal to their tribesmen to join their side. All these issues were uncovered, but perhaps unsurprising, given the huge numbers of militias from the rebellions in Greater Upper Nile that were absorbed into the SPLA.

The government of Salva Kiir Mayardit reasoned, quite admirably, that absorbing the militias and rewarding their leaders with high military rank was a reasonable price to pay for stability. But this policy quickly became much more costly than anticipated, on three counts. First, the absorption disproportionately swelled the army's ranks with members of one ethnic group, the Nuer; they eventually made up over half of the national defense force. In practice, the problem was not that the Nuer militias were absorbed in large numbers. Rather, it was the haphazard manner in which they were absorbed, with no real integration.[10] Second, the SPLA officer corps was unhappy at being out-ranked by former rebel leaders. Most of the rebel leaders were illiterate, and the degree to which they were capable of becoming professional officers was limited. For example, many senior officers only spoke Nuer and could not command multi-ethnic units. For their part, the senior militia commanders felt slighted; included in the national army but not really integrated into the system. They had rank, money and huge forces under their command, but were not part of the military hierarchy. This pushed many of them into the arms of Riek Machar when the rebellion started. Third, it provided an incentive for soldiers to rebel, to register their grievances against the government in the hope they would be offered an amnesty and a reintegration package.

The post-war and post-independence security situation in the country put the government on the horns of a serious dilemma. On the one hand, the multiplicity of militia forces, particularly those from Unity and Jonglei states, meant that there was no opportunity to build peace, reconcile the country and focus on developing resources for the benefit of the population. Striking peace deals with the militias was the only immediately viable way forward. On the other hand, inviting them into the national army compromised the endeavor to professionalize the armed forces. This was a guerrilla army seeking to transform itself into a credible professional one but some members of the militia lacked the basic military discipline, and indeed the basic training, to be part of a professional national defense force. They simply saw the army as the quickest way to salaried employment; many young people joined militia groups on the eve of absorption, taking advantage of the opportunity to join the army without having any understanding of military discipline. The result was an army that was an amalgam of previously warring factions, with no shared institutional culture or common ethos.

There was no coherent or unified command structure, and no respect for a central command. The policy of absorption split public opinion. Some saw it as a viable response to the complex security conditions of a country emerging from prolonged militarization; a minor price to pay for stability. Others saw it as a liability, both in terms of the cost of a constantly increasing army and in terms of the security consequences of such a mismatched army.

These issues may not have caused the violence of the next few years, but they certainly increased it. The escalation of violence could have been prevented if the security situation had been given the attention that many people had called for. Since the CPA, local analysts had warned that poor management of security, a failure to reckon with a history of ethnic relations wrecked by long liberation wars, ignoring the swelling ranks of the unemployed youth and retaining the urban bias that left the rural population unable to share in peace dividends, left the government in a parlous state. These issues were the mechanics of a ticking bomb whose explosion could rapidly unravel the gains of independence.[11] What was the trigger that sparked the explosion of Sunday December 15th?

The Citizen newspaper reported it held evidence that Riek Machar Teny had been planning to take power in Juba since 2005. He had long seen himself as more qualified for the top job than President Salva Kiir Mayar. His return to the SPLM after thirteen years of rebellion and collaboration with Khartoum was made possible by his vision of a rise to the top. He started planning his rise in the context of his efforts to mediate in the conflict between the LRA and the Ugandan government, forging secret deals within the region and beyond. What shocked most people, however, was that despite the fact that Machar was no stranger to using violence to gain power, he was prepared to turn to violence after spending the previous year talking about national reconciliation and peace-building. It was also particularly puzzling to many that Machar and his colleagues, most of whom were arrested in the wake of the outbreak of violence, began their quest for political change peacefully, holding a rally on December 6, 2013, but then turned to conflict.

POWER POLITICS OR TRIBAL WARS?

For the journalists and analysts who covered the tragedy unfolding in South Sudan, the most bewildering question was whether or not the situation had anything to do with ethnicity or tribal hatreds. While ethnic politics in South Sudan are complex, and undeniably part of everyday socio-political life, there is no doubt their role has sometimes been overstated. The real question was not so much about whether ethnic identity was fueling the violence but how were ethnic relations deployed in the contest among members of the political class. Were ethnic identities politicized or political competitions ethnicized?

Historically, conflict within South Sudan has followed three streams. First, the north-south liberation wars in the old Sudan; second, ethnic feuds over resources, especially among cattle-herding communities; and third, rivalries between political leaders. Independence ended the liberation wars. Ethnic feuds, despite occasionally stamping politics with an ethnic hue, remain relatively easy to reconcile in the context of traditional culture, as they are often confined to the groups directly involved and rarely affect the rest of the country. This leaves political wrangling, whether at national or state level, as the strongest stream. Desperate politicians are sometimes unable or unwilling to use ideas to gain political power. They reach for the ethnic card, drawing their kin into conflict by putting the survival of the group at stake. This link between political rivalry and ethnicity is at the root of the events that started in Juba on December 15, rapidly spread to other states, and left behind disunity, instability and unreconciled differences. Undoubtedly, some people held badly misconceived ideas about why the fighting started. Some deliberately exploited the violence for political gain, escalating the political mistrust that fueled the war; deliberate acts that fanned the flames of destruction for two years. Seizing on fragile ethnic relations already badly damaged by decades of war made the process of reconciliation and building stability all the more difficult. This situation is very likely to remain for the foreseeable future.

The context in which people can commit ethnic-based atrocities, or order others to commit them, is born of ethnic double standards and hypocrisy among many South Sudanese. Between 1991 and 1998, vast numbers of Dinka people were killed by order of some of the rebel leaders. Their justification was that the Dinka were defending John Garang's tight and undemocratic control of the SPLA/M and needed to be removed if Garang were to be toppled. When the SPLM was reconciled and reunited after the CPA, it created the façade that historical atrocities would be buried in the interests of stability. Riek Machar Teny, the architect of those massacres, became the vice president, raising hopes that everyone could look past their tragic history and focus on a brighter future of national unity and ethnic coexistence. But that was not to be. When the fighting started on December 15, some of the Dinka soldiers who remembered 1991 unleashed their misconceptions of what the new fighting meant, and went on a rampage, killing scores of Nuer people, innocent and guilty alike.

When Riek Machar Teny and Taban Deng Gai joined Peter Yak Gatdet in Jonglei state some time around December 19, their first order of business was to avenge events in Juba. Gatdet, the commander of Division 8, stationed at Bor, had a record of rebellion and return under amnesty as long as the Silk Road. He joined this episode of revolt in support of Machar by executing his deputy,

Major General Ajak Alier, going on to execute scores of subordinate Dinka officers. He may have eliminated these officers as a purely military calculation, but his action was read around the country as ethnically motivated revenge for what happened in Juba. Whatever Gatdet's rationale, his actions deepened the cantankerous ethnic mood, and offered the Dinka a position from which they could have their revenge.

Attempts were made to put together detailed reports of the atrocities committed by individual soldiers, particularly the Dinka soldiers during the Juba fighting. The government investigated allegations of deliberate targeting of Nuer, and scores of suspects were quickly arrested. Despite these efforts, shocking revenge attacks by Nuer on Dinka in Bor, Bentiu and Malakal continued; attacks that might have caused the Dinka in Juba not to cooperate with the investigations into killings of Nuer. When the ethnic group whose members were victimized at the start of the crisis was too angry to wait for investigation, and instead itself indiscriminately avenged the atrocities, any hopes of stopping the violence by revealing the truth and calling for calm were entirely dashed. No one had the courage to stand up, choke back the prevailing ethnic chauvinism and call for an end to the cycle of violence and counter-violence. Ethnic violence escalated to nearly unprecedented levels for the next few years.

It takes leadership on the scale of what happened in South Africa, Rwanda, Sierra Leone and Liberia, where prominent leaders stood against the tide of the African ethnic double standard and said "enough is enough," to sever the cycle of violence. But there was no evidence of such leadership in South Sudan when it was vitally needed; emotion overtook reason. The combination of hypocrisy, its leaders' political promiscuity and its people's citizenship being invested in ethnicity rather than the nation, left South Sudan a long way away from the cohesive and stable nation so many people had yearned for. This instability was amplified by a lack of investment in, and commitment to, the strengthening of social cohesion, underpinning of reconciliation and peace-building through conversations about the discord among ethnic groups.

South Sudan's return to war fits a pattern that has been observed in many countries that had endured protracted wars. Countries that have recently emerged from protracted wars are often so fragile that a return to war within a few years of peace agreements and other political transitions is the most likely post-war outcome.[12] The legacy of war, disagreements over political settlements, unfulfilled promises, unrealistic and poorly-managed expectations, competition over peace dividends,[13] and poorly-implemented peace accords inevitably threaten a stable peace. But the most significant factor in the relapse to war is the failure of security arrangements and security sector development following the agreement. If the country cannot come up with a credible plan to deal with all the armed men who fought during the war and help them transition to civilian life and do so in ways that grant them dignity and decent life, return to violence within the communities or to a renewed war is often most likely.

After the CPA, the South Sudanese people's expectations for independence were extremely high, and extremely poorly managed by their leaders. People expected safety, basic services, the rule of law and an efficient justice system, a constitution that respected the basic rights of the citizen and above all, food security.[14] But instead their leaders added another layer of the conflict and misery to their lives. Vast numbers of people were made bitter by increased inequality, corruption in state institutions, the theft of public resources, sectarian divides, nepotism and the mismanagement and appropriation of state authority.

The people of South Sudan, and some of the international allies that tried to help them, expected nation-building to go hand-in-hand with state-building; a horizontal, people-centered approach to post-war rebuilding, rather than the vertical, state-focused programs that dominated the period following the CPA and independence. The country's leadership did not give the pertinent question of collective citizenship in the nation its due weight. Instead, the people saw a divide between the élite that ran the country, who felt a sense of entitlement to state services because they had liberated the country, and the mass of the people who were either entirely excluded from the gains of independence, or only marginally included amid regionalism, ethnic loyalties, nepotism and corruption. This divide manifested itself in the widespread unhappiness of the young people, ethnic minorities and women, who felt particularly flagrantly excluded from the post-war opportunities. The youth were particularly an area of concern that needed much attention, especially in the area of skills development, employment opportunities and grounding of civic responsibilities, respect for diversity and peace. Unfortunately, most leaders saw the youth as a liability, a problem to address, rather than an asset.

It is fair to say that the sentiment most widely applied to the new war, even among the fighters, was a massive sense of disappointment. The vicious violence of this war, especially in the first five months, was commonly described as unprecedented. The South Sudanese had known nothing like this, even in the times when the government of Sudan had fought proxy wars, recruiting and arming militias from the south and pitting them against southern opposition movements. In the new war, the South Sudanese reflected their disappointment against the liberation philosophy that had united them against northern Sudan. Then, the southern Sudanese had a common and important cause that forced them to sweep aside or patch up local differences in the interests of unity and a unified front against Khartoum. After a fifty year fight for freedom, no one wanted to believe they could inflict such horrors on each other. As one distraught person wrote on a social media platform:

> What we have now done to ourselves, to our sense of freedom, our independent state will take years to recover from … We have exhibited to one another such vile hate and violence that some among us will say were similar or worse than what our most vicious enemy, the Sudanese government, had done during the north-south war.

It is worth noting that the new war coincided with the rapid growth of social media networks. Twitter, Facebook and the web quickly became a place where all manner of hurt, hate, threats, ethnic chauvinism and calls to war were displayed, to the disgust of South Sudanese and outside observers. Social media became the new frontier of the propagation of violence, as radio had been in the mass killings of Tutsis by Hutus in Rwanda in 1994.[15] The country is currently faced with real problems of ethnic hate being peddled on social media. In early November 2016, the UN Secretary General's Special Advisor for the Prevention of Genocide, Adama Dieng, warned that the country was in danger of sliding into a genocide if measures were not taken to rein in the growing hate speech and stop the atrocious attacks that target members of specific communities and ethnic groups. Government officials downplayed the significance of this finding. While such warnings are very important in a world ripe in violence and mass atrocity, the conclusion in this case was probably premature and caused more fear in the local communities than built confidence for reconciliation, the government said. But the opposition and civil society activists embraced the UN envoy's analysis, conclusion and recommendation.

Enlightened interpretations of the nature of ethnic conflict in South Sudan is often missing from these kinds of UN reports. The government also missed opportunities to keep ethnic conflict in check. Those South Sudanese who did not wish to take sides, wanted only an end to the conflict and peace and stability, called for the people to use their liberation history as a source of national unity and collective identity. But this history could also be a liability, a reminder of the atrocities that had been committed against their communities. But the opportunity to use history to create national cohesion was disastrously missed. Many people I interviewed immediately after the violence erupted argued that the people's horrific experiences of the liberation wars, and the long journey to independent nationhood, were not enough to create a collective national identity rather than a tribal citizenship. This sense of disappointment was not new; the hopes of a better, more secure and more prosperous life pinned to independence were slowly and steadily lost to corruption, nepotism, and exclusion. But these hopes were even more desperately shattered by the renewed vicious conflict, which was locally seen as emblematic of how little the "liberators" cared about the country and the people they claim to have liberated.

Just a month into the conflict, the country appeared to be heading toward civil war; a catastrophic prospect that devastated the post-independence aspirations invigorated by the end of the north-south war. The clash between Salva Kiir and Riek Machar, president and vice president, men likely to swap in and out of those seats at the right moment, could not have been more disastrous. "I feel ashamed when I see our people dying only because of two people, and find myself asking whether these people really value the lives of our people," said one interviewee.[16]

The frustrated people of South Sudan, made cynical by the national politics of failure, ethnic division and leadership crisis, asked themselves a stream of questions about the new war. "What was it that so many of our loved ones died for in the liberation wars?" "Why is it that Riek Machar could not wait for the 2015 elections if he wanted to become president?" "Why was President Kiir so unwilling to dialogue with his opponents in the ruling party who wanted to challenge him, to the extent of pushing them into a rebellion?" "Do these leaders not care about the millions they have now subjected to suffering?" "Why is the rest of the world slow to condemn this war and force the competing leaders to end the violence?" "What causes ordinary rural people, far disconnected from the politics of power at the national level, to champion a cause whose fruits will hardly be reflected in their own daily lives?" Their answers revealed both shock felt in the country and the helplessness felt by ordinary people. They suggest an inability either to unite in collective action and force the leadership to end the war or to deny the warring factions the capacity to use ethnicity to galvanize support. In short, the South Sudanese, divided along ethnic lines, were too weak to influence the war's dynamics toward peace; they were only capable of being deployed to support a war on all sides. The war morphed into a matter of ethnic pride and the determination to stick to defending the leaders, away from any real issues.

The South Sudanese, and outsiders, were especially baffled by how quickly the fighting took on an ethnic dimension. This was the element that most perplexed analysts, journalists, ordinary people on both sides and even the fighters. In the international media, some were tempted to rush to a conclusion that ethnic hatred was rearing its ugly head once again in Africa; one more case of pointless human cruelty; one more problem the world was too handicapped to do anything about. There were calls for caution against the temptation to rehash the primordial ethnic hatred of past decades; appeals for more nuanced analysis of how ethnic politics operated in South Sudan, its complexity and why it should not be overemphasized as the single most important explanation for the war.

The interviews and discussions that I have conducted reveal a very complex picture in which ethnicity is only one of a host of factors that helped in the quick spread of the violence. The Dinka and the Nuer have always had violent encounters, especially over cattle and grazing, but never anything of this magnitude. Such destruction of property, killing of children and attacking and raping of women has never been recorded in their histories. Many simply did not believe that the political rivalry between Riek and Kiir could draw their respective ethnic communities so rapidly into such a ghastly war, and many local analysts denied that ethnicity was a factor, a claim that has some truth.

But ethnicity was the most visible issue to the outside world. Ethnicity formed the basis for the exchange of hate messages on social media, especially from the south Sudanese diaspora; messages that many fear fed into the violence and may have been partly responsible for the hardened political positions at every level of society and continuation of violence. It is this conviction about ethnic positions, especially the perceived level of victimization and the desire to avenge it, which has made it very difficult to achieve compromise agreements or to cut down the level of violence.

It was ironic that the images of the Dinka and Nuer painted by colonial-era anthropologists, images that depicted them as "war-like," "good fighters," "brave" and "violent" were re-appropriated on social media, highlighted in military leaders' speeches and deployed to spur young people to join the war. The Nuer used social media to claim: "We the Nuer are the best fighters," "The White Army are coming, Dinka you should be afraid," and "Jieng are cowards." Others called upon the Nuer to demonstrate their bravery and their supposedly "great skills at fighting to restore the honor of our people who were humiliated in Juba." In return, the Dinka challenged the Nuer to "come to Bahr el Ghazal so we can show you how fighting is done." On both sides, writers called for the extermination of the other, using the language of mass murder.

The language of ethnic divide played a considerable role in the incitement of violence, and many suspect it was encouraged by ethnic stereotyping. There were shocking incidents in which ethnicity played a part once the fighting had started, but ethnicity was definitely not the cause. In Juba, at the start of the conflict, although many soldiers died on both sides, scores of Nuer, perhaps hundreds, were killed by Dinka soldiers and police officers, either because of their ethnic identity or from suspicion that they would support Riek Machar. When the rebels took control of the town of Bor, the capital of Jonglei state, and later Akobo, Malakal and Bentiu in Upper Nile and Unity states, the Nuer killed hundreds of Dinka in revenge for the Juba massacres.

The fighting spiraled into a merciless cycle of ethnic revenge and counter-revenge. And the mayhem included atrocities of a kind never seen before in Nuer–Dinka conflict. Although there had been sexual violence and rape of women and girls in the liberation wars and the post-war ethnic conflicts, it was largely unsystematic, and usually committed either by the Sudanese army in garrison towns, or as isolated cases involving members of the SPLA. The use of rape as a weapon in the new conflict was another sign of the depth of antagonism between the cultural siblings.

Many governments in the western world were shocked by the violence. The USA, Norway and several European countries had supported South Sudan's quest for independent statehood, investing huge sums of money and much diplomatic energy to ensure the conduct of the referendum and worked for the country's viability. Their leaders were extremely frustrated that the South Sudanese leaders had not heeded myriad warnings from the global north about the gathering storm of failure in South Sudan. But activists and law makers in the USA were also quick to blame their government, both for not acting sooner to prevent the tragic plunge into war of a country whose independence they had done so much to make possible, and for their slow reaction to the signs of impending ethnic violence. In April 2014, as the world commemorated the twentieth anniversary of the 1994 Rwandan genocide, there was a particularly vicious episode of ethnic targeting by rebels occupying Bentiu, the capital of Unity state. The fear of a repeat of Rwanda grew stronger in Washington, spurring President Barak Obama's government into action. Activists in the USA, including the *Enough Project*, a human rights and genocide prevention organization whose members included celebrities such as George Clooney and Don Cheadle, called on the president to not allow another Rwanda to happen in South Sudan.

Whether warnings of genocide were needed, or whether the activists used the term to provoke rapid action, the cumulative result of this and other pressures was that the USA took two important, albeit weak, policy decisions. The first was to send a special envoy to engage with east African leaders to find a route to peaceful settlement; the second was a White House executive order that threatened sanctions against those on either side who proved intransigent about the peace negotiations. In principle, these were significant steps; in practice, they were woefully weak tools.

The east African nations, especially Ethiopia, Kenya and Uganda were also alarmed and frustrated. They had hosted thousands of south Sudanese refugees during the liberation wars, and been immensely affected by the impact of war on their territories. They did not want to see history repeating itself. Supporting the refugees had placed a heavy burden on their countries' meager resources, and their help had been offered at a cost to their citizens, who had to compete with the refugees for educational services, health care and food. When South Sudan became independent, the citizens and governments of many of these countries saw opportunities.

They hoped the goodwill they had shown toward the south Sudanese would be returned, and the new country would allow them to run businesses and offer jobs to their skilled workers. Huge numbers of workers and investors poured into South Sudan after 2005. In 2013, there were 45,000 Ugandan citizens working in South Sudan, 25,000 Kenyans, 20,000 Ethiopians and about 15,000 Eritreans. These migrants worked all over the country in a variety of industries, in small enterprises and medium-sized businesses, in NGOs, with the UN, as day laborers, domestic servants and sex workers.

Within a few days of the start of the conflict, heads of state from Kenya, Uganda and Ethiopia descended on Juba to try to mediate and arrest the escalating violence as quickly as possible. They were highly conscious of what another war in South Sudan meant for the security of their territories, but they were also conscious of the loss of remittances sent back by migrant workers. Businesses owned by foreign citizens were being destroyed, shops looted, and banks burned. The Prime Minister of the Federal Democratic Republic of Ethiopia, Hailemariam Desalegn, and President Uhuru Kenyatta of Kenya insisted on immediate dialogue between Riek Machar and Salva Kiir, but Uganda's Yuweri Musevni instantly threatened the use of force if Machar proved intransigent. Uganda sent its armed forces to South Sudan, initially to "help evacuate its citizens," but they quickly became involved on the government side, protecting Juba airport and helping the government regain control of Bor town, the capital of Jonglei state, which had gone under rebel control when Peter Gatdet Yak switched sides.

Two hundred thousand people had fled Bor, crossing the River Nile into Awerial County in the neighboring Lakes state. They were living in desperate circumstances of humanitarian disaster: women and children, the wounded, the elderly and the sick were camped under trees, with only the clothes on their backs. Disease threatened; living among the trees unleashed malaria, South Sudan's leading cause of death, and unclean drinking water caused deadly diarrheal diseases, especially among the children.

The battle for Bor was deadly. When the government "liberated" it after nearly a month in rebel hands, the level of violence against the Dinka ethnic group and the sheer destruction of the town's facilities the SPLA discovered were staggering. The images that emerged from Bor were horrific and heartbreaking; unbearable to watch on television screens, read in newspapers, or hear about in mobile-phone conversations. In the town's hospital, patients had been shot in their hospital beds, women, including an old blind woman, had been raped. But there was worse to come. More gruesome images would emerge a few weeks later, mainly from Malakal, the capital of Upper Nile state, and from Bentiu, capital of Unity state, where rebel attacks wreaked havoc in these towns.

Historically, Dinka-Nuer conflicts, devastating as they might be, observed a basic etiquette that, for instance, discouraged attacks on women, children and the elderly. Even young men overwhelmed by battle, although labeled as cowards, were not pursued. The traditional goal was not necessarily to exterminate the enemy, but to demonstrate fighting prowess and loot the enemies' cattle.[17] But the concept of mercy towards the "enemy" seemed to have lost its currency. Signs of change, of the development of a gruesome quality to ethnic violence, first showed in the 1990s. Although there is disagreement about the factors behind this shift in values, the change has stunned everyone, including the fighters themselves.

Although war is drawn as having clear lines and divides and well-defined protagonists, on the ground any conflict is messier than it appears to those looking at it from the outside. There is more to war than the visible confrontations between the fighting forces, the destruction of property and the pain of death. In the shadows beneath the visible lie the hidden; the sexual violence, the suspension of historical restraints and the evisceration of social order. And the violence of war is often reproduced within families and communities, who pay the costs of war in insidious ways not often reported in the media or human rights reports. The daily decisions that families have to make, often under extreme circumstances, to enable them to survive and protect themselves against violence and hunger, also lie hidden. Families are forced to take immeasurable risks to save woefully little, and must continue to do so in the face of diminishing options.

These are the consequences of war that live on long after the guns have gone silent. Consequences that affect communities in ways that very few peace agreements can resolve. Consequences that spoil political settlements and become the root cause of the next war.

In conclusion, the new civil war in South Sudan was shocking, disappointing and destructive. It took lives, laid waste to property, set back national cohesion, wrecked ethnic relations and shook the confidence of the citizens in their new state and its leadership. Although it was politically settled after two years, the civil war has left lingering questions both about the ability of the South Sudanese leaders to steer the country to prosperity and also about the viability of South Sudan itself. The war brought to the country a global reputation that will take many years to restore. Internationally, even South Sudan's closest friends condemned it, understandable condemnation, given that the global community had recognized the struggles of the people of South Sudan and put their weight behind them over many long years. It is hard to understand why the leaders of South Sudan were so willing to waste their international goodwill, what the South Sudanese lost in order to be independent and how the people kept their resilience through the most testing of times.

The liberation wars left a huge burden on the country's shoulders; a burden that was not relieved by peace and independence. In this chapter, I have tried to show how the memories of long wars of liberation, the competition between South Sudan's leaders to capture the apparatus of the new state and control its resources, the exclusion of young people from the prizes of independence, a weak national security system, an unprofessional army, corruption and disregard for the rule of law were the factors that sparked the outbreak of the new civil war.

The shocking speed at which the civil war spread across a third of the country was born of simmering grievances that had not been given sufficient attention by the country's politico-military leadership. Many people had been urged for the start of a twin project of nation-building and state-building. Nation-building was needed to offer justice for atrocities and support national reconciliation to repair community relations destroyed by splits in the SPLA and Khartoum's counter-insurgency tactics. State-building was needed to restore the country's institutions and build new ones, professionalize the national defense force, provide basic goods and services, create a strong judiciary, responsible financial institutions and reliable infrastructure and, above all, encourage private enterprise and job creation. The near-collapse of South Sudan in 2013 was explained through the government's failure to promote these crucial dual elements for national stabilization and social cohesion.

5

REPORTING SUDAN'S WARS:
THE MEDIA AND THE BLURRED LINE
BETWEEN INFORMING AND INCITING

During South Sudan's long journey of liberation through the second half of the twentieth century, accurate war reporting faced serious challenges. Life was almost as hard and dangerous for the reporters as for the fighters. The war started simmering in 1947 but the trigger that set it going was the 1955 mutiny at Torit (now the capital of Eastern Equatoria state) involving southern Sudanese members of the SAF's Equatorial Corps. These men were ordered north, a move they refused, seeing it as an attempt to neutralize them and remove their support from the increasing clamor of southern dissent.

At this time, for all practical purposes, south Sudan existed in a news blackout except for a few, dedicated southern print journalists from newspapers such as *The Vigilant* and *The Grass Curtain*, who committed themselves to bringing news from the region to the rest of the world. The war in southern Sudan did not get the same international attention as other conflicts on the continent, for example the secession war in Biafra, in the south-east of Nigeria.

Southern Sudan, unfortunately, had no well-known champions on the global stage, as Biafra had in Chinwa Achebe and others. *The Vigilant* and *The Grass Curtain* dedicated themselves to recording the atrocities perpetrated by members of the SAF stationed in the southern garrison towns including Juba, Bor, Malakal, Wau, Aweil and others. Journalists documented – or tried to – stories of chiefs massacred in Bor, families attacked at a wedding in Wau, attempts to exterminate all the educated southern Sudanese in Juba, mass burials in wells and multiple drownings in rivers across southern Sudan. Southerners suspected of having links with, or aiding, the rebels of the southern Sudan liberation movement and the Anya-nya, often "disappeared" from their homes at night. Many were detained for long periods, some were summarily executed and others disappeared completely. Families and neighborhoods faced daily harassment and humiliation; any suspicion of unwillingness to report rebel activities was a sign they supported the rebel movement against the government.

In 1964, Sadiq al-Mahdi, head of the Umma Party, was elected prime minister in the wake of a popular uprising that toppled General Ibrahim Aboud. There was much for the southern Sudanese journalists to report but their activities were curtailed both by the Sudanese security agencies and the financial environment in which they operated. Technology was poor, the rate of illiteracy high and newspaper distribution was confined to a few educated southerners and foreign diplomats. Few laws protected journalists, and those that existed were ignored in favor of national security and the intelligence services' resolve to keep atrocities out of the limelight. The suppression of news was born of Khartoum's determination to prosecute a "scorched earth" war, of embarrassment about the news coming out of Sudan and the racist rhetoric which mobilized the northern Sudanese against southern grievances.

Despite their modest nature and restricted distribution, the news media demonstrated the utmost professionalism in recording civilian killings, abuse and humiliation. Their standards would rival those of any modern news organization, and what has been preserved of their output remains a very valuable historical record to date. They laid a strong foundation for a culture of bearing witness to human tragedy both for human rights activism and the benefit of generations to come. Reports made by foreign visitors, Christian missionaries and aid workers offer an additional glimpse at life in southern Sudan during the first civil war, a time that saw almost unprecedented levels of displacement, disease and malnutrition.

When the first phase of the war ended in 1972, southern Sudan became autonomous under a High Executive Council. Journalists such as Bona Malwal Madut Ring, Atem Yaak Atem, Ambrose Wol Dhal and Alfred Taban endeavored to continue their war-time commitment to witness, in the hope the southern government would maintain the culture and influence events in the north. Between 1972 and 1983 attempts were made to improve journalism and keep the public informed. *Radio Juba* was established, and the *Nile Mirror* newspaper was created and funded by the High Executive Council. But their efforts came to an end with the renewed outbreak of war in 1983. Some journalists joined the SPLA, some went into exile and some stayed in Khartoum to continue telling the story of the new war as seen from the north.

The world heard very little of the humanitarian crises and Khartoum's atrocities during the civil war. Under cover of the world's ignorance about the tragedies, and amid little sympathy for the south Sudanese, the Sudanese government bullied, humiliated and killed with impunity. Very few foreign journalists and other observers went beyond the standard reduction of the war's story to religious, racial and ethnic differences, writing very little about the political economy of the war, the drivers of the conflict, how it brought the country's limited infrastructure to its knees and affected the lives of everyone, soldier and civilian alike. But the ignorance was not quite complete; the history of events was recorded by courageous southern Sudanese who carried documentation out of the country. These documents have allowed historians to piece together a credible story of what happened in people's daily lives, and set their suffering in context. These examples of documentary media coverage of the old wars show the extent of the brutality, and the level of suffering inflicted on the civilians matched against the sheer resourcefulness of the southern separatist fighters. One example is a film made in Equatoria and Bahr el Ghazal by Allan Reed, an American working for the United States Agency for International Development (USAID) in 1971. This record makes it clear how far back the Sudanese counter-insurgency went, a practice that was refined, expanded and became more rampant and more vicious during the last phase of the north-south civil war. No matter how hostile the media climate was, trying to muzzle the voices of activists often seemed to push them to document more of the brutality of the state.

The documentation of war crimes is a very difficult endeavor, but one that needs to be done if future generations are to forge a positive future for their nations. History, carefully pieced together, survives the intense scrutiny and censorship of warring parties. Careful and accurate journalism can support peace-building and the establishing of national unity, even amid differences. For example, one of the marked differences between the Anya-nya and the SPLM/A was that they gave far more weight to ideas and collective southern nationalism than to ethnic background. During the first war, despite the unity of purpose among the southern Sudanese, there were always local rivalries and jockeying for control among the fighting forces and political leaders. But despite these disagreements, unlike the situation in subsequent conflicts, the leaders knew space needed to be made for future reconciliation and national cohesion, no matter how intense the dispute.

On the ground, the leaders' ability to rally the masses was hindered by communication challenges but the limited access to mass media and a strong sense of commitment to unity of purpose combined to keep southern Sudan relatively coherent politically during the first war. In hindsight, it is possible to say that lack of easy access to the media was a blessing in disguise, because it prevented political differences being inflamed by ambitious individuals. Throughout the 1960s, disagreements were frequent, not just between leaders of different movements, but even within them, although these tended to focus on ideological disparities and leaders' approaches. One point of issue concerned whether to wage a political campaign from within Sudan in pursuit of southern independence, or to pursue an armed struggle. This was the major cause of the Sudan African National Union's (SANU) split into external and internal fronts. But there was never much dispute over the right of southern Sudan to self-determination, a position refined over many years since 1947, with options of federalism on the table, all culminating in a strong sentiment for separation.

The near media blackout that had been a feature of previous wars was evident to the end of the civil war. The autonomous government of southern Sudan had just a single state-owned radio station, *Radio Juba*, a single newspaper, *The Nile Mirror*, and a few mobile loudspeaker units through which to disseminate information about health, security and other subjects. Although based in southern Sudan, and under the supervision of the High Executive Council, these media outlets were owned and censored by the Khartoum government and subject to Khartoum's media regulations. This changed very little during the second civil war, although the SPLA was well aware of the importance of the media. Soon after the SPLA/M was established it set up its own radio station, *Radio SPLA*, and broadcast into Sudan from Ethiopia in Arabic, English and some south Sudanese indigenous languages. Earlier generations' reliance on the word of mouth or on foreign media to spread the message of the revolution was no more. The BBC, Voice of America, CNN and other outside media outlets were certainly important to the liberation effort, but chiefly for their role in making the SPLA's case in foreign capitals.

During the post-independence South Sudanese civil war, the situation was significantly different, not just because of the nature of the war itself but also because of the massive changes in technology and access to information in the twenty-first century. The media became a double-edged sword. Used to belittle, vilify and show opponents in the worst light possible, they create animosities that could last for generations. Practiced professionally, they might just save the country from its perpetual cycle of violence. Strong, independent media can counter warring parties' divisive positions and sow the seeds of future reconciliation.

In this chapter, I shall consider how and when wars are covered in the media, by researchers and by humanitarian agencies. It is not easy to report from the midst of violence but the reporting of conflict in many parts of Africa is sometimes so generalized as to amount to a pornography of sympathy. Images of almost-naked, emaciated people scrambling for humanitarian relief, of malnourished or sick black children in the arms of white aid workers, captured on cameras they scarcely saw, were common in the coverage of South Sudan's civil war. Aid workers' good intentions aside, these images speak more about power relations between the global north and south, than of humanity and humanitarian generosity.

Reporting of mass atrocities, sexual violence and other forms of abuse and humiliation in South Sudan was often superficial. Coverage was largely without context, unverified, random and generalized. This is one way to make the case against war, making it seem unnecessary for anyone reporting it to seek a complete picture. Sexual violence is a ghastly crime, but reports of cases have received more attention than other, equally horrible acts of brutality, making it appear as though the war is all about gender-based violence. This is partly because sexual violence is an international war crime, but also because it has become a commonplace in reporting African wars, perhaps as a way to show war as meaningless political rivalries that have no regard for the sanctity of human life.

Both Sudan and South Sudan have had their fair share of media coverage over the last forty years. While some of this reporting, especially the human rights documentation of atrocities, is well-intentioned, extremely important and perhaps even credible, its methodology is problematic. Highly nuanced social and cultural issues surround the behavior of soldiers, which, if not fully accounted for by reporters, could paint a picture of their communities that not even the victims would agree with. Some of the reporting from South Sudan and Sudan aimed to spur global support for humanitarian interventions in refugee crises, put diplomatic pressure on the warring parties and supply information on the dynamics of the war, but even these noble aims were written from the perspective of the reporters, with very little analysis from victims and perpetrators. The rest of the media coverage was largely sensational, inaccurate propaganda, biased and motivated by political games and military purposes.

There is a noticeable lack of understanding of the socio-cultural and historical context, especially contexts that give prominence to the voices of the people, in accounts of Sudan's wars. War is a difficult context to study, not just because of difficulties in security and access, but also because its complexities are beyond the reach of journalists who are "on the ground" for just a few hours or a few days. The temptation to grab a sound bite and run is common, and understandable. The biggest and most obvious challenges to understanding contexts are the difficulties in obtaining interviews and the corroboration of evidence. Both are born of the brevity of time that can be spent on the ground. This became much harder in the civil war; the South Sudanese were so divided that it became impossible for journalists to believe anyone, lest they merely used the perspective of one party as the whole war experience.

To cover conflicts, in sufficient depth, a reporter needs to understand how families live, what they eat, how they protect themselves, who has died and how much they have lost. That level of detail requires spending time with people, something that is often logistically challenging, if not impossible. How people remember, reproduce and recount their experiences is fraught with trauma, tainted by rumors they have heard, and framed by their personal philosophies and ethnic perceptions. While it is not the responsibility of the journalist or researcher to solve the crisis they report on, a researcher who genuinely aims to do justice to people's experience, and help them, must deal sensitively with how people think they might be depicted. But war defies well-tested social science research methods; it is not possible to be a participant observant of hunger, or spend time developing a rapport with people displaced from their homes. There are ways to do it, such as drawing on highly educated members of war-engulfed communities as researchers, as well as informants.

Since the renewal of conflict in South Sudan, in December 2013, reporting both by media and human rights agencies has inadvertently prolonged the conflict as much as it has disseminated its messages. The reporting of violence and war-related humanitarian crises, and coverage of peace processes and the human rights issues has been done to keep the people informed, but there has been a growing concern about the role of the media in the incitement and promotion of violence, especially along sectarian divides. In South Sudan, one person's reporting of news is another person's call to war.

The media played both a positive and negative role in highlighting the tragedy of gender-based violence, and in promoting it. When the opposition force occupied Bentiu in April 2014, some of its elements broadcast calls for the rape of non-Nuer women in the area. Accusations abound about how the government used state-owned television and radio to defend its image and portray the opposition in a negative light. The line separating the provision of information and misleading consumers became ever more blurred.

The media has also been used to manage the relationship between South Sudan's leadership and the international community. At times, this has served to expose the misunderstanding and acrimony that exists in this relationship, to the detriment of cooperation on peace-related issues. The government has long viewed UNMISS with suspicion since the start of the conflict, sometimes directly accusing the world body of meddling in favor of the armed rebellion. In response, UNMISS raised serious concerns about the government's use of the national media to rally the people against the UN mission. This confrontation came to a head in early 2014, amid accusations that UNMISS in Lakes state had delivered weapons to the armed rebellion in Bentiu. On national television, the minister for information vented the government's frustration and anger, despite assurance from the UN that this incident was no more than a simple misunderstanding. The weapons were accidentally mislabeled and were in fact destined for the new Ghanian contingent of UNMISS, and the objects the minister claimed were bombs were actually gas masks for the peacekeepers. The government continued to show the gas masks on television for quite some time, insisting that they were weapons, thereby suggesting to the public that the UN was not only politicking against the government, but actively working against the people of South Sudan.

The media have long been objects of both suspicion and desire on all sides. The opposition used its online publications and social media as a conduit for messages of war, resource collection and recruitment, especially their opportunistic use of the events of December 2013 in Juba to portray the government as a killer of its own citizens. Supporters of the armed opposition have since focused on this incident, but mainly with a view to gaining political and military objectives rather than to show a commitment to documenting the tragedy to ensure future justice and accountability. At the beginning of the war, the SPLM-IO championed accountability as the major issue they would never compromise on, but in the peace deal signed in August 2015, they relegated it to the bottom of their list of demands.[1] The armed opposition fell short of pursuing the issue of justice in favor of immediate compromises with the party they accused of atrocities.

The massacre of Nuer people in Juba, in what appeared to be ethnically targeted killings, became a recruitment tool for the rebellion. Many disaffected Nuer youth read the reporting and flocked to the cause. This painful human rights tragedy undoubtedly needed to be properly investigated and widely reported, and much work was done on this by both local and international news agencies, but it is not lost to many people's minds that the armed opposition took advantage of the incident to swell its military ranks by appealing to the urge of the Nuer people to avenge their loved ones. The Juba killings were manipulated by media reporting that widened sectarian rifts, and drew a vast swath of people into the war.[2] To capitalize on Nuer anger, the opposition spoke of genocide, of as many as 20,000 dead, and of a government extermination plot. There was very little evidence to support such claims, and yet the messages, disseminated by the media, caused the violence far and wide at a speed that shocked everyone. The tragic incident was swiftly used by Riek Machar and his lieutenants. As one opposition supporter remarked, Machar had been "milking the suffering of Nuer people for his political goals … although we know he will drop the issue of justice for them the minute he gains access to power." What could have been a genuine civil revolt against the leadership was subverted by the politicians and used to very different ends.

The government, on the other hand, viewed the national media coverage of "rebel" activity as an unlawful broadcast of the voices of the armed opposition. To counter the opposition's messages, it used government-owned media such as South Sudan TV to debunk their arguments, together with national security legislation to threaten journalists with arrest or violence to counter the opposition messages. The minister of information declared that interviewing rebel leaders by any South Sudanese national or national publication was in violation of national security regulations and tantamount to a criminal offense. It was also alleged that the government closed down two English-language publications. There were, however, mixed reports about this story, especially regarding the *Citizen*. Journalists linked to the publications claimed that they were ordered to shut down by National Security, due to what the government saw as subversive reporting, but some insiders suggest that the newspapers used the security threats as a pretext; they actually closed down because of financial struggles and lack of access to foreign currency. But access to, or denial of, foreign currency is a power national security agents have previously exercised, closing some media businesses. Whatever the truth may be, South Sudan has a toxic media environment, with a tense relationship between the media and the government. This became evident as time progressed and the government became even more hostile to the media. In November 2016, amidst growing violence, famine, ethnic targeting, two radio stations reporting these issues were shut by the National Security Service, causing condemnation of the government from many corners of the globe.

To summarize, all the parties to the conflict, while calling on the public to use a rhetoric of peace, were also engaged in war propaganda, especially pertaining to the violations of the cease-fire agreement reached as part of the compromise peace deal. The warring parties' propaganda reached new heights in June and July of 2016, when they took and re-took towns in Upper Nile, devastating the region, especially the area around Malakal, the state capital. This was as much a media war as a field battle. Each side wanted to trumpet the victories it scored and the humiliating defeats it inflicted.

The role of the media is not just about what information people get, but also how they get it. In South Sudan, the most common news medium is the radio, especially the small FM stations scattered throughout the country, followed by newspapers, and then by South Sudan Television, especially for government news and information. These sources are confined to the urban population and the few literate people living in rural areas and small towns who can access services in foreign languages such as English and Arabic. Some of the FM stations broadcast in local languages but they are few and far between.

There are four mobile telecommunication networks currently operating in the country (Zain, Vivacell, MTN and Gemtel), competing for consumers' attention, trying to out-perform the others and provide the strongest signal and the best Internet-enabled network. As better services spread to the furthest reaches of the country, more people are able to read Internet-based news services, publish blogs, engage through social media such as Facebook and Twitter, and simply communicate more easily with family and friends. However, with the exception of voice calls, these media demand a literate audience, which many of the people of South

Sudan are not. For the illiterate, news still travels by word of mouth, when they meet at social gatherings, funerals, weddings and church services.

In South Sudan as elsewhere, the Internet presents both challenges and opportunities for news reporting and journalism. Formal, trusted and well-established media face steep competition from informal communication, blogs, social media and online publications. Every citizen can be a reporter. Foreign publications, including major newspapers such the *New York Times* or the (UK) *Guardian* can be read on a mobile phone; major television stations such as the BBC and Al-Jazeera can be watched, and links to programs or news articles can be sent far and wide on Facebook or Twitter. The minute a piece of news is produced, it is published. Once published, it can reach all corners of the country almost instantaneously. However, South Sudan has no concept of the impact access to the Internet could have on its social landscape; its peace, its coexistence and its national unity. It has no policies, and no legal framework to assess the serious implications of rapidly-developing communication technologies.

Professional journalists subscribe to a code of quality, ethical reporting and presenting a balanced and objective analysis. No such codes apply to "citizen journalists" online. Technology has made it easy to fabricate news and facilitate subjective reporting, which in South Sudan fosters dangerous divisions along sectarian lines. Opposition-related online publications, such as *Nyamilepedia, Upper Nile Times* or *South Sudan TV in Opposition,* have all churned out news reports that have proved unverifiable or entirely false. Reports of this kind rapidly become the subject of heated discussions in social media networks. They can quickly be discredited by people who want to inform themselves about the war but they remain important platforms for people who want to believe anything that praises their side. The rifts between online communities mirror those on the ground; there is a clash between those who want to establish or maintain credibility through accurate reporting, and those who want to maintain the morale of their fighting forces by portraying them as invincible fighters.

But truth and accuracy is not their aim; they exist as propaganda mouthpieces of the opposition and government. They report the movement of opposition troops, attacks and capture of government-controlled towns, military equipment destroyed or "captured in good condition," and personnel killed. Their reporting borrows its language from liberation war reporting in the old Sudan. A "tactical withdrawal" from a town actually means that the force was defeated, but the opposition forces dare not admit it, lest the resolve and confidence of their support base is shaken. For the government, the phrase "we are fighting the rebels on the outskirts of town," is also a euphemism for defeat.

All sides are guilty of slanted reporting and managing information; battles are fought in people's minds, as well as on the field. Malak Ayuen Ajok's army program on South Sudan TV is reminiscent of Khartoum's televised army programs broadcast in the 1990s, especially *Sahat al-Fida* (Fields of Sacrifice). Many South Sudanese found it shocking to see their national army adopting the language of the north. Vilifying the "enemy" and boosting the morale of the fighting forces and their support base among the public seemed to be the main objectives of those in charge of war-related information management. This produced two very important outcomes. The first was that the media were used to reporting the military confrontations along the increasingly hardened ethnic divide and to managing the war through speculating on sectarian relationships. The second was that this condemnatory attitude, some of which spilled over into generalized vilification of entire "tribes," was self-perpetuating, feeding a vicious cycle of hatred, and adding to the already strained relationships in the country.

The media, despite their potential to be strong vehicles for peace-making, have actually widened the wedge between ethnic communities whose views of each other were already badly affected by militarized language.

WAR AND SEXUAL VIOLENCE

Three important historical moments help shed light on the question of the use of sexual violence in the wars in South Sudan. The first was the north-south war, in both its first and second phases. There is no question that sexual violence was used against both men and women as a weapon of war, to humiliate and cow the enemy. Northern Sudanese soldiers stationed in garrison towns throughout southern Sudan seemed to calculate that abuse of this nature was a way to strike at the confidence of the people. Southern Sudanese society has a specific and unique moral philosophy, which puts women and children at the center of social structures; hitting at these groups meant the impact of the war was felt more painfully.

Northern officers were permitted to arrest women suspected of harboring rebels, or being in possession of intelligence information. During their interrogation, they were threatened by or subjected to sexual assault to extract the information. It was common to hear of people taken from their homes in Wau, Juba, Malakal and other towns in the dead of night, captured by night patrols, or taken in the chaos of battle and incarcerated in military barracks for days on end. The fortunate were released with stern warnings never to speak of their experiences; many simply disappeared, thrown down wells or dumped into rivers, or dumped in shallow mass graves.

Sexual violence was not confined to women. Men and boys were sodomized and raped while in military detention, in deliberate acts of humiliation. To add to their pain, they were told the sexual violence demonstrated the manhood of the northerners compared to southerners, of the Sudanese army to opposition fighters, and of Arabs compared to blacks. This was an attempt to de-masculinize the people, for a people rendered feminine could no longer be expected to win a war. This language is often so flagrantly racist as to be unbelievable. It shocks many non-Sudanese when South Sudanese speak of it, as if it was made up to simply tarnish the reputation of the northern Sudanese.

Survivors of sexual assault, even those who spoke about it, have never received justice. The men who carried out these acts were rarely identified and the victims (or rather survivors), were also aware that there was very little point in embarking on a quest for justice, given that the governments of Sudan had always been quick to dismiss such acts as occurring in the madness of war rather than being deliberate war crimes. In other words, they were part of neither government's policy. The way Khartoum dealt with the cases of sexual violence in Darfur after 2003 is testament to the doomed fate of justice in Sudan. The victims cut their losses and lived with their pain, rather than subject themselves to the humiliation of pursuing justice from an unresponsive state.

Poor levels of record-keeping and reporting contributed to Sudan's ability to evade responsibility for their soldiers' actions. The names of the officers involved were never recorded, and the quick turnover of command and transfer of soldiers to multiple war fronts within short periods, made documentation extremely difficult. South Sudan fell into the same trap, making efforts to cover up soldiers' actions to avoid being prosecuted for war crimes. The civil war left behind much undocumented suffering, inflicted both by the state as well as by armed opposition groups. With no credible documentation and a highly contested war history, the victims of South Sudan's civil war will simply be added to the long list of Sudan's uninvestigated atrocities against the South

Sudanese, challenging the notion of freedom that independence brought.

The second moment was the reproduction of sexual violence in families and communities in South Sudan.[3] This was not a weapon of war, but it was a product of a prolonged and oppressive culture of violence. The young men inducted into the military culture of the SPLA were pumped up with messages of revolution and the obligation of every southern Sudanese to contribute to it. They also realized they somehow needed to keep fighting but at the same time leave heirs. As the young men became conditioned to violence, using force to get their "manly" rights came to seem normal.[4] Living far away from their wives in their villages, often for prolonged and agonizing lengths of time, fighters took additional wives from the communities where they served. Men forced young women into "marriages," sometimes with total disregard for the local communities" norms governing marriage, sexuality and childbirth. This had serious consequences for the women's reproductive health as they lost a measure of control over their bodies and over the decision how far apart to space their children.

Even in marriage, let alone in forced relationships, the reconfiguration of sexual norms leads to an increase in the incidence of induced abortions. Some women felt that they were not ready to bear a child whose father could be called to the war front any day. They were forced to make drastic decisions, often under duress, and use risky and dangerous methods to terminate their pregnancies.[5] Taking wives from another ethnic group also meant that marriages did not always conform to the norms of local society, further blurring the line between marriage and forced marriage. Even in consensual relationships, there is intense discussion about whether it is acceptable for a man to force his wife to have sex. Sexual politics even affected the new constitution of the country, with individual rights set against supposed cultural norms that allow men to consider sex a "husbandly right" and a wife a mere appendage to her husband.

Changing sexual realities were a product of two war-time realities. One was the war-time militarist culture that promoted high birthrates as a way to "birth the nation" decimated by war. The other was the social practices that gave men the right to decide when sex happens. In post-war and post-independence South Sudan, the response to sexual violence depended on the willingness and ability of the women to challenge the violence, and the ability and willingness of courts to put individual constitutional rights above the moral views of society.[6] How soon these gender dynamics will shift, allowing men and women equal citizenship rights, remains highly contested.

Sexual violence in the war was insufficiently reported, almost invisible in human rights work and journalism. It was studied by academics but, when considering the results, we must keep in mind that sexual abuse, whether inside or outside marriage, is extremely difficult to study in a society in which sex and sexuality are not easily accessible, where morality trumps law, and where women are regarded as material assets of their natal or marital families.[7]

The third moment is the outcome of civil war in South Sudan. All the warring parties, the government of South Sudan and the opposition SPLA/M-IO, both reportedly committed terrible acts of sexual violence to humiliate the communities they deemed to be supporting their opponents. There were claims of sexual violence in Juba at the start of the conflict, and against women from the Nuer community at the hands of the government soldiers. These were followed by claims that the opposition, once it organized into a unified rebel movement under Riek Machar, took revenge on the Dinka in Bor town. Shocking acts of rape of women, including a particularly vicious rape of a blind elderly woman inside a church, were reported following Machar's occupation of Bor town. This atrocity remains uninvestigated and any evidence will most likely be swept away by other events.

Despite global efforts to report these terrible acts, in the hope the leaders would be shamed into rethinking their actions and rein in their fighters or seek peaceful reconciliation, as the war intensified more reports of ghastly acts of violence and atrocity continued to appear. Revenge attacks escalated to become formal military practices. One gruesome case occurred in April 2014, four months into the conflict, when a pregnant Dinka woman in Pariang town was killed by SPLA-IO and her fetus removed and chopped up. When the SPLM/A-IO took control of Bentiu, they were widely reported to have broadcast messages calling for the rape of all non-Nuer women. The media reported UN estimates that hundreds of people were killed in Bentiu, between April 15 and 16, including many civilians. Mass killings took place at a mosque, in a hospital, along roadsides and elsewhere.[8]

These seemed to be South Sudan's darkest days. People wondered how South Sudan could emerge from the abyss.[9] A sense of reflection entered the public psyche, and the South Sudanese began to speak about being one people. Calls for reconciliation to be built into the then ongoing IGAD-led peace process in Addis Ababa, Ethiopia, became louder and louder.

In March 2015, the UN secretary general reported to the UN Security Council on the sexual violence in South Sudan. His preface read:

> Sexual violence remains prevalent in South Sudan, exacerbated by impunity and a militarized society in which gender inequality is pronounced. Factors such as forced disarmament, the circulation of illegal arms, mass displacement, cattle raiding, intercommunal violence and food insecurity have increased the vulnerability of women and girls to sexual violence.

The secretary general also noted that "Such violence is, however, trivialized by law enforcement officials and by the community, with survivors often forced to marry perpetrators as a 'remedy.'"[10] A year later, in March 2016, the UN Human Rights Commission, Amnesty International and other rights groups issued a joint report stating that the SPLA, in the course of the war against the rebel forces, had committed brutal acts of sexual violence and other gruesome violations that could amount to war crimes and crimes against humanity.

The South Sudanese could not explain this almost unprecedented level of violence. Had this war, and the ones before it, caused the suspension of norms that prevented such acts in the past? Or have acts of war-related sexual violence become more vicious and therefore more visible? What do men who commit such violence say about the damage it causes to society? There are no easy answers to these questions but they do reveal one important reality: the importance of joint efforts by men and women in fighting this scourge.

Nothing in this particular war sharpened the role of the media as a force for good as well as evil more than the Bentiu incident. But the irony of South Sudanese episodes of violence, or perhaps their saving grace, is that despite the cruelty they reveal, there is always some positive aspect on which reconciliation efforts can be built. The Report of the UN Secretary General noted:

> The mass killings took place in Bentiu immediately after the capture of the town by rebel forces loyal to SPLM/A-in-Opposition leader Riek Machar, under the command of the defected SPLA general James Koang Chol. Survivors identify these forces – "rebels" – as the perpetrators of the mass killings. However, survivor accounts also suggest that some of the rebel forces intervened to stop the killings. In at least one of the mass killings, a group of perpetrators

described as "rebels" was stopped midway through a massacre by another group also described as "rebels."[11]

There was no question that these reports shocked everyone. They also showed the South Sudanese how much ethnic animosity revealed the artificiality of the claim that the South Sudanese were one people.

But it is important to understand the social norms and war ethos of the local communities. The Nuer and Dinka have historic rivalries over resources but violent conflict was regulated by a common ethos. As far as we know, these communities have never been known to engage in violence against women and children. The goal of resource conflicts was to show prowess, to defeat, not to annihilate. What purpose could sexual violence serve for the Dinka and Nuer? Was it possible that the South Sudanese had become so frustrated by violence that they gave up their historic ethnic coexistence and forewent living in harmony? Had the aspiration for power of the South Sudanese political and military leaders resulted in the disintegration of the notion of South Sudanese-ness, and dismemberment of a collective national identity?

There were several very high profile reports about the use of sexual violence. The first was the Human Rights Watch report of April 2014, which covered the initial incident in Juba, and later violence in other areas, including Bentiu.[12] The second was the report from the UN Secretary General's Special Envoy on Sexual Violence, Zainab Bangura, which said that women and children in South Sudan were the victims of the worst sexual violence she had ever seen. "In all my life, my experience of nearly thirty years in public service and in the UN and as a government minister, I have never seen what I have seen today," said the envoy after visiting the UN camp in Bentiu. "I come from Sierra Leone," Bangura said:

> I had the war. I was in the capital city when it fell. We picked
> bodies from streets and buried them ... I worked in Liberia for
> two years ... I have gone to Somalia, I have gone to DRC, I have
> gone to the Central African Republic and I have gone to Bosnia ...
> but I have never seen what I saw today,

Bengura's report, published in May 2015, was based on visits to Juba
and Bentiu at the end of a one-week visit to South Sudan. During
her visit, Bangura met officials, including President Salva Kiir,
and civil society organizations, including women's and faith-based
groups. She traveled to trouble-spots, and met ordinary people.[13]
Her comments, based on a brief visit and discussions with officials,
are insufficient as a basis for such a strongly worded conclusion;
a statement from such a high-profile UN person would create an
image the country would not be able to counter. Her report serves
only one purpose: to show solidarity with the victims of sexual
violence. Disparaging the warring parties could only lead to them
doing everything they could to defend their position.

The third and most extensive report in its coverage and detail
was the report of the AUCISS for South Sudan, a body set up
by the AU Peace and Security Council chairperson, Nkosazana
Dlamini-Zuma, soon after the outbreak of violence in Juba. When
the report came out, in early 2015, nearly a year after the inquiry
was convened, the country was in the middle of a promising peace
negotiation and the AU decided to postpone the release in case it
prompted the warring parties to shy away from the agreement. The
report was eventually made public in October.

The commission of inquiry interviewed a wide cross-section
of South Sudanese people: government officials, military personnel, opposition leaders, members of civil society, academics
and internally displaced people, including those inside the UN
camp. The report did include a brief history of the country, but

the data from these interviews were simply presented as statements, heard and recorded. The inquiry reported the political perspectives of many of those interviewed, and it seems that the interviewees recorded their largely unsubstantiated perceptions and interpretations of events they did not necessarily witness, as well as first-hand accounts. For example, to assert that President Salva Kiir was culpable in the Juba massacres, and had formed a private militia to defend himself and his power, many interviewees discussed a speech he had purportedly made in Warrap, his home state, a year earlier to the effect that he had. The report lacked analysis and contextualization of events against the wider political, ethnic, security and military climate. The result was a list of incidents from the moment the violence sparked on the evening of December 15 and following the course over the war over the next few months.

The report discussed incidents covered in the Human Rights Watch report.[14] There were descriptions of door-to-door hunting of people of Nuer descent, forced cannibalism and the execution of some two hundred men at a detention center. But few of the "witnesses" had actually seen the massacres themselves; they were basing their accounts on what they had seen in the media, but their evidence was presented in the report as eyewitness accounts. (The exception was the accounts of the IDPs, many of whom had fled from the sites of battles and had most likely witnessed the killings. They were interviewed inside UN Protection of Civilians sites.) Real and credible first-hand accounts, inflated numbers of deaths, the political/ethnic perspective, unconfirmed media reports and myths about a government that had run amok, were mixed together and offered as a credible document that could be used as a basis for punishment of abuses. Unfortunately, the perspective of the members of the commission came out more strongly than the facts of the situation.

The report could be a valuable record in a future search for justice. Families, with the help of legal experts, might be able to use it to craft cases in a court of law, especially against the state for its failure to live up to its basic responsibility to protect its citizens. The report also sets a precedent in the country's development of a culture of documentation of rights abuses, intolerance for impunity and citizens' willingness to speak up for one another when the state uses illegitimate violence or fails to provide protection.

But the AUCISS report failed the people of South Sudan on several accounts, especially in its recommendations for action. These included the recommendation that the principal leaders of the warring parties, President Salva Kiir Mayardit and former Vice President Riek Machar Teny, who ultimately bore the responsibility for plunging the country into a civil war, should be excluded from any future government arrangement that might result from the IGAD negotiations. How IGAD, the AU, or the rest of the international community were to bring peace by pleading with these powerful men while also telling them they must give up power and face the law was unclear. How were the mediators going to force them to do so? Was it not the fear of them walking away from the peace process that caused the AU to postpone the official publication of the report? And wasn't the conflict about keeping or taking power and all the resources that come with it? It was very clear from these recommendations that this was a process of appearing to do something; the African leaders behind the report knew from the beginning that it would not produce justice for the victims.

The horrific atrocities deserved a better investigation than this report was able to achieve. The report discussed political culpability but failed to pin the criminal aspects of these actions to a person and make a case for political accountability. It made general statements about the role of the nation's military, leaving the victims' families nothing to support their pursuit of justice. This report was prejudiced toward the nation's political class, seeking their removal from office even if none of them were held to account for the deaths and abuses. To go from accusations of political failure to govern and protect civilians to holding the president responsible for massacre, based on a rumor that he had been planning a massacre for two years, was an illogical leap.

This report was widely analyzed by the news media, and debated in public forums and on social media. South Sudanese groups and individuals reacted in disparate ways, almost as if they were not reading from the same pages. Supporters of the opposition and people of Nuer background, for example, applauded the report, as having categorically demonstrated the president's role in the Juba massacres. But many others saw that President Kiir was not any more liable for the events in Juba than Riek Machar was responsible for those in Bor, Bentiu, Malakal, Akobo and Bailiet.

The value of the report was reduced by the culture of moral equivalence that prevails in South Sudan. Supporters of the government seemed willing to accept that some responsibility be placed on the president for some actions, if the leader of the opposition took responsibility for other atrocities. And the converse was also true. The debate was not about the atrocities and who committed them, but about measuring the political cost of the war and determining who should be punished by exclusion from power.

This has left the dead unaccounted for. They were sacrificed for political expediency, which can never be a strong foundation for peace. The aggrieved will always search for ways to get justice, including revenge. If the peace agreement of August 2015 is implemented properly, and holds the key requirements for its success, and for the overall stability of South Sudan, there will be full accountability for crimes, and justice for the victims as the foundation for reconciliation, particularly between the Dinka and Nuer. For such accountability and reconciliation to be trusted by all sides, a credible justice system will be needed, whether that is a hybrid court involving international experts, national justices and local customary practices, or an independent and transparent South Sudanese tribunal.

DISPLACEMENT AND SOCIAL LIFE

Within a year of the start of the civil war in South Sudan, Human Rights Watch reported that, mostly in the three states of Greater Upper Nile:

> ...an estimated 2 million people were forced to flee their homes. Large parts of key towns and essential civilian infrastructure such as clinics, hospitals, and schools were looted, destroyed, and abandoned. Tens of thousands of people were still sheltering in United Nations compounds, too afraid to return home. Lack of accountability for decades of violence during Sudan's long civil war had helped fuel the conflict. Military and political leaders on all sides had failed to make any serious attempt to reduce abuses committed by their forces, or to hold them to account.[15]

Since the report was issued, millions of IDPs have remained in UN camps, in other IDP camps across the country, or in refuge in Sudan, Ethiopia, Kenya and Uganda. News reports about these people almost all focused on the conditions of the displaced but said very little about why they were displaced.

Most reports simply say the IDPs were victims of political rivalry between the leaders but offer very little about the history of previous wars and how they influenced the decisions of the fighters, or the decision of the civilian population to flee or stay. These reports did not mention the IDPs' opinions about the war and which side they supported, making them somewhat partisan. When SPLA-IO captured Bentiu, the Nuer IDPs inside UNMISS in Bor celebrated, clearly showing that they were supporters of the rebel movement. As a result, they were attacked by local people, who remembered how, early in the war, SPLA-IO had participated in the vicious assault on Bor that killed so many Dinka and destroyed the town, reducing it to ashes. News reports of the attack on the Bor UNMISS camp might have been tempted to characterize the attackers as inhuman beings who attacked women and children, ignoring the fact that the local Bor population strongly believed that many of the people sheltering in UNMISS at the time had participated in the attack on the town. Some of them had weapons inside the UN camp and so were hardly uninvolved in the conflict.

The huge cost of war and the burden it placed on the country's economy meant it was not just the people living in war zones who suffered. People in towns and cities, including state capitals, also suffered immensely from the influx of IDPs seeking respite from the war, and food, health care and education for their children. For nearly quarter of a century, between the early 1980s and early 2000s, Sudan was reported to have the world's largest population of IDPs. The story of the displaced was not just a continuation of five decades of violence in greater Sudan, but also a reminder that the CPA had certainly brushed over explosive issues in both countries, most especially in South Sudan. To conclude, the manner in which conflicts in Africa, and in the wider developing world, are reported in the media by humanitarian workers or by human rights agencies can be a double-edged sword. Reporting can be a tool to raise awareness and help the victims of conflict, but coverage can vary from a positive response from the global community to inciting more violence, hardening the positions of the warring parties and dehumanizing local people into hapless victims with no agency. In this chapter, I have tried to describe how South Sudan and Sudan's wars

have been reported over the years. The media were used very negatively by South Sudan's warring parties and their competing camps,
sometimes to recruit for the war, sometimes to vilify the "enemy,"
and incite people against one another along ethnic lines. The main
issues that I have highlighted include the dual war strategy of military confrontations and information production and dissemination
to glorify military successes, emphasize opponents' losses, mobilize
fighting forces and maintain morale.

Media and human rights reporting of these conflicts, as well as
recording events for the sake of generations to come, has aimed to
spur international action against perpetrators and in the interest
of victims, whether in terms of humanitarian intervention, peace
efforts or the application of instruments of international law. The
problem is that the reporting was neither balanced, objective, nor
measured either in its understanding of local context or in terms
of minimizing the potential negative use of information to pursue
more violence. This was important in conflicts such as South Sudan's
civil war, with its ethnic dimension. Slanted coverage often results in
many negative outcomes. In South Sudan, reporting became a tool
for inciting more violence and reducing the possibility of reconciliation and peace-building. The nature of South Sudan's civil war
resulted in news reporting contributing to the hardening of divides
and ethnic hatred. It also compromised the ethics, professionalism
and objectivity of journalists. Reporting was seriously challenged
by the complex, culturally sensitive and ghastly nature of sexual
violence as used in the civil war and others before it. The real stories
of the atrocities, the identities of the perpetrators and the shifts in
social fabric that allowed such heinous acts to be committed, are yet
to be sufficiently investigated, made public and prosecuted.

6

MIXED ECONOMIES, CORRUPTION
AND SOCIAL DISPARITY

South Sudan is likely to remain in turmoil for the foreseeable future, although the drivers of violence will be different. The new drivers will be more political and socio-economic; economic disparities born of corruption, diversion of national resources, the unresponsiveness of the top political leadership to local everyday concerns, the failure of local traditional economies to sustain large rural populations and the growing size of the poor urban population. Unrest in urban centers will also be driven by absence of opportunities for young people who migrate into the towns without skills for employment.

In the two decades between 1983 and 2005, South Sudan lost a fifth of its population through the direct and indirect consequences of the north-south war. Another third was displaced from their homes, mostly to become IDPs in what was northern Sudan, or refugees in neighboring countries, mainly Kenya, Ethiopia and Uganda. Its infrastructure, to the extent it existed, was wiped out. Ethnic groups were pitted against one another by the Khartoum regime's brutal counter-insurgency policies used to undermine the SPLA.

These problems produced what UN officials would later describe as "scary statistics." South Sudan had one of the lowest life expectancies in the developing world, the world's worst maternal and infant mortality, literacy rates, immunization rates and level of awareness of HIV/AIDS. There was a high incidence of malaria, huge gender inequality, dreadful water quality and poor sanitation. As the traditional economies crumbled under the weight of war, its population was driven into a grinding poverty almost unparalleled since the era of the slave trade. Much of the remaining population was forced to rely on international humanitarian largesse.[1]

Many citizens I have interviewed about this situation have described this period as the most "humiliating" experience in living memory. A village chief in western Dinka told me:

> To admit to poverty in order to qualify for humanitarian aid, or to watch your child waste away from hunger and there is nothing you can about it, or to abandon your home and be a displaced person near a relief center, or to eat leaves to survive … the sense of utter helplessness and humiliation that comes with such a situation is just about the most painful wound of war … and we continue to walk around with that heavy burden on our shoulders.

Another man, interviewed in January 2011 following the announcement of the results of the referendum, said:

> And yet we had knotted our hearts all that time and pushed ahead with the liberation effort knowing that the time will come when all that would be smoothed away by our independent state, by our own government … and that is why we are now celebrating, even if we cannot be certain what the period ahead will bring.

This was the backdrop to the post-war reconstruction efforts, an attempt to honor and uphold the promises of this new political transition made by the government and the international community.[2] These issues, made more deeply rooted by the prolonged war, could be expected to endure long after the return of peace. However, the way the CPA ended the war and distributed power entrenched them further.

The CPA gave total control of the state to the SPLM in South Sudan and to the NCP in Sudan. But despite its apparent populism, the SPLM proved unwilling to engage the different views of groups around the country for state and nation-building. It lost direction, and the country veered from the policies that could have confronted the serious challenges that the country inherited at independence. The political leadership continued to echo the liberation-era concept of "freedom," which included not just separation from the north, but freedom to exercise individual enterprise, and freedom from state control and violence.

A song by a famous 1970s traditional musical band, *Rong Awai* (Dinka for "nugget of salt"), depicted the concept of freedom very succinctly. Independence brought the song back to people's minds. Rong Awai sang *"piny len ci piath ago ngek acath kuen girienyde ku lut yecin jiebic"* (a country at peace where everyone walks around counting his own money and slips his hand in his own pocket). This song described the situation after the 1955–72 war, but there was no such thing in the wake of the new liberation war. That war delivered an independent country, but nothing else, unfortunately.

That background, the destruction, the post-war expectations and the remaining burden of that war define the challenges of development in the new country to this day. The time between the CPA and separation was fraught with euphoria and expectation. Oil revenues seemed unlimited, and public employees were still eager to serve. However, any successes that were achieved in the endeavor to respond to people's heightened expectations largely depended on state agencies' clear understanding of the complex situations, the capacity of agency personnel and, above all, on the existence of clear policies, good planning, sufficient funding and efficient budgeting, fiscal responsibility and capable project management. The desire to maximize personal gains was often tempered by the promise of continued flow of resources, and even would-be corrupt officials did not see the need to accelerate the speed of gains, or that some significant contributions to the people's welfare could be realized quite quickly. Road construction was commissioned in all states. Responses to hunger, to lack of health centers and schools, and to security concerns in rural areas, especially in areas bordering Sudan, were swift, at least in some states. But the initial momentum and success were short-lived and the state largely failed to meet the people's needs, demands and expectations from the moment public officials switched from a focus on public service to a scramble for self-enrichment. This switch intensified within two years into the CPA era.

The failures and wastage that were experienced generally resulted from a lack of capacity to manage resources at the national level, from inadequate security and lack of regard for the rule of law, and from poor coordination between agencies, the government and the donor community. The diversion of resources, which gathered momentum from the second half of 2006, changed the future of South Sudan and became the most serious source of state failure. The country was no longer able to honor its promises, and with that came several negative narratives. The state's failure influenced the degree to which citizens felt they had a stake in the state, and demonstrated the importance of ethnic identity, of citizenship in the tribe rather than in the nation.

This time also revealed that many leaders were not confident of the future success and viability of the state of South Sudan, and many diverted resources, sending them out of the country. In this regard, South Sudan's story of corruption is starkly different from that of other countries in the region. In most of east Africa, corrupt officials famously keep their spoils in their own countries, and invest in the employment of their people. In South Sudan, the corrupt leaders, perhaps afraid that the new country would take time to become stable and secure, refused to invest their ill-gotten assets in the country, denying employment to local people and failing to keep the machinery of the local economy oiled. They essentially removed the profits that propped the state and left the state without much to invest in citizen-centered development and service programs.

In this chapter, I shall look at South Sudan's governance structures, democracy, rule of law, corruption, human rights situation, development programs, service provision, and how the people's expectations have far outweighed the abilities and willingness of government officials to respond adequately. It will also explore the growing class and economic disparities between the small group of people who run the state and the large majority of the people, who live far away from the corridors of power. I will argue that the disconnection between what the citizens expected their country to do and what the government has actually done is partly responsible for the country's fragility in the face of the December 2013 conflict. These issues provide an opportunity to reflect on the concept of the state, how a comparative perspective on the functions of a viable state might apply in sizing up South Sudan against other states, and to probe the questions of state-building in relation to programs of nation-building.

THE DECENTRALIZED SYSTEM OF GOVERNMENT AND ITS SHORTFALLS

The South Sudanese have been engaged in a serious debate about how the country can simply implement its current system of governance, a decentralized presidential structure that divides the country into ten semi-federal states,[3] seventy-nine counties, hundreds of sub-county level structures (*payams*) and thousands of the lower units (*bomas*).[4]

The idea of this federal structure and devolution of power was developed by the NCP, and modified by the SPLM's John Garang, for the southern states, on the basis of how the "liberated" areas were ordered and run during the war.[5] This became the centerpiece of the transitional constitution in 2011; it was intended to bring government closer to the areas where majority of the citizens lived: the rural areas and small towns. It was thought this structure would give the ruling party's liberation mantra of "taking the towns to the villages" real meaning, enshrining democracy, using local taxes for local development, distributing oil revenues equitably and making service delivery a local affair. In late 2015, however, the president issued a controversial executive order creating twenty-eight states from the existing ten. This threw the country's governance into a quandary, because of the vast increase – almost to the point of bankruptcy – in the salaries, benefits and expensive equipment needed to run the new states and almost countless number of local government units.

Neither this new structure nor the decentralization policy were subject to any discussion or opinion surveys. Although the system of government was grounded in the interim constitution, it was never a widely disseminated document and did not have the benefit of contributions from the people. Many of the problems that citizens experienced were not subject to scrutiny and only a few citizens have had the opportunity to challenge or condone the system, as that would have amounted to challenging the constitution itself, and the SPLM way of doing things. If the war had not broken out in 2013, it is assumed that a review of the constitution would have taken place, although the commission in charge of this project had been at work for over two years without managing to take it to the people for consultation, let alone produce a permanent constitution. Resources were wasted in the wait for the commission to embark on the review. Foreign donor agencies put in large sums of money, but the commission dragged on and was caught by war and by the tragic death of its chair person, one of the most revered legal minds in the country, Akolda Tier.

The constitution review process was plagued by the diversion of resources, lack of coordination and legislative oversight, and the heavy domination of the process by the executive branch of the government; the same hurdles that barred the way to improvement in the social service sector. The new country was run and ordered on the basis of the hastily constructed constitution written to recognize the transition to independent statehood and create a semblance of law to help run the country until the country's founding document was revised. But the political leadership, both in its effort to hold on to public office and to effectively govern, failed to strictly adhere to the transitional constitution. The competition for power and the schemes to undermine opponents, most of which circumvented the constitution, instead undermined the stability of the whole country.

This erosion of public trust in the letter and spirit of the constitution can be seen in the way the state has failed to adhere to the very document that gives the state its existence. In everyday governance, all levels of government except the civil service, the judiciary and the army, were supposed to be elected, but no elections have been held since 2010. However, it could be said that the deteriorating political and economic circumstances of the country can be blamed for this constitutional oversight. But then the state institutions' disregard for constitutional requirements could be blamed for the political and economic crises, a cycle that will be very hard to break.

Did the country edge towards collapse because the constitution was delayed and disregarded or did disregard for the law cause the near collapse of the state? In terms of closeness to the people, the most crucial level of government is the county. County commissioners are supposed to be chosen by their constituents, but in fact have always been nominated by the governor and endorsed by the president. In turn, the governor is an elected position but he or she can be appointed and fired by the president. This has happened in several cases, when the president has used powers granted by the constitution when there is a national security imperative. This system makes the holders of public office more accountable to those above them, and not to the people they govern. South Sudan was rendered ungovernable when the liberation war ended, which eventually almost led to its collapse, as public officials spent most of their time trying to please their superiors rather than on the business of governing, and resources at state or local level were used to buy political loyalties at the bottom. This, combined with a lack of accountability, has led to a ubiquitous absence of government in most rural areas.

When the new civil war broke out in 2013, most people I interviewed said they saw it coming. They based their view on the muddle of governing that had eroded the foundation of the state before its construction began. Not only was the state absent from the lives of most citizens, it actively contributed to people's suffering where it existed. The laws and structures meant to bring the state into the lives of everyday people were disregarded and thrown away by the very people supposed to enforce them. In the end, the citizens followed suit. No tickets for traffic violations were enforced, no murder changes were brought against suspects in hundreds and thousands of cases, not a single public official was sent to jail for embezzlement and not a single South Sudanese pound was sent to a child in rural South Sudan in fulfillment of a mandate to provide cash transfers to children under five years old.

Breaking the law became the rule, not the exception. It was unclear how the leadership thought how long a country that could not do such simple things, let alone provide security, paved roads, electricity, good schools and healthcare facilities would endure before the citizens withdrew their loyalty.

MIXED ECONOMIES, SOCIAL DISPARITIES, CONFLICT AND THE ROLE OF CORRUPTION

It is difficult to reduce the spread of violence and conflict in South Sudan to a single explanation but it is safe to say that the socio-economic circumstances of many communities have played a substantial role in the demise of security in the last four decades. Some of the disparities are inherent in how traditional livelihoods operate but more recent inequalities are due to the injustice born of corruption in the management of national resources.

The use of public office to grant access to some and totally exclude the rest directly played into the discontent among certain sectors of the population, especially disaffected young people, who were a real source of unrest. Nearly all the barely organized fighting forces spoke of exclusion, mainly in economic terms, as the main reason why they formed and why they chose to fight the government. To give one concrete example, although the civil war was concentrated in Greater Upper Nile, there were several small rebellions in other parts of the country, including one in northern Bahr el Ghazal. The small number of desperate young fighters who joined it eventually rallied behind Dau Aturjong and joined Riek Machar's SPLM/A-IO. Another rebellion occurred in Nimule, under the command of Martin Kenyi, who also joined

SPLM/A-IO. A rebel movement in Western Equatoria state, which styled itself the South Sudan National Liberation Movement, eventually signed a separate peace agreement with the government to end their insurgency. One of their representatives to the peace talks, Victor Wanga, said: "We did not leave our homes to enter the bush to fight the government but to draw the attention of the government to listen to our complaints and we are not fighting any tribe."

This is not economic determinism, however. It is simply that changes in traditional economies, shifts born of the realities of conflict, can amount to serious social upheavals. In South Sudan, class divisions were comparatively minimal, especially as many decades of conflict had robbed communities, families and individuals of their traditional wealth and primary modes of production. Even senior government officials, and business-owners between the 1970s and early 1980s were rendered poor by the civil war. By the time South Sudan started to re-create its economy after the end of the second civil war, it seemed the field had been leveled. Most people existed at a similar level of wealth, except for a very few in the rebel military and the political élite, who benefited from the corrosive and predatory war economies that prevailed during the liberation period.

South Sudan's economy has five main pillars: small-scale rain-fed farming, livestock-keeping, fishing, small businesses and public sector employment. South Sudan has the largest concentration of livestock on the African continent, and cattle-keeping is the largest sector of the economy in terms of the percentage of the population involved. All ten regions/states, except for Western Equatoria, have varying degrees of animal production. In a climate of political instability, however, livestock can be subject to raiding, theft and confiscation by armed groups, as a way to tax the local population. What makes livestock so valuable, socio-culturally and economically, is also what makes them an extremely vulnerable and risky asset. But they do have the valuable quality that they can be moved when the population has to move. Farming is also a major contributor to the welfare of the population, especially to meet dietary needs, with the other three sectors playing supplementary roles. Most communities combine these activities, and some are seasonal anyway.

This economic system has always meant that a very few people control large amounts of wealth, but the notion of wealth is a relative concept; people moved in and out of a particular socio-economic state depending on their ability to combine the different sectors. A government employee whose family keeps livestock up-country might use some of their earnings to buy more cattle, thereby making their family visibly better off in terms of animal wealth. The family might be able to consume more, perhaps importing food and luxury items from a nearby town or from abroad. But such wealth often does not translate into better living conditions for the whole family, especially if we consider food consumption to be a measure of wealth, that is, that the family eats well-balanced meals and its children and elderly are well-fed. If wealth or poverty are measured by daily energy intake, most South Sudanese would be considered quite poor, despite many having massive animal assets. The children who travel long distances every day with the cattle to grazing pastures and in search of water can go for up to ten hours without eating until they return home with the herd in the evening. The cattle wealth that a family owns has very little bearing on what it eats; at certain times of the year, milk might be the only foodstuff. Cattle are rarely sold or slaughtered for meat, not even in times of famine; some families would rather starve to death than face such shame. Most cattle keepers do not produce milk products such as cheese, butter or yogurt, and have no refrigerators to keep milk fresh. South Sudan imports meat, powdered milk and many other animal products from abroad, a real quandary for the economists. In the absence of a government policy to introduce efficient means for the use of cattle resources, rural populations are likely to be locked into historical practices for some time, increasing the marginalization of a vast swathe of the population. Although rural communities have always sustained the balance of their activities and are unworried by the difficulties and content with their lifestyle, it is unquestionable that such livelihoods may no longer be sustainable in a rapidly changing world.

The majority of South Sudan's population, more than 83%, lives in rural areas and follows a traditional livelihood; the average person spends most of their time and labor in food production. Most rural South Sudanese in cattle-herding states are often hungry day-to-day and have many seasonal nutritional deficits. Humanitarian workers and development specialists call these periods of deficit hunger "gaps" or "lean seasons." Despite the involvement of cattle-keepers in peasant farming, the absence of a mixed food culture including vegetables, fruits and legumes is a major dietary problem, one that state institutions have yet to regard as a priority. Among the Naath/ Nuer and Jieng/Dinka, there is a cultural belief that certain plants, especially green vegetables, are not real foods and are unworthy of men; only suitable for poor, non-cattle-owning people. Of course, these notions lose ground in times of severe food shortages, such as the many famines that have sporadically afflicted South Sudan over the years, when a variety of wild foods, including green leaves, were consumed. Having to resort to these food sources to fill the gap is often included in descriptions of the humiliation that war has brought upon people. Some of these food cultures can appear irrational in an economic sense but are difficult to write off, as they provide an emotional and psychological bulwark against modernity and globalization. Livestock will remain central to the lives of herding populations for as long as instability remains a feature of South Sudan's political landscape. There is also debate about whether this culture is sustainable where it cannot satisfy the basic requirements of a healthy life. It will necessarily be changed by urbanization, demand for farmland, state development projects and other external forces, and when the children who normally look after the cattle are sent to school.

The boys and young men who traditionally tended the cattle are now more interested in attending school, and then go into paid employment, rather than spending their entire lives in a precarious and anxiety-ridden profession. There is considerable debate between those who see cattle-keeping as being a sustainable component of a modern way of life, built around a value system that must not be compromised, and those who see it as something that has run its course which the forces of social change will sweep aside. Complex cultural debates aside, the only way cattle-herding can continue as a major means of livelihood is if the entire cattle economy is overhauled and incorporated into the national economy. But to achieve this, both the government and private enterprise will have to lead the process of commercialization and demonstrate to the herders that the "cattle complex" can only be sustained if it is allowed to become more efficient, to keep pace with the rapidly changing world.

The culture that underpins the place of cattle in people's social and economic lives is undergoing rapid transformation, and is beset by multiple challenges related to education, overgrazing and diminishing pastures, climate change and rain patterns, urbanization and the precarious nature of cattle-keeping. The plains are becoming overgrazed, cattle-rustling is becoming ever more deadly, the old norms that deterred cattle theft are being eroded and young people are leaving for towns and cities in ever larger numbers. Some join the armed forces some start small businesses, some find employment as day laborers, and some loiter in urban slums, either becoming a burden on their few employed relatives or ending up in a life of crime. Some wealthy families hire herders from poorer families, but that is also unsustainable in the long term. Only people who cannot afford or are unwilling to send their children to school will be able to continue traditional herding. Some families divide the children, sending some to school and others to the cattle camp, although this has been known to create rifts between siblings. Those kept at home eventually come to begrudge the learned ones when the benefits of formal education become evident. Though no one can tell how long it will take for herding as we know it to die out or be abandoned, there is no argument that new forms of economic activity will take over.

The rising rate of migration of young people from rural areas to the cities is steadily becoming both a political liability and a potential resource. The existence of a large but unemployed population of young people living in cities is a major driver of violence and crime. Some young people, frustrated by the endless struggles associated with life in towns, and lacking the skills needed for city jobs, return home disgruntled and ready to join any armed group that may be recruiting. But young urbanites are a vibrant labor resource that could benefit the national economy, were there a policy that could tap it. Offering young people opportunities, through targeted skills training, could transform the national economy and be an important part of stabilizing and building the nation, imbuing young people with a sense of belonging to and pride in the nation; citizens of a nation, not of an ethnic group. It also provides young people with a sense of investment in themselves, giving them a future to live for. It is especially important for young men to feel they have a lot to lose if they are tempted to join a non-state fighting force.

However, the country currently approaches the issue of young people as a problem rather than an opportunity. This perspective has added to the factors that drive young people away from seeing themselves as people with a stake in the state and into the – often violent – embrace of politicians and military leaders. Additionally, the young people themselves have often been disorganized, divided along ethnic lines and unable to rally in huge numbers to engage politically. In the absence of real student unions and lack of independent youth leadership, and amid ethnic polarization, it has been easy for young people to be taken advantage of and deployed for others' political gains.

It is safe to say that the spread of violence, especially after 2013, is at least partly born of changing rural economic circumstances, and the lack of alternatives offered by the state. The formerly relatively classless societies of South Sudan have changed, shown by the rapid growth of economic disparity since 2005. This disparity was driven by five major factors: a predatory war economy that placed military commanders above everyone else; displacement of people from their homes for long periods; lack of opportunity and skills training for young people; and gender inequality. Above all, disparity arises from the corrupt practices of government officials; large sums of public money have been diverted to individuals through shoddy government contracts amid lack of oversight and accountability. The institutions that should oversee accountability and transparency, including the legislature, the judiciary and the anti-corruption agency, have been culpable in, if not party to, such activities. South Sudanese people have repeatedly mentioned in interviews and opinion surveys their disappointment over the mismanagement and theft of public resources, especially monies earmarked for food purchases, infrastructure and the health and education sectors.

Corruption in the infrastructure sector is one of the glaring challenges that have outraged citizens. In January 2011, when the country had voted to secede, the then government of Southern Sudan proposed and funded the construction of a new airport terminal in Juba, the completion of which was timed to coincide with independence. That deadline slipped, the independence celebrations came and went, and foreign dignitaries were received in the dilapidated old terminal. Everyone understood: the South Sudanese were focused on their celebrations and visitors forgave the young country for not having had enough time to rebuild its infrastructure after a long, destructive and deadly liberation war. But to everyone's shock, the money was gone. Work did not resume after independence and no one was held to account. The only action taken was that the minister in charge was fired in a cabinet reshuffle and no further questions asked. That minister is now said to be one of the wealthiest people in the country.

More funds were subsequently released but that money went too. The terminal remained a construction site for several years, despite a third release of more funds. Five years on (at the time of writing) the old terminal is still the only facility in use. This building, which has not been updated since 1982, has virtually fallen apart. The South Sudanese are highly embarrassed that foreign visitors' first view of their country is of a hot and crowded arrival hall, and their first breath in South Sudan is filled with the stench of broken and waterless toilets. That no one in the entire government has asked a question about this, not the legislators who approve the money, not the cabinet ministers who endorsed the project and not the anti-corruption czar, all of whom travel through this airport, is a mystery to many citizens.

Most South Sudanese recognize corruption as a source of injustice and therefore of instability. One of the strongest links between corruption and economic desperation in rural areas is the diversion of money from road construction. Between 2006 and 2012 huge budgets were allocated to construct feeder roads to connect Juba to the capitals of all ten states but the only paved highway, which connects South Sudan's capital to the Ugandan border, was funded by a US$240 million grant from USAID. Some seasonal road maintenance was carried out, using a fraction of the local funds to put together a patchwork of gravel and mud roads that are washed away by the annual rains, and the rest of the money went into corrupt pockets.

There are many ways to divert resources. The authorities in state capitals and national government officials in far-away Juba sign the contracts, and huge sums are handed over without any inspection to verify the existence or the quality of the work. The outcome is very poorly constructed roads, with no drainage and no bridges. Sometimes this is deliberate, in exchange for bribes; sometimes it is because the capacity of the national supervisory staff is weak and their level of motivation low. There are also cases where qualified government engineers are bribed, co-opted and silenced by contractors.

The lack of proper roads means the regions of the country remain essentially isolated, unable to benefit from trade and social intercourse. Western Equatoria state, by far the most agriculturally productive region, due to its skilled and self-reliant farming communities, fertile soils, lush vegetation and adequate rainfall, does not have an efficient road network that would enable it to supply produce to other parts of the country. The result is that its maize, fruits and vegetables go to waste if the farmers produce more than they, their families and local markets can consume. And so a region that could produce commercial quantities of food is forced to remain a subsistence economy. Western Equatorians need animal products, which they could buy in Unity state if they could travel and move their goods without hindrance. Similarly, the northern parts of Upper Nile are legendary for the amount of sorghum they produce, but people in other parts of the same state are annually at risk of famine, even as sorghum rots in Renk town. But policy-makers, and the political leadership of the country, see food insecurity, poor road infrastructure, the diversion of public funds, high unemployment, the humiliation of hunger and political instability as independent factors, not as a connected web that can only be tackled by a comprehensive approach.

Today, a few politically well-placed people, both in the public and private sectors, continue to directly steal from public coffers, rendering themselves and the state unable to meet their obligations and keeping the country in a state of perpetual unrest. If the stolen money leaves the country, the government will always be financially insecure and short of foreign exchange capacity. There will be no private sector to speak of, especially not one that is capable of employing a sizable portion of the population. The lack of employment means few people able to pay taxes, and so the country remains beholden to the oil industry. The oil industry is almost naturally antithetical to open democracy and public scrutiny, especially in the developing world. If Nigeria, Gabon, Equatorial Guinea and Angola are any example, nothing riles citizens more than knowing that their country is generating huge revenues from extractive industries without accruing any benefits. Unlike tax-based public spending, which the citizens can scrutinize, oil-based economies are rarely subject to citizen demands for transparency. Corruption in the oil industry is a direct source of instability, not just because of the disparities it produces in society, but also because oil revenues cause many African governments to become even more autocratic and kleptomaniac; a recipe for serious unrest, as attested by the situation in the Niger Delta, Nigeria.

Corruption in the financial sector is probably where South Sudan has suffered the most, especially in the Ministry of Finance. Unlike most countries', South Sudan's Ministry of Finance is not just in charge of economic and fiscal policy, but also of monetary policy, approving and disbursing funds to various government agencies, issuing letters of credit to private companies for the purchase of imports, signing government contracts, payment for contracts, sometimes issuing loans to individuals and businesses without requiring guarantees and holding of assets as collateral with no proof of their capacity to repay. That is too much power in a single institution that has become increasingly averse to parliamentary oversight, and where no one has the strong political will to demand annual audits. The senior management of the Ministry, from the director general, the undersecretaries, deputy ministers and the minister more or less dips a free and unquestionable hand in the national coffers.

One of the most outrageous deals the Ministry of Finance made was in 2007. The Council of Ministers resolved that traders and suppliers of foods should bid for contracts from the Ministry of Finance to import huge amounts of sorghum, the staple food of southern Sudan, and stockpile it around the region against anticipated famine. The contracts to deliver the grain became a free-for-all; having a certificate of registration as a business in South Sudan was the only criteria for qualification to become a government contractor. Hundreds of business owners applied, well beyond what was needed, and all were approved. People with no business experience, no registered business and without a single penny of guarantee, rushed to register companies. Many government officials knew it was a fraud but went ahead with it, knowing that they stood to reap handsome rewards through a chain of deals involving traders, state authorities, senior management in the Ministry of Finance and brokers.

The idea was that once the grain was delivered, and stored somewhere in the country, the contractors would have their waybills signed by the state government, and the central government would buy the grain. The government would sell the grain to the public at a subsidized rate, recouping nearly half the money. The subsidy was seen and justified as a peace dividend. Unfortunately, many contractors did not deliver any grain but presented fake waybills, agreeing with the local governor to take a "cut" of the value of the invoice in exchange for their signature. Corrupt governors signed these waybills, fully aware that they were fraudulent. The most painful, though comical, elements were the brokers, who offered to help traders get their contract paid quickly, usually in exchange for a percentage (usually 10%) of the final payment. Traders, who had no access inside the Ministry of Finance, where the payment process was controlled, handed over their papers to the broker. The broker, who might be a friend or relation of a Ministry official, took the papers in for approval and the money was transferred into the trader's private bank account. Everyone took a cut along the way. Even if a trader gave away half of what they gathered, they could be quite happy. Huge sums of money were paid, everyone involved became wealthy overnight but no grain was delivered, no lives were saved and the country was not protected against mass hunger. Grand theft became legitimate business and state officials with fiduciary responsibilities became the architects of a heist.

Even when it became public knowledge that the grain contracts were a hoax and the country was being robbed in broad day, no one was willing to stop it and the fake contracts continued to be paid. Public officials sometimes could not be paid due to shortage of funds and communities were denied their rightful services but contractually, the government was obliged to pay. Showing that the traders had not delivered the grain could implicate the entire government. The sums handed over have not been tallied to this day but are estimated to be about US$4 billion. These stolen millions are a strong driver of social disparity and have earned senior government officials and overnight "business people" a terrible reputation. Snickering behind the back of some of these people was the only recourse the people had for their stolen public resources.

One minister became known as "Mr. Ten Percent," for the bribe he frequently demanded to facilitate quick action. The whole episode demonstrates, in no uncertain terms, that the challenge of curbing corruption is perhaps second only to the question of insecurity and abuse of citizens' rights. Together, they create a strong and escalating corruption-insecurity nexus.[6]

One disappointed young man had this to say:

> I usually almost shed tears when I remember the liberation days in the 1990s when some of our current leaders and military generals would come to our villages and mark with charcoal every homestead they wanted food collected from and with soldiers arriving in the evenings to take away the food, which people gave up, begrudgingly but gave up nevertheless as their contribution to the war ... and now that we have achieved our goal through everyone's contribution, they throw that history into the dustbin, turning their backs on us.

Corruption is broadly defined as the exercise of public power for private gain, including both "petty" and "grand" corruption, as well as the capture of state activities by the élite for its own interests and profit. In South Sudan, "corruption" covers the direct theft of public money, bribery, cheating in contracts, nepotism, all forms of advantage that accrue to an individual by virtue of their position in the government and, above all, the fact that people are rarely convicted for even flagrant abuse of public office for personal gain. Corruption is not restricted to high-level government positions but pervades all levels of society, from mechanics, plumbers, teachers, civil servants, to the top layers of government. Corruption in South Sudan has become commonly condoned, as it entangles many people, even those who only benefit from it by virtue of being related to a public official.

The most dangerous thing is that corruption has developed into a sub-culture in which public property is seen as fair game. Those who have done well for themselves while holding public office are often applauded as intelligent and savvy and those who leave office empty-handed derided as inept good to their relatives for nothing. It is common to hear people commenting negatively about those in high level government positions who remain financially modest when they leave office, or positively about those who do well while in office. When a person who has misbehaved fiscally is reprimanded, it is not uncommon to hear them suggest that such behavior is acceptable, because what they have taken "is government property not your mother's." When theft appears to be condoned, and the institutions that should be monitoring it appear unable or unwilling to take it seriously, or are possibly even complicit in it, corruption becomes a vice that everyone abhors but to whose eradication no one is willing to commit.

Inadequate accountability and transparency lead to poor governance, often manifested via misappropriation of public resources. Bad governance retards public opportunities and promotes greater injustice. Good governance, in contrast, produces desired outcomes: economic, social, security and more.[7] Good values do not arrive by accident; they are taught, promoted and enforced by the law and social mechanisms. The concept of good governance means full respect for human rights and the rule of law, effective participation, multi-actor partnerships, political pluralism, transparent and accountable processes and institutions, an efficient and effective public sector, state and government legitimacy, open access to knowledge, information and education, political empowerment of people, equity, sustainability, and attitudes and values that foster responsibility, solidarity and tolerance. A country thus governed acknowledges its shortfalls, promotes those who have sustained these values as role models and punishes those who work against them.

States enact anti-corruption, accountability and transparency laws and regulations to engender and sustain good governance. However, their outcome largely depends on the level of enforcement, itself a consequence of political will and institutional strength. In developing countries, where weak institutions and lack of political will combine to degrade the ability of the political system to deliver its core functions, poor outcomes are often a consequence. In South Sudan, possibly owing to such ills, corruption and lack of transparency seem entrenched in the public sector; in 2014, Transparency International ranked South Sudan 171 out of 175 countries. The weakness of state institutions is one of the many challenges facing South Sudan; research shows that corruption flourishes in states with limited legal and administrative capacity.

South Sudan has a number of laws that forbid corruption, promote transparency and sanction public scrutiny of the state activities. The Penal Code Act of 2008 (sections 87, 91, 92, 94, and 95), prohibits bribery and mandates serious consequences for offenders of up to ten years' imprisonment. The South Sudan Anti-Corruption Commission Act of 2009 authorizes the commission to investigate and refer cases of corruption to the Ministry of Justice. Yet the war on corruption remains highly personalized. Instead of supporting the laws and strengthening institutions such as the national audit chamber, the anti-corruption commission and parliamentary committees to carry out their constitutional mandates, individual people, such as the head of state occasionally intervene to fire officials who have been accused of financial misdeeds, or form investigation committees to respond to major incidents of theft. If the accountability institutions were strengthened and mandated to fight graft, there would be no need for the president's personal involvement; the institutions would just carry out their mandate. Just as the president appoints and dismisses at will, they are also able to pardon corrupt people who have committed serious crimes that threaten to bankrupt the country and tarnish its reputation.

If those in public office are seen to escape the consequences of serious financial misconduct, it is unsurprising that ordinary citizens feel they too can engage in these terrible behaviors with very little consequence. One example concerned the Office of the President. Two senior officials stole large amounts of cash in 2014, claiming there had been a break-in. They were suspended, pending a high-level investigation involving the chief of anti-corruption and the Ministry of Justice, a first step of its kind. This allowed the public to hope that the president was acting seriously for once, but no report was ever published and the two officials were quietly reinstated after a while. After about a year, the same two officials, along with a few more others, repeated their crime, taking even larger sums. They were again suspended but this time not reinstated in office. However, they were not forced to return the money. Although not wholly satisfactory, this incident marked the first time in the country's short history when criminals were tried. Eventually, some sixteen people were indicted and taken to court in a trial that lasted several months, although speculation that they would again be released was rife. In fact, they were all found guilty of larceny and sentenced to life imprisonment. This caused shock and jubilation in equal measure, even though there were concerns about how the legal procedures were followed and suspicion about how all sixteen could receive the same sentence, despite their varying degrees of gravity and involvement in the crime.

President Kiir, although he often spoke out against the corruption he believed was rampant during the war among military officers, long before the CPA was signed, was timid in his war against civic corruption. It remains to be seen if this case was a sign of the president launching a serious war on corruption, or a whitewashing that will result in future pardons and quiet releases. In any case, it may well be too little too late. Large sums, of the order of four billion dollars, were removed from public coffers, rendering them unable to fulfill the liberators' promises of prosperity. The public perception remains that the country's leadership is unserious about fighting graft and corruption.

The lack of accountability for financial crimes, the view that corruption is increasingly condoned and the fight against it being personal rather than institutional, has major consequences on whether future programs to minimize or stem corruption will be successful, even if new officials are in power and the anti-corruption institutions are strengthened. A subculture that has emerged in the wake of corruption is an hypocrisy in which everyone decries the horrific levels of corruption in the abstract, and politicization or ethnicization of anti-corruption measures when it is closer to home. Members of an accused person's family, clan, ethnic or political group will scramble to their defense, occasionally forcing the government to drop its case. They do this because they see injustice when some people are charged with an offense or fired from their jobs, and others are allowed to get away with the crime. When accusations of corruption come knocking on the door of their own kin, it becomes a witch-hunt. This might be so, but it makes it difficult to form a unified public front against vice. Selective justice is a major part of the weakness of the accountability institutions and with it come social inequities that feed into conflict.

This is partly how the gap grew between public sector employees and those in the private sector on the one hand, and the rest of the public on the other. Corruption became the source of the ugliest form of injustice and the ghastly beginning of a class system that was foreign a decade ago. The citizens who suffer the consequences are left with no recourse other than to withdraw their trust or write off the whole government as uncaring. And when corruption follows ethnic lines, depending on the background of the person who controls financial resources or holds a key decision-making position, people retreat to the familiar, to ethnic or regional loyalties, for protection and access.

This makes the creation of a loyal citizenry, people who are proud to belong to a political entity, a nation-state, difficult to achieve. The nation-building project is defeated and a citizenry created that is quick to turn to its ethnicity in times of need, when violence breaks out, when political parties are created or elections take place. Corruption divides the nation, at first along class divides but, since economics and politics in this part of the world remain local, ultimately into ethnic or regional politics, as Bayart's *State in Africa* and Michela Wrong's *It's Our Turn to Eat* attest.

GOVERNANCE AND THE ROLE OF POLICY RESEARCH

The depraved and blatant theft of public resources is directly linked to the plight of many South Sudanese. But the failure of governance, and increasing inequality, cannot be blamed on the diversion of resources alone. Part of the problem is that the political structures and governance institutions, and the people who lead those institutions seem unresponsive to the cries of ordinary people. Whether their suffering is related to rampant insecurity, state violation of basic constitutionally protected rights, lack of basic social services, continued underdevelopment or the role of corruption, part of the reason their voices seem inaudible is that there is a gap between policy research, opinion surveys and field reports from local governments and the policy decision-making process.

Are political leaders unable or unwilling to respond? Are the challenges simply beyond the capacity of a young state? Are citizens' expectations unrealistically high in light of the destructive role of liberation wars? The reality is that there is a disconnection between the leaders' concerns, which are related to attaining and keeping political power and control of resources, and the mundane aspirations of ordinary people, focused on survival.

Politicians and state technocrats do not deny the seriousness of the problems, and it would be overly judgmental to suggest that they do not care. But there is no evidence that these problems are subject to the kind of credible data-gathering and analysis that would enable politicians to fully understand what is going on and formulate possible solutions. A review of the many development plans that the South Sudan government has produced over the years, often in collaboration with donor-supported "expert" consultants from the global north, reveals neither any serious new research nor evidence that policy-makers are using existing social science research. A cogent body of literature connects insecurity to poverty, increasing social inequality to xenophobia, the failure of state and local government to implement the local government act and prevent the interference of the central government, and also links corruption, especially the migration of stolen money to foreign banks, to the weakness of local private enterprise and the national economy.

The local dynamics that drive violence, the impact of youth unemployment on political stability, the role of women in rural economies and the social and economic impact of thirty years of war on local livelihoods have also been widely analyzed. Some of these analyses are produced by South Sudanese academics and practitioners from local research centers, both independent and based at national universities. There are of course excellent analyses produced by foreign academics and consultants who know the country well, but the local work derives its value from the researchers' indigenous knowledge attained by virtue of their intimate knowledge of the problems that face the country. But it seems that these researchers, national and foreign, are not communicating with policy-makers. There is no evidence that policy-makers read their work, understand it or use the recommendations when designing development policies. Much of the decision-making process still depends on the personal perspective of the official concerned, which might have little relevance to the problem. Even the design of individual projects, perhaps about where a new road should go, where a water project should be located, a new market be built, a police force stationed, a magistrate judge placed or a traditional chief's court be set up, do not seem to benefit from research.

What drives the disconnection between research and policy? It is not only born of limited awareness of the existence of research, the capacity of officials to understand the analysis, or even a lack of interest, but also derives from the accessibility of research. Most senior bureaucrats in central and state governments are older, from a generation that is not acquainted with the technologies that have eased access to information for so many people around the world, and in small towns even those who can use technology have limited Internet connectivity. It is also true that the ability and willingness of public officials to use research as a basis for public policy decisions is not a well-established institutional culture. Sometimes officials do not encourage research; many are suspicious about any form of knowledge-gathering and unwilling to share public records, amid concern that the researchers might find something that implicates them in corruption.

I interviewed many senior and mid-level government officials about their knowledge and receptivity to policy research, the degree to which they are comfortable sharing information about their work, how open they are to discussing research findings and how much they incorporate research into their decision-making. Most had never read a paper analyzing the political, economic or socio-cultural contexts of the country, and their policy design has largely been done without reference to research, even when analysis and data are available. This attitude among senior officials is the biggest obstacle to the production of knowledge and the ability to translate that knowledge into workable ideas for the nation's development.

To produce knowledge, many countries have a national commitment to fund institutes of higher education and government-affiliated think tanks, and to develop a reservoir of qualified people who either work directly for the government or as private consultants. The knowledge-generation system in South Sudan has multiple levels of weakness. The production of knowledge itself is at one level, and there is no credible commitment to facilitate it, as evidenced by a lack of funding for research and reliance on donor support for local institutions. The second level is the dearth of qualified researchers; the few available are so under-funded that they often resort to working for NGOs and foreign donor and development agencies. There is no clear commitment to producing a skilled workforce, and the field of knowledge production will most likely remain under-populated by South Sudanese researchers for the foreseeable future. This weakness is linked to the lack of access to computers and information technology. Access to the Internet, where it exists, is extremely poor, and generally unavailable to most people. Without it, researchers are unable to read journals, web-based research products or communicate with their peers and counterparts abroad.

The third level concerns the channels through which knowledge is fed into policy decisions, and through which decision-makers can channel their questions. On the whole, such channels are non-existent, unclear or, where they exist, poorly communicated. The result is that major public policy decisions, that affect people's lives in major ways, are either made in a vacuum or based on the sentiments of public officials.

The fourth level is the coordination between the research agencies and knowledge producers, and policy-makers. This is partly born of lack of access to publication routes available to other researchers and partly due to what may be described as a "turf war" between the research and policy communities, which leads to wasteful duplication of research effort. Many think tank and university researchers complain that public institutions do not allow access to records and object to requests for interviews with public officials. This is a major hindrance to knowledge acquisition and the ability of institutions to learn about themselves, which obstructs the country's development agenda. Policy-makers do not feel the pulse of the citizenry; there is often no way for senior officials to understand people's perceptions about corruption, nepotism, growing disparities, the rural-urban divide and other brewing unrest. Without the capacity to gauge the level of unhappiness in the country, corruption and the disparities it produces become drivers of conflict without the leadership knowing that it is happening.

It would be safe to say that the country has not had enough time to develop a culture of research, analysis and use of knowledge as a basis for policy decisions, but there are few signs of such a culture developing in the near future. The political leadership would be well-advised to start developing this culture, or the country's policy designs will continue to be carried out on the basis of individual beliefs rather than through sound locally based research.

South Sudan, beset by insecurity, development needs, humanitarian issues, health problems, environmental issues, political violence, ethnic rivalries and resource-based ethnic violence is over-researched in these areas. But most of this research is conducted by foreign researchers, international NGOs and foreign consultants. The knowledge generated by this research is destined for foreign journals, NGO offices, UN and donor agencies, but is hardly ever used as a way to improve national public policy.

Using a very well-received journal article about the violence and counter-violence that had plagued Lakes state for years, written and published by a western anthropologist, I tested my suspicion that public officials do not use research. I took the article to every member of the state parliament, state cabinet members, the state governor, local government officials and the police commissioner. I asked everyone if they had seen this incredibly insightful piece about their state, and not a single official knew about it, even though they remembered the researcher conducting their field work.

Areas of need remain important as research themes for the government, and are on the radar screens of public and private national research bodies, even though the government does not actively fund research. But even NGOs that produce research do not keep it as part of their permanent institutional knowledge. Research is often project-specific and is either discarded at the end of the project or simply left in inaccessible storage. This, combined with the quick turnover of NGO staff, means new international staff often have to reinvent the wheel when they are deployed to South Sudan, making their learning curve about the local context all the more steep.

Some areas of need seem more important to the government than others, based on the amount of funding that the government and donor agencies put into research or the implementation of projects. Security, including the national defense force, the national security agencies and other organized forces, is the leading recipient of government funding; it is estimated that the government puts more than half the national expenditure, nearly US$500 million dollars annually, into this sector. How much of this goes into research, training and professionalization is not known, as the Ministry of Defense is very secretive about how it uses public funds. (Much about war and security in the country remains under-investigated; for example, the death toll of the last civil war with Sudan remains unquantified to this day, with only unreliable estimates of two to three million people. The new civil war raged for more than two years and no one knows exactly its cost in human lives, material resources or wrecked ethnic relations, although such knowledge would be useful in reconstruction, reconstitution of the army and rebuilding ethnic relations.)

Economic development and the provision of public goods and services follows, in terms of government investment and expenditure. Most citizens, having been deprived of these services in the old Sudan, expected and demanded immediate action to improve security after the end of the civil war. Whether the government has lived up to the expectations of the public is open to debate. The politically connected few have done very well, while the majority with no access to the corridors of power feel entirely excluded from the gains of independence. The disparity of opinion between the new rich minority and the marginalized majority, and the debate that goes on around this, is most intense in the areas of security and safety, healthcare, educational services, food security, telecommunications and infrastructure. Whatever physical infrastructure existed was destroyed in the quarter-century of war, and the lack of progress in this area has heightened the level of disappointment and unhappiness toward the state and the government.

The burden of the liberation wars, ethnic violence and the unrestrained use of state violence to deal with tribal militia issues, have created an environment in which the state is increasingly seen by citizens, especially rural people, as a party to the violence, not the solution. An area of great importance with regard to understanding how the citizen relates to the state is peace-building and reconciliation to mend ethnic relations affected by conflict, including human rights abuses, demands for accountability, justice and reparations for victims of sexual violence, mass atrocities, the targeting of non-combatants and the destruction or theft of property. South Sudan's political leadership has promised to conduct reconciliation and peace-building, but this has not happened, mainly due to political rivalry between the leaders and the diversion of funds by the people in charge of the programs. If the fear of research continues, ethnic relations will remain strained, and a random incident could trigger the outbreak of another war.

Unemployment or marginal employment, especially of young people, is a major aspect of growing socio-economic disparity and socio-political unrest. South Sudan is one of the most youthful countries in the world; 73% of its population was below the age of thirty in the 2010 national census and household survey. This makes the need for a clear policy on how to tackle the demands on and pressures from young people unmistakable. The areas of the economy that would address the challenges of youth unemployment include food security, especially the development of agriculture, livestock and fisheries, and ways to wean the country from its unhealthy dependence on oil. Although oil is a highly technical sector that employs only a very small number of people, its revenues could be used to create major capital projects in transport, electricity generation and food production, which would employ millions of citizens.

Agriculture, in all its forms from plant to animal to fish, is the major trade and pillar of traditional livelihoods. With more than 83% of the population living in rural areas and reliant on peasant farming, properly investing in and developing agriculture could be the most sustainable source of income for the country and loosen its dependence on oil. A finite resource that is at the mercy of unpredictable global markets and a source of undemocratic practices and political instability, oil is not a reliable resource. But how can agriculture be developed if decision-makers are not engaging with locally produced research, or research discussing the experiences of other countries in similar situations? South Sudan has fertile soils, varied climates and adequate rainfall. The Nile is an abundant source of fish, and the country has Africa's densest concentration of livestock. With more than twelve million head of cattle, sheep and goat, South Sudan has more livestock than people, yet the country imports meat, yoghurt, butter and other milk products; research could show how to turn this anomaly around.

The country's wildlife is also legendary; the antelope migrations along the Boma plateau in the south-east of the country are second only to the Serengeti in Kenya and Tanzania. How to conserve their majestic animals, support the people's stake in conservation and maintain the delicate ecological balance sustained by generations of South Sudanese is a challenge that transcends the country's borders. Tourism could be a major area of research, investment and development, with the potential to economically engage people living in or near game parks. But over the last ten years, the diversion of allocated budgets, the swelling of the ranks of the wildlife protection and conservation force by large number of ex-combatants with very little experience in wildlife protection, and a consequent increase in the salary bill, have stood in the way of the development of this sector. However, no one is willing to feed this knowledge into policy decisions.

Health and education stand out as important areas in which research has been insufficiently used to help policy design, although they are priorities for both the government and citizens. Although the health sector enjoys a high profile in government rhetoric, the government allocates only a miniscule percentage of the national budget to it, but this is an area that both receives a great deal of foreign funding. The reason why it is so important is that South Sudan has some of the world's worst health indicators. The health system is weak in many areas, including poor immunization coverage, and control of malaria and tuberculosis and chronic non-communicable diseases, such as heart disease, diabetes and cancer.

Poor nutrition and famine complicate the health of the South Sudanese, as they compromise the person's level of resistance to the above diseases.

Health care is also the area most revealing of socio-economic disparity. The wealthy can use private clinics or travel abroad for health care, mainly to Kenya and Uganda, but also to Egypt, Jordan, India and Thailand, often at public expense if they are politically connected or hold public office. The fact that the country's élite and their families seek health care in foreign countries shows not only that they do not trust the national hospitals, but also that they do not feel the urgent need to invest public money in local health facilities. If ministers or governors, or their wives, do not have their babies in local maternity hospitals, they cannot know what the service is like. Citizens who watch their loved ones die in local hospitals from avoidable causes such as childhood diseases preventable by vaccination, insufficient blood in the blood bank, lack of electricity which prevents oxygen being given or halts an operation, are naturally bitter. Too many people die in South Sudan because of lack of access, cost or poor level of service, all connected to the diversion of public resources and the absence of credible research in the corridors of power.

To conclude, much of what I have considered in this chapter is the subject of anthropological research and development studies, and is well known. But I have discussed it here to make clear the point about the disconnection between research and policy-making at all levels of government, which is a serious problem. Most, if not all, important policy decision-making is based on the whim of the person in charge of a government agency and does not benefit from research. There is a tendency among the leaders of South Sudan to see social science research as a luxury, the domain of anthropologists and sociologists, a thing that could be interesting to read when the opportunity presents, rather than a significant form of knowledge that could be used in policy design. Some are enthusiastic about seeing their own communities written about, sometimes adopting the anthropological interpretation of cultures, social organization and family dynamics to describe their own society and sub-culture; a fun way to record and preserve culture, but something with limited relationship to government decisions.

This has meant that the major policies that affect people's lives are made in a knowledge vacuum, with little recognition of the changes that are occurring in society, and no attempt to make the connection between such changes and the state's inability to provide an alternative to political turmoil. When violence breaks out, crime increases and young people demonstrate their unrest, which comes as a surprise and shock to the country's senior leadership. If those leaders paid attention to research results, or conducted their own research and analysis, they would realize that there is a strong link between corruption, youth unemployment, increasing poverty, feeling of exclusion and violence. And they could possibly anticipate unrest or perhaps even pre-empt it. However, this begs the question of whether social science, a traditional western way of knowledge generation, and a tradition once rooted in colonialism, has not gained traction as basis for policy decisions in Africa in its hundred-year history, does it stand a real chance of becoming useful to key African decision-makers in the future?

The combination of the decline of rural economies and livelihoods, lack of state intervention and the increasing diversion of public resources to personal and family use has increased the socio-economic disparity, which is so dangerous for the unity and stability of the country. The growing corruption-inequity-instability nexus has become more evident in the last ten years, and an additional factor in increasing insecurity. This nexus has not been dispersed, as it is in many countries, by the use of research and policy analysis to understand the pulse of the country and disarm disaffected segments of the population.

In this chapter, I have described the flagrant and insidious growth of corruption, which is causing citizens to inadvertently applaud the vice, even as they abhor and complain about it. To prevent the widening socio-economic gap, reduce the likelihood of violent ethnic feuds, increase respect for the rule of law and build a strong culture of civic responsibility, it is important that the government of South Sudan, civil society and political parties collectively fight the corruption that has driven a wedge between the excluded rural and urban poor and the politically well-placed few who control state power and the resources.

A successful war on corruption is a function of strong laws, determined enforcement and general civic awareness. Standing up against this ill, as a community, is a form of nationalism as important for the good of the country as the war of liberation. Allowing corruption to thrive will feed inequality and class divisions, which in turn drive the bitterness that results in unrest and violence.

7

ETHNIC RELATIONS, THE NEW WAR AND THE (DIS)UNITY OF SOUTH SUDAN

The unity of the former southern Sudan, and the degree of social cohesion that exists among its people have historically, at least for the last sixty years, been propelled by a single issue: the question of secession and the unity of Sudan. This was a long-pursued quest, but one in which there was little articulation of what would happen after independence was achieved, how the country would be governed and what challenges it would face. In the 1980s, many South Sudanese, thousands of Dinka and large numbers of Nuer, especially from the Gajaak section, died in fighting over this question, as the contending sides allowed it to fray into massively violent confrontations. Thousands of deaths in pursuit of an issue later viewed as totally unnecessary and completely avertable; historical oneness had often existed side-by-side with disagreements among the south Sudanese.

While the dispute continued, leaders changed sides and moved in and out of positions. The unity of Sudan versus southern separation was not always a black and white issue, at least not for all the southern Sudanese. Some people saw advantages in Sudan remaining unified, and separation as a potential liability. Others saw separation as the panacea for Sudan's protracted political woes, categorically the only option, preferring whatever challenges the south might face to the horrors of second class citizenship in a united Sudan. In the end, the people of southern Sudan were always in favor of separation, notwithstanding the challenges of creating a viable state. But there was little discussion about what would keep the southern Sudanese together afterwards.

A few people looked past the day of separation. The leading thinker, John Garang, who had the audacity to think publicly and the capacity to think in terms of practical policies, was a unionist who never openly admitted that separation could be a fall-back position should all else fail. South Sudan therefore became independent before anyone considered what an independent South Sudan should be, what ethnic-based divisions would look like when the unifying factors were removed, what would happen when there was no Khartoum to blame. In short, what the shape of a unity-in-diversity project should be.

Throughout the post-colonial history of Sudan, there were signs that disagreements were confined to debates between southern and northern Sudanese about the nature of the state. But after 2005, when the post-CPA calm ran out of steam, other divisions within were revealed. These divisions were rooted in rivalries among the separatist politico-military leadership, and were manifest in rebellions against the Juba government triggered by perceptions that political power was heavily dominated by a few ethnic groups and the SPLA/M. The list of grievances – tribalism, nepotism and the concentration of power in a few hands – that caused the volatility varied depending on who was the accuser.

In a pattern that seriously affected the country's security, unity, stability and resource management, senior army officers who were unhappy about integration, or felt sidelined, frequently rebelled, hoping they would be re-integrated with an inflated rank and sizeable monetary compensation. These episodes of competition, rivalry and rebellions quickly began to take on an ethnic dimension, as the leaders used their ethnicity to attract supporters or to defend their seat in government. What would happen to a nation thus divided did not seem to cross their minds.

The unity of purpose that the people of southern Sudan demonstrated during the liberation and referendum, despite localized violence, ethnic divisions and political rivalries in the SPLM, seems to have misled the leadership into thinking that solidarity could be translated into a strong foundation for the new nation. But when South Sudan became independent, after almost 190 years of struggle, its leaders were quickly made aware of the colossal challenges ahead. They had to work out how to transform their shared history of destruction and death into an asset for unity. They may have worked together to achieve the monumental goal of independence, but political separation was not enough to keep the people glued together, and loyal to their country. It became evident that South Sudanese-ness was more an "imagined community," as Benedict Anderson (see bibliography) described it, than a ready-formed entity.

The government of the new state inherited a country without a single inch of paved road, a literacy rate of less than 27%, and the worst childhood immunization rates in Africa. A country in which only one out of ten women had their baby under the care of trained healthcare workers and a 14-year old girl was more likely to die in childbirth than graduate from high school. The UN's "scary statistics" were not abstract numbers; they clearly delineated the gigantic tasks the new country's leaders faced. No one anticipated that these leaders would almost lose sight of what had fueled the liberation efforts. Some of South Sudan's leaders thought the people's shared experience of destruction and suffering could become a basis for oneness and national belonging. Every passing day of delay in the country's ability to address its problems in a timely manner reduced people's trust in the state and the government, and their excitement about belonging to a new country.

With more than sixty ethnic groups within its borders, South Sudan is one of the most ethnically diverse countries in Africa. Some saw this diversity as a challenge to its ability to become a cohesive, unified and stable country, but others saw its cultural richness as an asset that could be harnessed to create an exemplary African nation. "Unity in diversity" became the preferred phrase to describe how South Sudan would stabilize itself. The SPLM's vision for stability-building, although initially conceived for all Sudan, contained programs that would reward the people for their hard work on liberation that could be tweaked to fit the circumstances of separation. "Taking towns to the villages," which John Garang eloquently described, was one approach; it called for the extension of development services to rural areas and also the distribution of power and government.

The vision also contained elements of statecraft to celebrate the rich history of the country and reflect its many heritages, so that every citizen and community could see themselves represented in the nation's story. In theory, the vision aimed to create a national identity to which every citizen could subscribe, to see themselves as belonging to the nation and not to a tribe; to create the political stability that emanates from people's graduation from strong tribal or sectarian affinities and into the wider national body politic.[1]

Unfortunately the SPLM's vision, despite the recognition of its elements' centrality to the stability, viability and prosperity of South Sudan, was not converted into the practical policies needed to shield the country against the challenges that threaten new states. The lack of implementation of these programs exposed the ruling party to piercing criticism that it had lost its vision and the increasing amount of dissatisfaction with the SPLM led to its disintegration and fed into the factors that drove the country into a new civil war. Gradually, as the leaders scrambled for power and resource control instead of prioritizing nation-building and assisting communities to rise above the horrific memories of past wars, the vision ran into serious challenges.

People's expectations were high; the lack of state-building capacity and policies to manage these expectations made the SPLM's vision seem an empty promise, especially to the rural population and urban poor whose expectations focused on services they were denied under Khartoum. Observers remarked on the loss of direction among the SPLM leaders; it seemed only its lofty slogans remained. Freedom, Justice, Equality, Democracy and Prosperity were beginning to ring hollow. Analysts and independent observers warned that allowing negative popular perceptions of the SPLM to flare could throw the ruling party and the whole country into turmoil. Some accepted this criticism, including members of the political bureau, who requested a review of the vision in consultation with the party membership in the country.

Riek Machar, vice president and deputy chairman of the party led a delegation touring the country "to thank the people of South Sudan for their contribution to the liberation" and take the pulse of the nation. They found a population that was very angry about what many saw as a total disconnection between the leadership and the citizens still waiting for the ethos of liberation to be translated into welfare. The findings of this tour became part of the disagreement within the party, as some senior members of the party saw the criticisms as facile assessments and some dismissed them as doomsday predictions; some demanded immediate action to rectify the imbalance and others saw it as a "blame game." Unfortunately, many of the observations about the loss of direction, the people's diminishing confidence in the state, their complaints about lack of good governance and corruption, and above all how these developments threatened the stability of the country, were correct.

The outbreak of war in 2013, although rooted in political disagreements, destroyed property, diminished security, halted development and foreign investment, and imposed a financial cost the country could not afford. The war shattered the country's global image and threatened its most important resource and foundation: the lives of its people and their ethnic unity. It was obvious that the conflict would be resolved sooner or later, but the question was how the South Sudanese would view each other afterwards, and what that would mean in terms of how the country maintained its territorial integrity. These questions will remain a concern for some time to come and their answers will be determined by how the leadership tackles the vile actions ethnic groups have meted out against one another at the behest of political leaders.

With the various ethnic groups at loggerheads over ethnic pride, the distribution of the national pie, political power, disputed memories of violence and accountability for war crimes, the unity project and the growth of a national identity will remain fragile and tenuous. The ability of the state to cohere will remain challenged by the disconnection between citizens and the state, partly due to the inability of the state to provide security, justice and accountability, the most strongly anticipated independence prizes.

In this chapter, my goal is to present an analysis of the extent to which the South Sudanese leaders had attempted – or not – to think ahead as they prepared for independence. How did they intend to transform their young state from a political and geographic entity into a nation? How did they propose to "make South Sudanese"? I shall describe some of the obstacles to national unity and the development of a collective national identity that placed pride and loyalty in the nation first and ethnic identity second. I shall also consider whether there was actually a foundation on which they could build such a transformative project. In a sense, there was political recognition that a nation did not exist just because the new state of South Sudan was established, an understanding that "nations are made, not born." The challenge of crafting a nation requires a clear and home-grown roadmap, a commitment to a program of action, an investment of political will and adequate financial resources.

The chapter also focuses on how the new civil war increasingly took on an ethnic hue, pitting the Nuer/Naath against the Dinka/ Jieng. It also explores how the civilians of the two ethnic groups, whether they fought on the side of the SPLM/A-IO or the government, or were simply caught in its midst, navigated the treacherous waters of this most vicious of conflicts.

OBSTACLES TO COLLECTIVE BELONGING

Anyone who knew anything about the new country's recent past in the fifty or so years before its creation could tell that it stood on shaky ground in terms of unity and peace. The country needed a plan that combated the obstacles to nationhood and invested in and promoted the opportunities offered by the shared history of liberation struggle as a basis for the state and nation-building projects.

At independence, people's recognition of the role of state in their life was tied to the services that the state offered. When the state delivered, people were strongly South Sudanese; when it did not, they were Jieng or Zande. The program of nation-building needed to assert itself in promoting reasons for citizens to see themselves as represented in the body politic, with a stake in their nation and less in their tribe. This endeavor needed not to be empty rhetoric but goal-oriented and executed with the utmost commitment and transparency.

During the liberation wars, however, as the South Sudanese committed to the collective effort to challenge Khartoum, which translated into a tenuous unity, the region was beleaguered by the destabilizing counter-insurgency tactics of the Sudanese government that pitted the South Sudanese against one another along ethnic lines. Many leaders saw these Khartoum-sponsored confrontations as temporary results of the burden and pressures of war that would not stand the test of time. They believed that when some of these "bought" South Sudanese realized where their real interests lay, they would come to their senses and the unity project would forge ahead.

However, the global community that supported South Sudan was sometimes unsure about the logic of the splits within the ranks of the southern front. Outsiders could not understand why Riek Machar allied himself to Khartoum after splitting from the SPLA in 1991, what Paulino Matiep Nhial of the SSDF was doing in Western Upper Nile, or Martin Kenyi in the Equatoria Defense Force. All these men had fought against the SPLA, with varying degrees of success, with the support of Khartoum – the enemy all southerners agreed they should collectively fight – in arms and intelligence. Were the splits and confrontations an indictment of the South Sudanese and their ability to present a united front against Khartoum? Many South Sudanese dismissed such accusations, saying that the splits were born of temporary lapses in judgment by a few people desperate for power and resources, and not evidence of the demise of their unity of purpose.

At independence, the nation-building project needed to debate these war-time squabbles so that they could no longer feed retaliation. Sadly, this debate was not conducted, although everyone in the leadership talked of its importance. The immediate result of Khartoum's policies, and the local competition for power that they inspired, was the continuation of intense and daunting ethnic conflict. Paulino Matiep and his SSDF, and numerous other militias with roots in the Any-nya II movement, wreaked so much havoc in Western Upper Nile and Bahr el Ghazal that the confrontation morphed from one between the Khartoum-linked SSDF and the SPLM into a Nuer-Dinka war, because the SSDF relied on cattle raids in Dinka areas to feed themselves. Although these were local dynamics in the manifestation of the major civil war between north and south Sudan, the ethnic dimensions of the conflicts caused real damage to ethnic relations and the South Sudanese sense of collective belonging both before and after independence.

In addition to Khartoum's sponsorship of these South Sudanese self-destruction projects, rivalries among southern leaders were often stoked by struggles for control of the opposition armies linked to political disagreements about liberation. Each leader thought control of the movement would allow them to push the version of liberation they wanted to advance. These political dis-agreements tended to follow sectarian fault lines, as breakaway leaders were only able to register their grievances by recruiting the support of their ethnic kin, drawing their communities into conflicts that were beyond the usual competition over livestock and grazing rights.

When Riek Machar and Lam Akol's 1991 attempted coup against John Garang, which failed to remove him from the helm of SPLA/M, resulted in the formation of the SPLA/M Nasir faction (named after the town in Upper Nile where the coup happened). This was by far the most destructive splintering; its eventual result was a prolonged violent conflict between the Dinka and the Nuer that lasted almost a decade. Another offshoot of Riek and Lam's revolt was a group led by one of the founding members of the SPLA, Kerubino Kuanyin Bol, from Twic, in what is now Warrap state. Kuanyin was a veteran liberation fighter from the first round of war who was absorbed into the SAF following the Addis Ababa

Agreement of 1972. As commander of Battalion 105, stationed in Bor, he was celebrated for "firing the first shot" that sparked the second liberation war in 1983.

Garang, Kuanyin, and another first war veteran, William Nyuon Bany, had established the SPLA in 1983 but their revolts were related to growing dissent within its ranks. John Garang was criticized for the iron-fist style with which he ran the SPLA. Kuanyin and Nyuon, although great field commanders whose prowess against Khartoum had earned them the respect of many southern Sudanese, were both known for the brutality and speed with which they punished soldiers and robbed civilians. They were also very ambitious and limited in how much they were willing be ordered by their commander in chief, John Garang. After Riek and Lam had failed in their coup, the two had various disagreements with John Garang. Some concerned their conduct as senior officers, both in the community and over strict military issues, while others centered on the debate over liberation of Sudan and independence for southern Sudan.

At different times in 1992 both Nyuon and Kuanyin were arrested and detained by Garang and both defected from the SPLA when they were released. Nyuon, celebrated for his command of Battalion 104, based at Ayot in Jonglei, was killed while fighting against the SPLA in Equatoria in 1996. Kuanyin defected to Khartoum, joining the NCP and committing to fighting John Garang by executing Khartoum's program of destabilization of the SPLA's civilian support base. He knew that the path to John Garang passed through a large swathe of territory where the SPLA enjoyed popular support, especially in Dinka areas, and so chose to fight in his home area of Bahr el Ghazal, especially Gogrial. Kuanyin wreaked almost unprecedented and massive havoc, greatly contributing to the deadly famine of 1998, which killed more than 60,000 people in Bahr el Ghazal in three months.[2] Kuanyin reasoned that while he did not intend to kill his own people, he was fighting Garang, and if the people who were supposed to support his cause instead chose to defend Garang, they could expect to suffer.[3]

Kuanyin's actions quickly proved how the South Sudanese remained flexible about which side they fought on when the contest was not clear cut. In 1998, in coordination with the SPLA, he attacked the SAF garrison in Wau town, seized control and declared he had decided to rejoin the SPLA under John Garang. Although the town was re-taken by the SAF some days later, the momentary seizure by the SPLA was greatly celebrated, boosting their morale, and Kuanyin did rejoin the SPLA and was moved to Nairobi shortly after, where he held talks with John Garang about his reintegration.

Unfortunately, over the next few months, due to Garang's suspicion about Kuanyin's motives, their reconciliation was never finalized. In September 1999, while traveling through Upper Nile trying to round up his former soldiers in the hope of reorganizing them to rejoin the SPLA, Kuanyin met his fate, killed under mysterious circumstances. Many fingers were pointed at Garang. Kuanyin, while a great and brave fighter, was a rather unruly soldier, with some mad militarist habits, and Garang may have thought his reinstatement to the SPLA presented unacceptable challenges to his leadership. Kuanyin's death remains a very sore point between leaders from Jongeli, John Garang's home, and the people of Bahr el Ghazal, Kuanyin's.

This incident, although it only involved people from one ethnic group, is a classic example of how such confrontations preoccupied much of the leaders' thinking. It left very little comfort about what would happen to South Sudan when it became a sovereign nation; how men with such acrimony between them could create a unified nation. If they could demonstrate such viciousness against one another while in the midst of the war against a savage foe, what would happen when their common enemy, the government of Sudan, was removed from the field?

For many South Sudanese, confronted with wartime realities, the common answer to this question was that Khartoum was to blame. These local conflicts were seen as a part of a divide-and-rule scheme, intended to weaken the southern resolve to liberate itself. This was a simplistic argument, but a convenient one. Even the fighters and their leaders, who had to turn their guns on their (supposedly) own people, were quick to use this argument, despite it flying in the face of the facts about the real driver: the leaders' greed for power.

This is not to say that Khartoum had no hand in events, as one of my interviewees pointed out:

> You mean you knew all along that Khartoum was playing you against your brethren and you complied, only for you to turn around and blame your self-destruction on the enemy whose goal has always been the destruction of you both, and you think you can make him look bad ... is that not admitting to your own stupidity [rather] than revealing the viciousness of your opponent?[4]

Few South Sudanese doubted Khartoum's role in their internal wars, but many questioned why their leaders allowed their collective enemy to pit them against one another.

Other equally, if not more, horrendous and abominable atrocities were committed by the South Sudanese against their own people, including Peter Gatdet's multiple defections, returns and re-defections from the SPLA throughout the 1990s and 2000s.[5] More recently, David Yau Yau and George Athor in Jongelei, Martin Kenyi Terensio in Equatoria and Garhoth Garkuoth of the SSDF opposed the SPLA at the behest of the Khartoum government. The SSDF had its origins in the territorial and tribal militias (particularly in Equatoria and Western Upper Nile) that resisted SPLM/A incursions during the late 1980s, and among the largely Nuer fighters who remained loyal to Riek Macher after his failed coup. The impact of these groups, and the leaders who championed them, can be measured as much for the rifts they created in the South Sudanese people's efforts to be a cohesive nation as in the material destruction they caused.

Notably, these groups strongly espoused self-determination for southern Sudan, but when they signed the Khartoum Agreement in 1997, they exposed themselves to the mockery of many South Sudanese. Many could not understand how they sought separation from Khartoum by joining their most vicious opponents, the Islamic radicalists that the South Sudanese abhorred. "To go and fight on the side of our enemy and then expect them to hand you separation, the very objective of the SPLM, which they have fought so vigorously to deny us all these years and to prevent it from ever being realized … I just do not understand that logic," remarked one South Sudanese person, distraught by the arguments used by Riek Machar to defend the Khartoum Peace Agreement as an avenue to self-determination. "Either these men were just covering up their surrender to Khartoum with this agreement or were entirely naively duped, revealing their inability to think, or they were simply out of ideas," said another interviewee.

The Khartoum Peace Agreement committed the government of Sudan to a self-determination referendum. But when the promised referendum did not materialize (Khartoum never really intended it to), Riek Machar returned to the SPLM/A in January 2002. Most of his forces, together with other militias that joined the SSDF in mid-2001, maintained their commitment to the Khartoum Agreement, holding out right up to the CPA. Martin Kenyi, Garhoth Gatkuoth and Paulino Matiep Nhial were among this group, so much so that when the CPA was being negotiated, Kenyi and Garkuoth represented Khartoum's armed forces in the discussion of security arrangements. After the CPA some, chiefly the SSDF under the command of Matiep, were invited into the SPLA by President Salva Kiir so they could face the referendum together.

Paulino Matiep became second-in-command of the newly established army of southern Sudan, under Kiir. He committed himself to the unity of southern Sudan in preparation for the referendum. He had long been committed to self-determination, if slightly illogical in his approach of demanding from within the belly of the enemy, so to speak. Peter Gatdet, Gatluak Gai and other militia leaders oscillated between joining the SPLA and staying as Khartoum's proxies, but Matiep kept to his word, and publicly committed himself to South Sudan's independence, a position he maintained until his death in August 2012. He described the potential achievement of independence, a year before his death, as his moment of most happiness, when I interviewed him in 2007. But for the others, there remained too much bad blood among the various forces that were reintegrated into the SPLA. This created a very volatile national army, where officers existed in ethnic cliques. The country's biggest institution, and the one that most reflected its ethnic diversity, was unable to function in one of its main roles and sow the seeds of national unity.

The gravity of the tensions within the army was demonstrated in 2013; when the country imploded, the army fell apart along old war-time, ethnic-based, faults. The former warlords and militia leaders, Riek Machar, Peter Gatdet, Mabor Dhol, Simon Gatwech Dual, Gabriel Tanginye and Garhoth Garkuoth, quickly became the leaders of the SPLA-IO. With their capacity to mobilize their ethnic group, the Nuer, these men led the war not just against the government but also against the state and against the Dinka. In essence, the war was executed with the intent to kill as many Dinka as possible, for they reasoned that the government in Juba was a Dinka government. The language of "Dinka government" continued even after the two sides signed the peace agreement of August 2015 and formed the government of national unity in April 2016, with Riek Machar reinstated as first vice president. In fact, this unity government quickly fell apart when the armies of Kirr and Machar started fighting in July, barely three months in, and Machar was forced to flee from Juba once again, back into exile, and moving from one country to the next.

When the war started in 2013, Riek Machar's fighting force was made up of early defectors from the national army of South Sudan, but they eventually organized into what became known as the SPLA/M-IO. Their early success, culminating in the rapid capture of Bor town a few days after the war began in Juba, threatening Juba in January 2013, and the occupation of Akobo and Bentiu later in April, was attributed to the sheer numbers of White Army members who flocked to Riek's side. The White Army was a civilian youth fighting force, mainly from Luo Nuer, that took its inspiration from a nineteenth-century prophet, Ngundeng. They rallied not to support Riek's political ambitions but supposedly to avenge the killing of hundreds of Nuer people in Juba, in what they were told were targeted killings carried out by Kiir Mayardit's Dinka.

Nothing more strongly demonstrates the use of ethnicity to mobilize for war than the list of generals Riek Machar gave command of his forces, which reads like a parade of warlords. They included Peter Gatdet, military governor of Unity state, Gabriel Tangiye, military commander of Upper Nile, Gathoth Gatkuoth, military governor of Upper Nile, Gabriel Duop La, military governor of Jonglei and James Koang Chuol, military governor of Unity state and later military commander in Jonglei. Most of these military generals had been instantaneously promoted to the ranks of lieutenant general and major general and their ascent led to generalized ethnic violence as they supervised the war on Riek

Machar's Nuer side. Unlike the national army, which was mixed and used either English or Arabic to give orders, the SPLA-IO was almost exclusively Nuer, and used the Nuer language on parade. As Riek shuffled and reshuffled the generals around the warzones controlled by the SPLA-IO, there were frequent squabbles, not just within the ranks of the rebel movement but also along sectional lines among the Nuer. The White Army, for example, who were largely from Lou Nuer to the east of Greater Upper Nile, objected to having Peter Gatdet, from Western Upper Nile, as their commander.

The speed at which these fighters gained territory against the government, and their vicious notoriety, were both attributed to the inspirational command of Gatdet and Gathoth. They shared a style of command and morale-boosting approach, feeding the fighters with phrases emphasizing the Nuer's warrior tradition, bravery and skills and increasing the hateful rhetoric against the Dinka: "Nuer are braver than Dinka," "Nuer defeated the British colonial army," "Nuer contributed the most to the liberation of the country." The Dinka responded, when they had the opportunity to speak freely, among themselves. But it was not long before the SPLA-IO splintered. Gatdet and Gathoth, true to their nature, broke away from Riek Machar and defected to Khartoum, claiming they were unhappy with how Riek Machar had run the rebellion and with way he was commanding the war. This greatly weakened the SPLA-IO, just as Riek's split from the SPLA in 1991 dealt it a nearly deadly blow to the whole southern Sudan cause.

The government in Juba regained control of much of the territory the rebels had occupied in the eighteen months before Gatdet and Gathoth left Riek. Their disagreements with Riek, and their defection from his camps, although it gave the government an upper hand in the war, remained a problem for South Sudan's stability. As South Sudan searched for ways to end the 2013 civil war, the breakaway groups continued to pose a threat to the peace process.

Indeed, the peace agreement between the government and the rebel movement, signed in August 2015, involved only part of the Nuer military leadership and excluded others.

An agreement signed in the midst of rebel volatility was inevitably shaky and the stability of the country was in jeopardy while rogue elements, such as Gatdet, remained outside it, hosted by Khartoum. The general stability of the whole country was challenged by the continuing multiplication of military factions, all needing to find reconciliation among themselves before each ethnic group could reconcile with the other nationalities. Splinter groups will naturally demand a share of whatever is available, and exclusion of the breakaway groups from the process by Riek and Kiir threatened that the peace deal would fall into the same traps as the CPA.

One obvious way in which the excluded groups threatened the stability of the country was their capacity to derail not only the peace agreement but also the success of the reconciliation efforts and nation-building projects that could form the foundation of South Sudan's peace and prosperity. But appeasing them, and absorbing them, in the superficial manner of the CPA set up the country for a return to conflict. Ending the cycle of violence required a decision either to keep them out of the army entirely, or integrate them into the armed forces, in the context of a comprehensive security sector overhaul.

The country had to find ways to avoid the confusion of the previous decade, when the lack of clarity over definitions and extent of security sector reform, disarmament, demilitarization and reintegration, and military integration, produced a security program that quickly crumbled. Lesley Anne Warner argued that the boundaries, philosophies and actions required for each of these programs must be clearly defined and separated to ensure success.[6] The experience of South Sudan was that, while amnesty and integration of armed contenders is a useful way to end conflict, it often leads to an unsustainable swelling of the armed forces and the encouragement of rebellion.

During the prolonged second liberation war between north and south, southern Sudan suffered from the ravages of the SPLA's conduct of that war. Ordinary people were expected to contribute hugely to the war effort, and soldiers' behavior inflicted damage on the social landscape of their own communities. The effects rippled across the nation's moral outlook and value systems, including the sense of civic responsibility and the willingness of individual citizens to see each other through a wider national lens. How the South Sudanese view each other today, across ethnic boundaries is still marred by the memories of wartime confrontations and the actions of the liberation leaders.

By the time it ended, the war had cost the people of South Sudan much more than lost human lives, damaged property and wrecked state institutions. It had caused an incalculable shift in social relations, cultural norms and attitudes to violence. Part of the glorification of violence was manifest in the ease with which fighters were mobilized for war. It was also shown in the targeting of people on the basis of their ethnicity, and revealed in the shrinking of public confidence in the ability of the "liberators" to govern the independent state. Violence halted or weakened the development of state institutions, leaving people more invested in ethnic or regional affinities than in the state. The multiple episodes of localized conflict were mostly swept under the carpet and not addressed on their own merit to find independent solutions, or allow people to come to terms with them. That made them strong drivers for the next round of conflicts.

As the region prepared for independent statehood, the unity of the people of South Sudan was grounded in their shared suffering from the liberation wars. The unity of the South Sudanese was unmistakable in many ways, and demonstrated by the overwhelming popular vote for what they saw as the start of political freedom. But this unity, expressed as rallying for a common cause rather than in credible collective symbols, was not enough to sustain the stability of the new state. In their determination to become independent, the South Sudanese overlooked differences among themselves in favor of a free South Sudan. But there is a huge difference between a popular decision made in response to collective protest against unity with the north, and the ability to turn a political construction into a viable nation.

Two monumental tasks confronted the leadership. One was to immediately build a strong state on the ashes of the war, a state capable of efficiently responding to the needs and expectations of the South Sudanese. The second was to transform the history of liberation wars into a rallying point for a collective national sentiment. In other words, to find the positive historical moments when most South Sudanese viewed their cause from a single vantage point that could be a foundation on which to build the nation. The horrific experiences of war needed to be addressed on a national platform, to help the country offload the burden of negative history through dialogue and recognition of mistakes, using justice, accountability and reconciliation to heal ethnic rifts torn by war.

PUBLIC GOODS AND SERVICES AS THE SUCCESS OF THE STATE

The state-building project needed to manage the people's expectations covered a broad spectrum: security, food production, health care, education, transportation, infrastructure, power, telecommunications, housing, the welfare of wounded veterans, orphans and widows, and the repatriation of refugees and IDPs. The vast rural population (more than 80% of the people) also expected attention to be paid to their unique problems: diminishing rural livelihoods, isolation because of poor infrastructure and poor basic services. And those living in the border areas had further problems, inherited from Sudan.

Whatever the nature of the problem confronting different communities, each saw the new state as the panacea; the natural gains from peace and independence. Communities had joined the liberation war to resolve local grievances and concerns, and so independence arrived already weighed down by expectations. It was crucial that services and investments were provided equitably across the country, to become the nucleus of the nation, as the people of South Sudan graduated from sectarianism and exclusive tribal identification to a more inclusive national character. The investments also needed to be made quickly; the longer it took for them to materialize the narrower was the window of opportunity in which the leaders could respond. Sadly, the state proved disastrously unsuccessful in these endeavors, and the people felt betrayed.

The South Sudanese were not naïve enough to think that benefits would accrue overnight, but they did expect to see signs that the government was working toward these goals. Neither did the people really think that the government could deliver these alone; the citizens knew that everyone had to play their part. But the country did need a development policy roadmap, an agenda in which the government could invite the public to take up the responsibilities of state-building. This, however, did not happen, at least not quickly or satisfactorily. Instead the people saw corruption, nepotism, competition for power among the ruling élite and politicians steering national resources towards their families, tribes and home regions. The miniscule health and education budgets, despite huge amounts of oil money, some US$ 19 billion over a decade, was the strongest indictment against the country's leadership.

The immediate result was a sense of disappointment, as the euphoria of independence quickly evaporated from all corners of the country. In the opinion surveys that were conducted by (among others) the International Republican Institute during the CPA interim and through to independence, young people said they were excluded by a system that prioritized the aspirations of the older generation. Minority ethnic groups protested against the domination of the two largest ethnic groups. And all across the country, people complained that the security services were heavy-handed, violent, abusive and ethnically biased.

The leadership was overwhelmed by what looked like a lack of strategic patience among the citizens. Having banked on the anger of the South Sudanese toward Sudan as being the most important factor gluing the people together, the SPLM and other political associations missed the point that, important as it was, it was not a foundation strong enough to build a nation on. The anger toward north Sudan, the collective suffering and the euphoria of independence could have been a rallying point; an opportunity to imbue pride and loyalty to South Sudan. But it was missed. A shared history is important for unity, but it must be used and celebrated if all are to see themselves in it, and therefore take pride in their contribution and recognition.

HISTORY AS THE FOUNDATION OF NATIONHOOD

South Sudan's political and military leadership, community leaders and civil society all talked of the importance of reconciliation as a foundation for stability and economic progress. The government created a cabinet-level Department for Peace and Reconciliation; there were parliamentary committees and special advisors. These recognized the importance of a commitment to justice, unearthing the truth about historical conflicts and the damage they caused to ethnic relations, and the role of reconciliation in the creation of a collective nationhood. Promises were made to mend past wounds and repair the ethnic relations that had been wrecked by the pressures of liberation. A national healing and reconciliation process was envisioned, a program of reform that would facilitate equal sharing of resources, reduce public expenditure and provide security, but this was not to be. The South Sudanese continued in their insecurity, facing ethnic feuds, rising urban crime and cattle-rustling. The leadership did not really understand that reconciliation can only be possible where there is at least a promise of justice, and some form of recompense and accountability. Reconciliation was pursued as a state project, making ordinary people less confident in its genuineness, given that the state was seen as party to the conflicts, not to be trusted as a credible mediator.

Furthermore, the heavy-handed and traumatized security forces were still in place and increasingly became sources of insecurity. The people of South Sudan had an army that was not confined to barracks, whose guns were not tagged, whose members publicly carried loaded guns, even when the country was not at war with itself. This was certainly not an army in whose hands civilians could feel safe. Effective military integration is a foundation for security reform, disarmament, demilitarization and reintegration. Unfortunately, the Juba government placed the cart before the horse, by attempting to professionalize the army too soon. Reintegration, DDR and training were a façade, not a genuine program of reintegration. The army needed background checks and a literacy training program to enable soldiers to read and understand the conduct manuals, human rights requirements and other documents that guide a professional force. South Sudan's national army was a disaster both in security and cost. The Department of Defense consumed around 50% of government expenditure.

Training was minimal, equipment purchases limited and there were no proper garrisons where soldiers could live dignified lives with their families.

As South Sudan prepared for independence, the question posed squarely in the minds of many of its citizens was that while they had created the state of South Sudan, how were they to create the South Sudanese identity? What stake did people have in South Sudan? What did the state need to do, or promise to do, to enable people to think nationally? The country did not have a citizenry that related to, was loyal to and expressed its citizenship to South Sudan, rather than to sectarian, ethnic or regional entities. What would make the people South Sudanese, rather than Nyangatom or Makaraka?

Partly due to the failure or weakness of the nation-building project, less than three years after gaining independence South Sudan was plunged into a new civil war. More than ten thousand were killed and more than two million displaced.[7] Political divisions quickly escalated into violence, prompting army defections and civilian mobilization. Former militia leaders and warlords reverted to tradition and quickly rebelled. Brutal targeting of civilians along ethnic lines was revived, and with it came the shattering of the hopes of a unified and stable South Sudan. This was the situation at the time of writing, in 2016.

The noble nation-building project, which depended on the nation's major institutions for its implementation, cracked with the disintegration of the national army under the weight of ethnic loyalties. The sudden return to war, after the sacrifice of so much to achieve the most celebrated political transition in the history of the country, can be partly explained by the political complacency after the CPA, especially when it had become evident that independence alone was not be a sufficient solution to centuries of marginalization.

Despite the recognition of the need to start laying the founda-
tions of national identity, an official complacency was evident in
the fact that the components of that identity were never articulated and disseminated on the national stage. High-profile leaders,
even the president himself, failed to show their commitment. The
old unity, created in the war against the north to keep the South
Sudanese focused on liberation, was no longer enough to create a
new identity. Whether through complacency or ignorance, there
was an assumption that the citizens did not need to be made
to relate to the nation. Their birth and physical presence within
the country, and the declaration of citizenship was assumed to
be enough to make people South Sudanese, with an intellectual,
emotional and physical attachment to the country and to one
another. It was unclear whether the failure to imbue citizens with
a sense of collective nationhood was born of the many pressures,
financial and otherwise, that the country faced immediately after
signing the CPA, or to the inability of government institutions to
coordinate nation-building. Before its destination of independence,
cohesion, stability and national pride South Sudan had dug itself
a hole, and it fell into it.

What was needed was the identification of commonalities
among the country's many nationalities, and their promotion as a
shared characteristic of a national culture; ways to celebrate their
heritages and give people the opportunity to learn about each other.
Differences used in the past to divide people – language, religion,
traditions, political ideologies and so on – also needed to be chronicled and discussed on the national stage, so that they could be seen
in context, not through a lens of negativity made more pronounced
by the war. The South Sudanese have always understood each other
through negative stereotypes, and not through solid knowledge
of each other's cultural characteristics. Individual characteristics,
negative or positive, are sometimes used to generalize about entire

ethnic groups. It is common to hear the South Sudanese say the Dinka are power hungry, the Nuer are violent, the Equatorians are cowards, the Azande are incestuous, the Murle are infertile child abductors and the Kuku are witches.

Poor infrastructure, especially bad road networks and widely distant markets, combined with the lack of access to news media in the rural areas, intensifies the distances between isolated rural communities. Language barriers remain a major obstacle to mutual understanding and national cohesion. Other than those in border communities, most rural South Sudanese can barely communicate with each other across ethnic lines. Those living in towns and cities, or those with formal education, communicate with each other using Arabic, English or Kiswahili (among those who lived in Kenya as refugees during the war). A clear government policy was needed, whether to promote all the national languages and teach them in schools as vehicles for cultural intercourse, or choose one language and teach it to everyone, to foster rapid linguistic unity, as happened in Indonesia and Tanzania.

The educational sector in general, beyond the language issue, is an area offering many opportunities for the growth of national identity. The creation of national boarding high schools, where young people have a chance to grow up thinking nationally, learning and appreciating the traditions of other groups from their peers and schoolmates, is one route. School sports tournaments, to teach young people the ethics of leadership, teamwork, tolerance and sportsmanship, which contribute greatly to the development of strong and tolerant people, are another. Teachers, together with civil servants, police and other organized forces, can be distributed to all corners of the country, according to their skills and the needs of different regions of the country. As they travel from their birth states to different corners of the country, they take their culture with them and transplant it to the communities they serve. In turn, they learn from the community in which they live and work.

South Sudan is a youthful country; over 70% of its population is under thirty years old. And this young generation has grown up knowing more about war and violence than anything else. South Sudan needed to invest in its young people quickly, so they had a sense of a future to live for. Engaging with young people, and investing in their welfare, is an investment in the security of the country and the creation of a collective national identity. Security, because a large young population that felt excluded from state protection is likely to seek unconstitutional means to register its grievances, joining militias, rebel movements and engaging in criminal activity. And national identity, because seizing young minds is a chance to instill the basic tenets of national culture, including love of country and shunning of sectarianism. Unfortunately, young people were excluded from the gains of independence, causing them to gravitate towards militia groups and engage in violence.

There was much brewing beneath the surface of independence. When, just a little over two years into independence, the political leaders started fighting over power and the resources that came with state capture, the people's anger found an outlet in the most ghastly form.

THE NEW CIVIL WAR AND PROSPECTS FOR A UNITED SOUTH SUDAN

With hindsight, we can see that the violence that erupted in South Sudan in December 2013 was inevitable, given the treacherous history that had given birth to the world's newest country. The civilians who joined the ethnicized conflict carried past conflicts in their mind, and the primary political contenders quickly turned political disagreements into matters of ethnic survival.

Though unsurprising, the violence shocked the country and the world by its brutality, how quickly it spread and how soon it followed ethnic fault lines. The Dinka and the Nuer seemed willing to unravel the country, despite their historic and jointly demonstrated commitment to a free South Sudan. This spoke loudly of the power of ethnic loyalty over national identity. It defied logic that the two biggest ethnic groups, who had joined hands with the rest of the south to fight the north, and agreed about the importance of separation and the push for self-determination together, butchered each other once they had achieved their goal. "Why?" asked ordinary people in villages across the country. "Why?" asked IDPs in the UN Protection of Civilians Sites. "Why?" asked international observers. And could the leadership have predicted and prevented it?

There were no easy answers to these questions. Suffice it to say that the near-collapse of South Sudan was not only understandable but inevitable given the history of state formation in Africa and beyond. History is replete with stories of war following the creation of states, whether because of what some scholars call the "liberation curse," or because of other burdens. This does not mean that it has to happen, but if we recognize that other new states have struggled with similar issues, a history lesson might avoid newer states falling into the same chaos.

The leaders of South Sudan did not do their homework efficiently. If from the start they had invested their efforts in the dual project of state and nation-building, South Sudan might have avoided the division between collective nationhood and tribal loyalties, which has proven the death knell of many African countries. Even when tribal loyalties do not break up a country, they can keep it under perpetual threat of collapse. After fifty years of independence, five decades of being Kenyan, not Kikuyu, Luo or

Kalengin, Kenya's plunge into post-election violence in 2007, which saw Kenyans hacking each other to death on a tribal basis, shows that tribal loyalties, even dormant ones, can be deadly. Under such circumstances, competition for public office, for example, remained a function of rallying one's ethnic voters, and in the process kill chances of real democratic transformation, where citizens vote on issues and not for their ethnic kin.

Many South Sudanese have suggested that South Sudan's experience between 2013 and 2015, gruesome and appalling as it was, offered the young state an important lesson in nation-building; that it was better that such divisions showed early, rather than allowing people to believe all was well for years and then face the kind of setback that happened in Kenya. Among people desperate for a light at the end of the tunnel, seeing a simple philosophy in the darkness was an interesting development. Hoping to find opportunities amid daunting destruction is an admirable, if at times exasperating, quality of the South Sudanese. They fight, yet among the rubble they find justifications for why they should be forging ahead with the creation of a nation-state. A South Sudanese national identity may be imaginary still, but it is something all seem to aspire to, despite their acrimony. When the current vicious civil war ends, it will be a test of this attitude and the desire to remain "one people, one nation," as the independence celebrations declared.

Although no two South Sudanese can agree exactly what triggered the violence of December 2013, there was no disagreement that it was the most gruesome and devastating of ethnic wars between the Dinka and Nuer. Neither was more victim than the other, but none could deny the damage the violence inflicted on the capacity of the South Sudanese to see each other as one. Many observers came to regard this episode as the first time every sense of humanity was disregarded and every known war ethos suspended. AUCISS, Human Rights Watch, Amnesty International and many

NGOs have investigated this conflict, and all recognize acts of atrocity that were almost unprecedented in living memory. Their conclusions, despite the possibility that they were reached haphazardly, from short visits and interviews with people whose objectivity was questionable, reveal what the conflict damaged, most importantly the sense of unity that South Sudan was desperate for.

Many explanations, none more credible than another, have been advanced. The government said it was an attempted *coup d'état* by senior members of the SPLM. The opposition believed that the president of the republic was to blame. Most of the country falls in the middle; some lean toward the government position, others more toward the opposition's explanation, and all points between. But whatever caused the country to unravel so quickly, the truth is that this conflict revealed the country had fragilities beyond its "ancient hatreds", contests for power, state capture or the liberator's curse.

The East African regional grouping, IGAD, moved quickly to halt the escalation of the situation into a civil war. A ceasefire was signed within one month of the fighting starting; a great step toward a peace deal. But the future welfare of the South Sudanese had not looked so bleak since 2005. There was no telling if the ceasefire would stick; there were many very angry people whose appetite for revenge might not allow them to respect it. The humanitarian needs of the 1.6 million IDPs and 600,000 refugees in neighboring countries were daunting. By the middle of 2016, the number of IDPs had surpassed two million and refugees one million. People would certainly die from competition and violence against and among IDPs, malnutrition, unclean drinking water and disease. The economy of the country, which relied on oil exports, and was already suffering from lack of diversification, suffered even more from the cost of rebuilding what the violence destroyed. Foreign investment, import of skilled labor from east African countries, development aid and social service delivery were hampered by insecurity and the shift in the foreign policy of donor countries. Above all, citizens' skepticism about the ability of the state to care for them, waning nationalism and the rifts that remain within the political class, set South Sudan back at least a decade. It will take many years to regain the people's trust and prove the country viable in the eyes of investors, donors and foreign experts.

The South Sudan peace settlement had to go beyond restoring the status quo to deal comprehensively with the social, political, economic and security problems that are the deep roots of the conflict. A deal that simply divides power between the contending political and military elite will only pause the conflict. These roots are strengthened by sectarianism, which is used by people in public office to channel the resources to kin, region or ethnic nation as a way to buy political capital, something akin to Jean-Francois Bayart's description of the Cameroonian phrase "the politics of the belly." The IGAD countries, together with the rest of the international community, aimed to help South Sudan set up a joint mechanism of South Sudanese and international actors to oversee specific institutions, to avoid misuse of resources and prevent ethnic bias. Countries emerging from prolonged wars have historically imported skilled people, especially at managerial level, to strengthen state institutions. Skilled people are needed in the judiciary, so that war crimes are investigated efficiently; in the constitutional review process that considers history, cultural diversity and future stability; in financial institutions, to prevent the siphoning off of public resources to foreign countries; in the re-creation of a professional military to enable it to reflect the ethnic diversity of the country and set up the basic prerequisites for qualification; and the police, to focus on literacy and a minimum knowledge of the local laws.

Nuer communities have mobilized civilians for war for generations, but the political economy of the civil wars and the large-scale violence of recent decades have altered leadership structures and fighting tactics. The continuing influence of traditional spiritual leaders within Nuer society has been used by political and military leaders to mobilize popular support, aided by politicized ethnic rhetoric that promoted the targeting of civilians and contributed to a cycle of revenge attacks. However, the warring parties and international community's overemphasis on historical grievances between the Dinka and Nuer disguises the complex relations within and between these groups. For instance, the spread of the civil war was partly promoted through propagation of the ideas of the prophet Ngundeng, whose prophecies allegedly included the identification of a Nuer son who would become president of South Sudan, someone whose characteristics, including attributes such as having a gap in his front teeth, being left-handed, and well-educated, were alleged to resemble those of Riek Machar.

Before the outbreak of the civil war, Ngungdeng and his ideas were revered across the country; a sign that most South Sudanese respected each other's heritages and identities. Ngundeng's prophecies were essentially messages of peace and justice. While they were certainly used by politicians or military commanders to manipulate young fighters to emulate his bravery, and that of his son Guek, who fought the British colonialist to the death, his stories of peace could have been applied very differently. When a wooden rod, known as a *dang* in the Nuer language, which had been taken to the United Kingdom in the early twentieth century, was acquired and returned to Juba in 2011 by Douglas Johnson, a scholar of Nuer history, Riek Machar, Nuer dignitaries and other South Sudanese rallied in a huge celebration, ushering in what could be described as a start of national pride in local culture. But this changed in the wake of the war, as Riek Machar and his followers publicly talked of being inspired by Ngundeng to fight this war. This talk became a source of mockery against Riek Machar, painting him as a man lost in the depth of superstition whose messages of leadership and political reforms should not be taken seriously. Once again, hope that a local cultural symbol of nationalism might multiply nation-wide was extinguished by individual political ambitions.

CULTURAL EXCLUSION COULD KEEP SOUTH SUDAN IN PERPETUAL CONFLICT

South Sudan, without a doubt, is one of the most ethno-culturally diverse countries in the world. Its 10 to 12 million people hail from more than sixty major ethnic nationalities. These groups have many similarities – and dissimilarities – in their cultural practices, such as marriage systems, folklore, arts, livelihoods and means of production, religious traditions and more. But whether they come from the plains of Bahr el Ghazal, the swamps of Upper Nile, the hills of Eastern and Central Equatoria or the thick forests of Western Equatoria, there is no question that they have one thing in common: they all belong to a single polity called South Sudan and it belongs to all of them.

Belonging to a nation comes with both rights and obligations. South Sudan has a long history of oneness; the shared experiences of slavery, colonization, exclusion, political marginalization, Khartoum's disdain for their cultural identities, forced Arabicization and Islamicization and their collective struggle against external domination, a struggle that spanned more than 190 years until it culminated in independence. The South Sudanese must now transform that shared history into a sense of nationhood, a guarantee for citizenship rights and source of pride for them all. There are several things that the political leadership, the civil service and civil society can do to promote this. They can start by avoiding the usual temptation of emerging states to think of development, infrastructure and the delivery of services as more important than a project to create a citizenry that is loyal to the nation. They can go on by cultivating a culture of dialogue between the citizens and their government.

To conclude, the government's need to respond to the people's expectations of the peace dividend is extremely important, but it is equally crucial to underline the fact that the leaders' success in serving their citizens hinges on the recognition of the importance of culture as the ingredient that can either stitch a nation together or can tear it apart. To forge a collective national identity, so that citizens are able to see their citizenship in the nation as more important than citizenship in ethnic nationalities, it is important to view cultural diversity as an asset that can build a colorful nation that each single citizen can see themselves reflected in and be proud of. To do this, the nation has to be inclusive in its promotion of its diverse cultural heritage, and take care not to forget that cultural marginalization was one of the main factors in the long liberation wars. The country must not repeat the practices that drove the people of South Sudan out of the union with the north. The entire country must be conscious of its diversity in daily policy decisions, so that no citizen or ethnic group feels unrepresented.

The realization that nations are made, not born, offers the chance to demonstrate to the world that ethno-cultural diversity does not have to be a disadvantage. Poorly managed, cultural diversity can contribute to conflict but when cultural commonalities are celebrated and differences are recognized, they can contribute to stability. To be inclusive, South Sudan must celebrate its diversity equitably on the national platform. National media outlets' programming should reflect the cultural mix that makes up South Sudan. All cultures should be considered national cultures; promoted, displayed and celebrated in museums, archives, memorials, cultural centers, music, film, arts and educational curricula. Failure to do this can only lead to citizens' discontent, risking ethnic discord and new civil wars. A glance at history reveals that exclusionary practices, such as those practiced by Khartoum, are unsustainable and can lead to break-up. The domination of one cultural or ethnic group at the expense of others will produce citizens who give no loyalty to the nation and who may turn to violence when they run out of options.

Beyond culture, there are other diversities that have to be recognized to construct a stable and harmonious society: sex, age, and profession. From the traditional cultural perspective, these differences tend to have negative effects. It does not take long before cultural marginalization translates into exclusion from services, jobs and citizenship rights and, before long, to conflict.

The involvement of armed groups in carrying out the atrocities seen in South Sudan's fratricidal civil war are rooted in the past failure of the state to protect people; people made the decision to join or to stay away from the war based on their memories of past actions by the state and by competing ethnic groups. Understanding these dynamics is crucial to efforts to mitigate the cycle of violence in the future. Transcending the divides through concerted programs that help people move away from loyalty to tribe in favor of loyalty to the nation is crucial, and requires serious leadership. But achieving such a goal depends on truth-finding, justice and reconciliation. It also depends on a dual project of state-building that creates infrastructure, develops institutions and provides services to the people so that they can feel they have a stake in the state, and nation-building that celebrates the heritage and histories of all the ethnic nationalities of the country. Such a program could have prevented the chaos of the civil war.

It will take at least a generation before programs to generate collective national belonging bear meaningful results, but such programs could have helped reduce the numbers of disgruntled young people who saw war as a cure for their grievances. Although they blamed the state for their grievances, the tribe should have been the obvious target, given that they saw the country's leaders as members of tribes rather than national leaders, so that fighting a political leader meant attacking their ethnic group. If South Sudan does not invest heavily in raising the value and importance of the nation in the lives, minds and hearts of younger generations this kind of attitude will remain a danger. Such a project requires political will, financial investment and coordination among government institutions, and the visible involvement of high-profile leaders.

But even as ordinary citizens, opposition political parties, faith communities and civil society plead for a program of nation-building to spare future generations the ravages of conflict, there is little certainty that the leaders of South Sudan will heed the advice or meaningfully respond to the pleas of their people. The dream of a unified nation, with a sense of pride in itself, may well remain a pipe dream for years to come.

8

CONCLUSION: THE FATES OF THE TWO SUDANS

This book is the story of the multiple, and multi-layered, violent political conflicts that cost Sudan its unity and plagued Sudan and South Sudan, and the historical, political, social and economic contexts in which these conflicts took place. I have chronicled the causes of the conflicts, what fueled them, the damage they caused and the fate of the efforts to resolve them. This chapter summarizes the main points, and provides recommendations on the way forward in South Sudan's efforts to reconcile its ethnic nations and build peace within and among them. Reconciliation and peace are vitally needed, to stabilize the country so that it can focus on economic development and service provision to its desperate people, who have known very little other than violence and conflict for the last sixty years.

Throughout this book, I have focused on the question of why a negotiated settlement for separation that hinged on both sides' aspirations for peace and harmony has ended up with almost the opposite, failing to meet its most popularly prized aim and uphold its principles. What does this mean for the future of relationships among the people who live along the two countries' borders or those from one side who are stranded in the other? How long will the two countries remain in a situation of no declared war but also no peace? How will the two Sudans overcome their impasse on the outstanding issues of separation, including the shoddy agreement on oil revenue sharing and other economic matters? How will they address the issues of nationality and citizenship, the movement of people, goods and services and, above all, the demarcation of their new and long international border? In this chapter, I will identify some pointers to the way forward, reflecting on whether the civil war that almost caused the complete collapse of South Sudan could be seen as an opportunity to craft a nation that will be more resistant to violent outbursts.

The secession of South Sudan in 2011 split Africa's largest country, the Republic of Sudan, in two. The split has been the subject of much analysis, particularly over the viability of the two countries and the benefits of mutual cordial relations. The secession followed a violent and protracted conflict over issues of distribution of national resources, struggle for state power, accusations of racism, religious differences, language biases, underdevelopment in the peripheral regions, claims of margin-alization, cultural exclusion and long-standing practices that gave the southern Sudanese a sense that they were treated as second-class citizens in the law and constitution. But throughout the conflict of 1983 to 2005, and despite its horrific violence, there was cause for hope in the philosophy of the SPLM. This group argued that Sudan's conflict was not about a north-south divide but the creation of a "new Sudan" in which race, religion, ethnicity and social differences did not affect citizenship and the protec-tion of rights.

There were numerous moments in that two-decade history when the determination to keep Sudan unified was asserted.

When the SPLA troops sang morale-boosting songs that said they had their eyes on Kosti and Khartoum, or when fighters from the north joined the SPLA in droves, these moments entirely changed old war dynamics and brought the conflict closer to the seat of power in Khartoum. There were also campaigns for peace, for example when women's groups from both sides came together to proclaim the obvious reality that no woman on either side would support the continued slaughter, especially those from the south, where state-sponsored violence had been more acute.

However, when the widely celebrated CPA was being negotiated, a compromise was reached. This forced the leaders of south Sudan to backtrack from the idea of a new, unified, open, democratic and secular society in a whole Sudan and instead work for a split. How this switch occurred puzzles and disappoints many Pan-Africanist and Pan-Sudanists to this day[1]. Some African leaders stood against it, some recognized that there had been too much bloodshed and it was too late for unity, others reasoned that a split might be necessary to give the Sudanese a chance to step back and experiment with the idea of two states in the hope of future re-unification, should it become clear to them that a unified Sudan was better than a split one.

But by the time the IGAD-led negotiations showed promise of an end to the war, the south Sudanese had made up their minds about leaving the union. The unity of Sudan died alongside the millions of people in south Sudan who died terrible deaths. It most definitely died with John Garang, when his helicopter crashed into the Eastern Equatoria mountains in July 2005, just thirty days after he had been sworn in as first vice president of Sudan and interim president of Southern Sudan.

When the moment of secession came, there was no mistaking its justice, if we judge by the euphoria expressed by the people of

South Sudan and their supporters. People waved the new flag of South Sudan, shouting "Freedom," and "thank you George Bush" (in recognition of the role the USA had played). A few people fainted when the flag was finally hoisted, perhaps from heat and dehydration, but maybe from happiness. Droves of foreign dignitaries came from all corners of the globe, including South Sudan's arch-opponent, Omer al-Bashir, president of Sudan. The visitors braved the hot African sun to celebrate with people who had fought long and hard to make this moment possible. The UN General Assembly President said of this moment: "This is a remarkable achievement, a long-standing conflict has been stopped."[2] But had it?

Despite the joy, the question of how the new state would relate to Sudan, its northern neighbor, lingered. Would the normal mistrust between the two countries remain entrenched, or would a new spirit of cooperation replace the history of acrimony? Would the issues of post-CPA wealth-sharing, cross-border trade and security become sources of continued confrontation? Would the border areas be contested? How would citizenship be settled, and how would the government of Sudan deal with south Sudanese people who had lived in the north for more than two decades and were now stateless almost overnight? There were numerous economic matters to be settled: Sudan's external debt, currency issues, distribution of state assets, the pensions of the South Sudanese who had been civil servants in the old Sudan. Above all, how could the young landlocked state export its oil through Sudan's oil facilities and how much would it cost?

None of these questions, collectively referred to as "outstanding CPA issues," were sufficiently worked out before the split. They were therefore certain to become a thorn in the side of the two countries' relationship, if not potential drivers of further conflicts.

LANDING ON HARD GROUND

South Sudan is a country born of war; a country that lived by and through war for many years. It was at war with northern Sudan for the better part of fifty years after Sudan attained its independence from Britain in 1956. In 2005, the world community pushed through the CPA, which ended a deadly civil war that had started in 1983. The CPA paved the way for separation, and after a referendum in which more than 98.8% of the people voted in favor of independence, the world's newest country was created in 2011.

By voting to leave Sudan, it seemed that the South Sudanese declared they had had enough of a life of war and vowed to bid farewell to it. Everywhere, there was hope that the region would make a quick transition to stability, development and prosperity. The country had significant oil reserves, it was expected that the immense oil revenues, used efficiently, would quickly improve the delivery of goods and services its people had been denied under Khartoum. With a history of its people's demand for democracy and civil liberties, and based on their history of collective resistance to everything Sudanese, the country seemed to have a recipe for success.

Unfortunately, the story of the new South Sudan quickly became a story of mismanagement of this huge wealth. Over ten years, some US$19 billion were diverted into personal foreign bank accounts, wasted in a bloated civil service and spent on a huge army. Oil became a curse, not a blessing. South Sudan was born into much wealth but its leaders had known only poverty for more than two decades; now was the time to pay themselves. They rolled in petrodollars, spending millions on private mansions, luxury cars and other goods in massive shopping sprees. While healthcare and educational services combined received a measly 7% of the budget, the Ministry of Finance and the Office of the President overspent their budgets by up to three times. A country that had US$150 million every month in oil revenues could not pay its teachers and doctors; soldiers starved while the Department of Defense claimed more than half of national expenditure. It was no longer a question of whether or not corruption was a serious issue in South Sudan. The question was where did the money go?

In 2016, nearly eleven years after the CPA, very few of the people's expectations and promises have been realized. By most accounts, things are worse. Human security, whether measured by personal safety, community security, improved livelihoods, positive health indicators or the overall stability of the country, deteriorated in the years leading up to independence, and continued to worsen afterwards. This decline was born of policy failures and poor implementation of government reform programs on the one hand, and the massive burden the liberation wars had left behind in South Sudan on the other. At independence, South Sudan, a huge country the size of many east African countries combined, was devastated by war. At independence, it had only 25 miles of paved roads, some of the world's worst human development indicators, and poverty levels almost unequalled on the African continent. Huge numbers of citizens owned guns, the rural population was cut off from basic services, the army was the nation's biggest, most dysfunctional and most expensive department, the bloated public sector massively outweighed the private sector, human resources were weak and ethnic relationships were shattered. The new state landed on shaky ground. The country had no political unity beyond its shared antipathy to the north, no vibrant civil society, corrupt political leadership, rampant armed militias and huge numbers of disaffected young people.

The people's shattered hopes and aspirations plunged the country into a new civil war in 2013. This came as a shock to everyone, given that South Sudanese had fought long and hard, as one people, to liberate their country. The humiliation of civil war tarnished the image of their country in the world. The competition for power within the ruling SPLM was allowed to escalate into a civil war, through mismanagement and the unwillingness of the politico-military élite to compromise. After it started in Juba, the war spread very quickly to cover nearly a third of the country in Greater Upper Nile region. In August 2015, under immense international pressure, a peace agreement was signed but its implementation remains fragile at the time of writing. The war cost the country an incalculable price in material, human lives, ethnic relations and the country's image abroad. Foreign aid was suspended and instead directed toward humanitarian assistance for war-affected people displaced from their homes, stripped of their assets and without health services.

Many questions were asked about why the war broke out, particularly why it wasn't seen coming and so prevented. UNMISS had been deployed after independence exactly to prevent this kind of war from happening. No one really thought UNMISS was capable of ensuring the security of citizens, but they could have seen the clearly visible signs to ask for more assistance. UNMISS was neither able to recognize the gathering storm nor to protect civilians, except for the 150,000 people who fled to its camps. The government's failure to predict and pre-empt the conflict was largely due to unwillingness of the leadership to heed policy advice based on research, which showed that renewed conflict was inevitable if nothing were done to fix the looming problems. If research and independent analysis had been incorporated into policies and decisions, this unenviable state of affairs might have been averted.

One of the major obstacles that obstructed state-building and provision of services was what most development experts refer to as "lack of capacity" in the country's human resources and institutions.

During the liberation war, most people had no access to education, except those who were living as refugees in neighboring countries or further afield, most of whom were unable or unwilling to return. The sense of entitlement among the liberators meant that people with no skills other than fighting were given public service jobs they could not perform. Resources were wasted due to mismanagement. Some skilled members of the diaspora returned home to help but many were shunned and derided as people who had run away to hide from the war and were now coming back to take up the jobs the liberators had made possible. Most became frustrated and returned to their adopted homelands. This lack of skills meant there was a limited capacity to create national policies, development plans and short-, medium- or long-term visions of how to transform the new country. The government proved unwilling to catch up to the rest of the world in terms of modern technologies; government departments do not have websites to this day. The question of how to build a sense of nationhood to go hand-in-hand with the development of state institutions was never asked, partly because the capacity to think "outside the box" was missing from most government institutions.

Experience from other countries that have emerged from similar circumstance suggest that to turn this situation around so that the new country could stabilize, develop its institutions and train its people, South Sudan needed to invest in higher education and technical training institutes, identify its natural resources and create special skills training programs. The Government of Southern Sudan, which was set up in 2005, strove to use research, policy planning and development vision, to design efficient methods for using its natural resources to the benefit of the whole country. It established research, training and analysis centers, some housed within major government departments and others as independent academic institutions. But this human resource was hardly ever used; heads of departments proved suspicious of research, data collection and analysis, fearing that such research could expose the mismanagement or theft of public property that contributed to the country's economic crisis and bankruptcy.

AMBIVALENT NEW NEIGHBORS

The secession of South Sudan might best be understood as a compromise between two extremes. On one side was the pursuit of the armed struggle to reformulate the Sudanese state into a democratic society, whose accompanying violence and destruction was tearing apart the fabric of a country whose leaders were trying to hold on to its unity and territorial integrity at any cost. On the other were the continuation of war, and the threat of violent disintegration into a Korea or Pakistan-India situation. The two sides found a middle ground in the CPA negotiations to end the war and establish a six-month interim period for reconstruction and the rebuilding of trust, after which the people of southern Sudan would hold a referendum on unity or separation. With the two sides seated at the negotiation table, the choice between the two extremes seems obvious: it would surely be better to have two states living in peace with each other than one country destroyed by war.[3]

In Sudan, the reactions to the splintering of the country were mixed. Sudanese officials, including President Omer Hassan al-Bashir, made it clear if South Sudan became independent, Sudan would become "100% Islamic and Arab," flying in the face of the reality of the country's religious and ethnic pluralism, but suggesting there would be a sense of relief if the part of Sudan that troubled the entire country departed.[4] Some of the staunch diehards of the NCP, such as al-Taib Mustafa, the president's uncle, celebrated the departure of the south. But a large swathe of Sudan's population mourned the break-up of their country.

Although the CPA and its subsequent creation of two states can be praised for bringing a lull to a nasty war, it must also be judged in terms of how much violence it removed from the region. Sadly, it did no such thing. On the contrary, it exacerbated the decline of security, whether judged by the level of political violence that continued in both countries, the bombing of South Sudan's territory in search of rebels, the level of institutionalized and state violence, the welfare of the people or by justice (or lack of it) for the crimes committed. Khartoum's commitment to a military solution to the conflicts in Blue Nile, the Nuba Mountains and Darfur, its unwillingness to tolerate dissenting voices, and the brutality with which protests were suppressed speak of a country that continued to prioritize violence over dialogue. The vigor with which the NCP continued to pursue an Islamist agenda indicates its clear commitment to the policies of cultural exclusion that drove the south away and its supposition that Sudan would become a more perfect Islamic and Arab country once the south departed.

As Sudan's leaders continued to speak the language of dialogue, making peace overtures here, signing piecemeal agreements there, to fracture the opposition and to buy themselves more time in power, the rhetoric of peace and dialogue competed with news of war for newspaper pages and media space. Large parts of Darfur, Blue Nile and the Nuba Mountains were essentially written out of state responsibility, and their inhabitants depicted as outlaws and menaces that had to be defeated. Even when Khartoum spoke the language of peace, it was with disdain toward the people of the "new south," as a country with whom peace would only be only possible after its armed opposition had been militarily defeated and its inhabitants cowed and undermined. President al-Bashir continued to object to the idea of national dialogue that involved meetings with the opposition movements outside Sudan, saying that SPLM-N in Blue Nile and the Nuba Mountains must come to Khartoum to register for the dialogue.

South Sudan did not perform better in terms of its approach to peace and stability. One approach was to attempt to deal with ethnic conflicts through disarmament, which simply escalated the violence. Having failed to rein in ethnic or militia violence, and unable to assert a monopoly over the use of force, the state found itself resorting to unconstitutional and abusive tactics that escalated into a war with the tribes. The support that the Juba government extended to SPLM-N remains a sore point in Sudan-South Sudan relations, influencing how Khartoum negotiates with Juba; when the South Sudan civil war began in late 2013, Sudan took the opportunity to reciprocate by extending support to the rebels led by Riek Machar Teny. This set the two countries on a path of accusation and counter-accusation as their leaders tried to undermine each other's territories. The alternative, much more placid approach to separation nevertheless threw up as many challenges as it resolved. One of these is the difficult relationship between the governments and between the people who must share space in a politically acrimonious, deeply mistrusting, religiously divided and fearful environment.

The situation that has prevailed since the split has not upheld the spirit and letter of the CPA. There is no question that the appearance of cooperation demonstrated by high level officials visits between Juba and Khartoum, polite words when officials meet, and the talk of peace, is little more than pretense, especially in light of Khartoum's aerial bombings inside South Sudan's northern borders, and Juba's hostility in shutting down oil production in early 2012, occupation of Panthou/Heglig and its relationship with SPLM-N. As a political compromise, the CPA hinged on one single promise: that there would be an opportunity to build two viable states living in peace and harmony with one another. But the low-key war waged along the border, the closure of borders, disputed border towns, banning of trade, restriction of movement of people and services, confiscation of property owned by South Sudanese people in Khartoum, issues of nationality and citizenship and the economic war between the two countries, starkly deviate from the promise of the CPA.[5]

Opportunities do exist that could transform this difficult relationship into mutual cooperation. One is the social and historical connection between the people of the two countries, especially the peoples of the border states. Twelve states lie along the border, five on the southern side and seven on the northern, and although not all are on cordial terms, the opportunities presented by cross-border trade and links through traditional livelihoods and cross-ethnic marriages hold the promise of a new foundation of coexistence. Without trying to reduce the burden the history of violence places on these relationships, the annual peace meetings between the Rizeiqat of South Darfur and the Malwal Dinka of northern Bahr el Ghazal, or between the Missiriyya of South Kordofan and the Dinka of Warrap and Abyei, as well the historic relationship between the Dinka and Shilluk of Upper Nile and the people of White Nile state, are fertile ground for peace, as long as the governments in Juba and Khartoum are willing to prioritize the aspirations of border people.

Looking back on what has happened since the break-up, the relationship between the states is characterized by the mutual mistrust and suspicion of their governments. The meddling in each other's domestic political turmoil and security challenges, the painful memories of the war, especially on the southern side, the utter animosity of Khartoum to the overwhelming majority for separation in the referendum; all these feed the climate of mistrust. We also see the hallmarks of suspicion in the continuing economic war waged by Khartoum against South Sudan; a war of empty pride rather than of economic sense. The pretense that South Sudan is not economically important to Sudan is countered by the huge amounts of goods smuggled from Sudan that fill the markets of Wau, Aweil and other towns in northern parts of South Sudan. This economic war hurts both sides. South Sudan is a nascent country that must build everything from scratch and import most of its consumer commodities; it was the biggest market for Sudanese-manufactured goods, especially food and construction materials. For Sudan to stop its traders selling their goods in their biggest, and geographically easiest to access, market seems like an exercise in spite against South Sudan. Perhaps Sudan hopes that this tactic will force South Sudan's hand in other negotiations, obliging South Sudan to negotiate from a position of weakness.

South Sudan has also engaged in badly thought-through economic decisions, some more driven by national pride than by economic sense, some aimed at undercutting Sudan that actually inflicted more pain on itself. The hasty introduction of a new currency, the South Sudan Pound, was more a symbolic expression of nationhood than a pursuit of a long-term vision. In response, Khartoum introduced a new Sudan Pound and refused to redeem old currency in circulation in South Sudan. It cost South Sudan almost US$1 billion to redeem all that Khartoum refused to take back. The decision in early 2012 to shut down oil production in protest against Khartoum's demand for exorbitant fees for the use of oil facilities, over which Sudan claimed exclusive rights, was another expensive political choice.

The relationship is also characterized by bitterness over nationality and citizenship, border demarcation, contested areas and border security. The agreements about the four freedoms were negotiated with a win-lose attitude and signed begrudgingly, leaving each side trying to avoid complying with its side of the bargain. Together, the oil revenue sharing arrangements and the security challenges have created the most stubborn obstacles to the cooperation that the CPA hoped to cultivate and nurture. The two countries exist in a tight space between the promise and opportunities for cooperation and peaceful coexistence on the one hand, and the challenges of overcoming built-up mistrust, aggression and negative perceptions on the other. In the decade since the CPA was signed, there has been a plenitude of both promises and challenges. Sudan and South Sudan are likely to remain in this uncertain space, playing the game of mutual cooperation, but holding their cards tightly to their chests. Only new events such as the fragile peace deal in South Sudan, or a change of government in Juba or Khartoum might be a tiebreaker. But futures are very difficult to predict in this region.

The two governments seem to be gambling on the possibility that time will resolve some of their issues. The leaderships see compromises as surrender and loss of face, so they kick difficult decisions down the road. Future generations of Sudanese and South Sudanese will have to deal with the legacy of their current governments. Will the passage of time allow the bitterness to be massaged away? Is a state of no war and no peace actually the best way to manage their relationship? Or do the governments and the people of the two Sudans need to act? The risk of delay is that the spirit of peaceful separation could be entirely compromised under the weight of immediate challenges. The risk of too-quick action is always that disagreements remind the two sides of their history of violence, and they fall back into war.

There are three choices. The first is to allow the memories of violent conflict to cloud relationships; the second is to make brave decisions to emphasize the peoples' experiences of mutual respect and benefits; the third is to make visible the historical, social and economic threads that link the people of the two countries and try to build a future on them. The first choice means continued conflict that would threaten the prosperity of both countries. it is propelled by the illusion that one stands a chance of winning against the other. The latter two choices offer the greatest opportunity for the peoples to move towards each other and a future of stability, cooperation and prosperity. There is little disagreement over the facts, but the history of fear, mistrust and the mindset of a win-lose negotiation have blinded politicians to realities of the situation, as well as to the people beholden to their leaders.[6]

A HISTORY OF VIOLENT INTERACTIONS OR A FUTURE OF LINKS?

In South Sudan, memories of war between north and south lie close to the surface. Those memories include the counter-insurgency of Sudan's armies in the south, of indiscriminate military activities in southern Sudan that seemed to have no purpose other than to humiliate the southern Sudanese into submission. The IDPs from southern Sudan who lived in Khartoum during the war have memories of how year after year they were evicted from their makeshift homes, pushing them into the edges of the desert. The people who were interviewed for this book remembered the destruction of their livelihoods, the loss of dignity and a social fabric eviscerated by the long history of Sudan's activities in the south. Structural violence at the hands of the Sudanese state, exclusion from national resources and the cultural and religious bigotry of some northern Sudanese groups are remembered by the South Sudanese as part of their lived experience, and part of how they relate to Sudan.

In a climate where such memories dominate the narrative of the relations, how to weigh the horrific memories of the liberation wars and the counter-insurgencies on the one hand, and the search for a future of harmonious coexistence on the other, is a crucial decision both sides must grapple with. It is challenging to imagine how such memories should be kept and honored while the two peoples search for a strong foundation for their future relations. Will the two peoples and their two states keep throwing the history of violence into each other's faces, or are they capable of an honest search for collaboration? Can the Sudanese people look beyond their terrible experiences and move forward? What will it take to promote their historical links over their memories of violence?

Although the momentum of independence in southern Sudan was built by many issues, such as the history of slavery and racial discrimination, state violence and inequitable distribution of the national resources were the major galvanizers of the liberation sentiments and struggle for independence. It was these sentiments and struggle that prevented almost everyone in South Sudan, whether government officials, civil society activists or individual citizens, from fully appreciating how negative Khartoum's reaction would be. The CPA's premise that the two countries should seek coexistence and the promotion of mutual interests gave false hope to Sudanese people on both sides. Everyone assumed that the move back to the south, supported by the governments of both countries, would be instantaneous, easy and relatively uncomplicated, emphasizing the historical connections between families and communities, especially those on the borders. Voices from the southern side of the new border spoke of the need for the two countries to recognize that, despite the horrors of war, political transitions should not disregard the bonds between individuals, families and communities.

In anticipation of, and campaigning for independence, the South Sudanese both at home and in the diaspora confidently expressed two hopes for that independence. One was an end to violence, after the violent armies of an oppressive state were no longer in South Sudan; the second was improved living and economic conditions when their resources, from oil reserves to agricultural land and to livestock, could be exploited exclusively for the development of South Sudan.[7] However, despite significant progress on delivery of services, at least between 2007 and 2012, the realities of the post-independence era were very different.

Almost everything that could go wrong in South Sudan went wrong. Too great a reliance on oil meant that the leadership of the new state did not invest in the diversification of the economy, so agriculture remained blighted. Violence continued, in different forms and by different actors. The attacks of the SAF and its proxies subsided greatly but the South Sudanese turned against each other, even as they sang songs of unity. The plunge into civil war almost entirely snuffed out the beam of hope sent out by independence and caused a return to the drawing board with regard to sovereignty. Independence, and the freedoms it brought, was celebrated but independence did not feed families or send children to school.

On the northern side of the border, loud and influential voices, such as the owners and editors of the *El-Intibaha* newspaper and the Just Peace Forum were heard. Several groupings within the ruling Islamic movement of Sudan exerted tremendous pressure on the government to expel anyone who either "looked" South Sudanese or supported the independence of South Sudan. For some of the northern Sudanese, the separation represented their best chance to create a more perfectly homogenous Arab and Islamic state that they believed had been hindered by the presence of the southern Sudanese. They argued that Sudan should focus on a person's religious and cultural identity when assigning rights such as nationality, not their birth, length of residence or marriage, as is the norm in many countries. By campaigning to create more rigid relations between the two states, it seemed they hoped to punish the South Sudanese for their decision to secede. There was lamentation and tears in Khartoum about the country's break-up, but there were also celebrations. For example, Al-Taib Mustafa and Ghazi Salah el-deen el-Atabani, the former senior political presidential advisor and a prominent figure in the ruling NCP,[8] saw South Sudan's independence as ridding them of the inconvenience of having to justify the Arab and Islamic identity of Sudan in the face of obvious ethnic and religious pluralism.[9] On the night South Sudan's referendum results were declared, Al-Taib Mustafa slaughtered a black bull in celebration, marking the end of racial and religious diversity of Sudan. "We can now breathe, and develop an Arab and Islamic nation," he remarked.[10]

The irony that some people within the regime wanted to punish the South Sudanese for voting to separate, while others celebrated the separation, was lost on no one. It revealed the lie that the new North Sudan would be more cohesive, homogenous and peaceful once the "South" had gone. Nothing revealed this delusion more clearly than the wars in Darfur, Blue Nile and Nuba Mountains. In stating that Sudan would become homogenous in the wake of South Sudan's separation, Khartoum may have momentarily forgotten that while these wars were fanned by economic exclusion, marginalization from power and state violence, there is no question that the exclusion of these regions' unique cultures was also a major driver. It is misguided to think that they can be aggressively suppressed in favor of cultural homogeneity; the more they are deliberately suppressed the more likely it is that Sudan will not see peace in these regions any time soon.

The reaction of the Sudanese government to the South Sudanese decision to vote for separation was not gentle. The Khartoum authorities seemed to believe that the South Sudanese must live with the consequences of their decision. The social and cultural relations among Sudanese people were dismantled through rushed programs of retaliation and vindictiveness. The government of Sudan threatened to expel the South Sudanese from Sudan, ignoring the moral and legal understandings of the transformation and regardless of whatever ties they may have created in the north, both to land and people. Hundreds of thousands of Sudanese on both sides were left without definite legal status, their circumstances rendered tenuous overnight.

Not until the second half of 2015, two years after South Sudan's civil war started, did harsh words coming out of Khartoum start to slow. Though they continued to reemerge from time to time, depending on other challenges confronting Khartoum, this reduction in the belligerent rhetoric was perhaps born of Khartoum's role in the IGAD peace mediation or might be related to the realization that South Sudan was no longer in a position to support the Sudanese rebel movements. It might also be the result of having gained the upper hand in the relationship, especially with regards to economic arrangements, security and contested borders, as Sudan is currently in control of all the disputed areas.

INVISIBLE CONNECTIONS AND THE PROMISE OF PEACEFUL CO-EXISTENCE

Two major political developments occurred within and between the two countries after the separation was effected. The first was the 2012 agreement between Juba and Khartoum on a variety of post-separation issues, among which was the "four freedoms agreement."[11] Though these have yet to be implemented to the letter, they created a climate conducive to the development of a culture of tolerance for the citizens of one country who live in the other. The other was the December 2013 outbreak of civil war in South Sudan, which sent nearly 400,000 refugees fleeing into Sudan, especially into White Nile state right across the border. This renewed the discussion about whether such migrants would be received as refugees or IDPs. Khartoum made strong overtures to the effect that the South Sudanese were welcome and would be treated as citizens in Sudan. In November 2015, on the occasion of a visit to Khartoum by Festus Mogae, former president of Botswana, who had just been appointed by IGAD as head of South Sudan's Joint Evaluation and Monitoring process for the implementation of the August 2015 peace agreement between the South Sudanese warring parties,[12] President Al-Bashir said what everyone had wanted to hear for quite some time; that the historic social links between the two peoples were strong, and that the mutual suspicion between the two countries was unwarranted. There was hope for renewed tolerance for each other's populations.

The Juba government had declared at the time of secession that any northern Sudanese living in the south could register as a legal resident and eventually become a citizen if they so chose. This was a clear suggestion that separation should be a gradual process, setting a good example to build on for a peaceful future between the two nations. By sorting out residency, movement of people and the return of confiscated property, the two countries could create a platform for conversations about future peaceful co-existence. For the political class, such issues may seem minor, but a symbolic gesture of good will can go a long way to assuage fear and mistrust among the ordinary people. People-to-people communication will sort out the question of residence, not rigid and poorly implemented laws that exclude and discriminate.[13]

When the NCP's security people began seizing property owned by the South Sudanese in Khartoum, many people found a way around the problem by handing over their houses to northern Sudanese friends to look after until the situation changed. Many South Sudanese who lived on the streets in Khartoum during this volatile moment actually owned houses, but dared not stay in them, lest the regime's supporters confiscated them. Similar informal arrangements were made in South Sudan, where business owners gave their properties to trusted associates and friends. As people began to trickle back to where they used to live to check on their property, the trips could be the start of the building of new social networks that might lead to cordial relations.

Cooperation is especially vital to the people who live along the long border between Sudan and South Sudan. The border states are the economic heartland of the two countries, and their most densely populated areas. Peace between the two countries rests on the ability of the people of the border zones to freely travel, trade, farm, move with their cattle, own property and work wherever they need in this vast territory. The links between the people of this region and the mutual benefits of easy social and cultural intercourse will far outweigh the states' drive for rigid borders.[14] Throughout human history, population mobility has been the single most important factor in the formation of communities, states and societies. If people have to move to survive, they will move, state restrictions or not. The quicker the two governments recognize the importance of movement in the lives of border populations, the sooner relationships between the people of the two countries will become sustainable, rather than a liability.

Beyond the border, other invisible lines connect the people of the two Sudans. Without reducing the horrific memories of war, the atrocities of the Sudanese state, the abuse of the displaced South Sudanese in the north and the mistrust that has built up over many decades, which are all very real, it is still plausible to suggest that friendships and family connections forged when southern Sudanese lived in the north can be a basis of coexistence beyond official agreements on economic cooperation, nationality, freedom of movement and trading links. These invisible lines of interconnectedness may well outlast agreements between politicians.[15]

To conclude, the decade since the CPA has shown that the two Sudans will probably remain in the uncertain space where war is likely but will always be averted by the realization that none can afford this acrimony. Sudan will most likely continue to bomb areas in South Sudan, allegedly searching for Sudanese rebels. As long as the NCP remains in power, Khartoum will also continue to oscillate between closing and opening borders. South Sudan might attack a border town inside Sudan, as it did in Panthou/Heglig, but such flare-ups will be smoothed out by diplomacy; all sides will quietly apologize and a major crisis will be averted. Security, border demarcation and control, mobility of citizens, contested areas and oil issues will remain potentially explosive points in the relationship, but neither country will be willing to escalate them to the level of all-out war. Mistrust, national pride, memories of atrocities, the support of opposition movements and on-again-off-again economic wars will continue, but these will be mediated by the leaderships or by outside friends.

If the two countries are able to rise above the personal pride of their leaders (or perhaps when current leaders have left office), stop politicizing the needs of their people and reach concrete agreements on borders, mobility and security, this could herald the beginning of new social networks that might lead to cordial relations. Intercommunal and interpersonal communication, not rigid, exclusionary, discriminatory, poorly implemented or disregarded laws will sort out issues of nationality, citizenship, borders and trade. An example of harsh citizenship issues that remain in Sudan is whether women will be allowed to pass Sudanese citizenship to their children whose fathers are South Sudanese. At the moment they cannot, even though the law allows it in the case of children fathered by nationals of other countries. To ensure that the laws that each country institutes are just and humane, and that they keep the rich history of their social connections in mind, calls for strong advocacy are being made to persuade the governments of the two countries to adopt treaties that establish principles and rules to reduce or eliminate arbitrariness and discrimination in the proof, acquisition, enjoyment, and loss of citizenship.

It would be best to refer such issues to the AUHIP, or any other such instruments that might come up in the future, but most of all to keep the dialogue going, so that Sudan and South Sudan do not become entrenched in a permanently acrimonious and volatile status quo.

NOTES

INTRODUCTION

1 de Waal, 1989.

2 de Waal, 1997.

3 Jok, 2007.

4 The most prominent of these being the agreement between Garang's SPLM and Muhamed al Mirghani of the Democratic Unionist Party, one of the main sectarian parties in Sudan at the time. In the agreement, made at Koda Dam, Ethiopia, in 1988, the two parties agreed to end the war on condition of self-determination for the south.

5 Very few of the "making unity attractive" programs were really implemented, and the result was that the South Sudanese never wholly trusted that north Sudan would be genuine in promoting unity. The South Sudanese all seemed to work toward separation during that period and when the plebiscite occurred, there was no doubt how they would vote.

6 Woodrow Wilson Center, 2008, *Implementing the Comprehensive Peace Agreement: Prospects and Challenges.* Washington, DC.

7 For example, South Africa's African National Congress (ANC) openly opposed the separation of South Sudan. Thabo Mbeki, the President of South Africa, went on record in support of unity and told the southern Sudanese leaders at the time that South Africa would not support their quest if they insisted on the break-up of the country.

8 Copnall, 2014.

9 See International Crisis Group, "Sudan and South Sudan's Merging Conflicts." *Africa Report No 223*, 2015.

10 Natsios, 2012, Copnall, 2014, Thomas, 2015.

11 Michael Onyiego, "Sudan-South Sudan War: Heglig, Disputed Town, Full Of Dead Bodies, Circling Antonovs." *Associated Press*, April 17, 2012.

12 Thomas, 2015.

13 See Jenik Radon and Sarah Logan "South Sudan: Governance Arrangements, War, And Peace." *Journal of International Affairs*, Fall and Winter 2014, Vol. 68, No. 1. Also see Alex de Waal, "When Kleptocracy becomes Insolvent: Brute causes of the civil war in South Sudan." In *African Affairs*, July 2014.

14 Zartman, 1995, Jok, 2007.

15 In the case of Sudan, this process was widely documented by human rights organizations and individual observers as the Sudan government's preferred method of counter-insurgency on the cheap and fighting a war by proxy. See *Bahr El Ghazal and the Famine of 1998*, 1999, Human Rights Watch.

16 Ferguson, 2006.

17 Edward Laws, "Political Settlements, Elite Pacts and Governments of National Unity: A Conceptual Study," *DPL Background Paper 10*, 2012.

18 Young, 2012.

19 See "Civil Wars: The Picture in Africa." *The Economist*, Baobab Africa, November 13, 2013.

20 See Paul Collier and Nicholas Sambanis (eds.) 2005, *Understanding Civil War: Africa*. Volume 1. The World Bank: Washington DC.

21 The last phase of this war is estimated to have caused the death of three million people in the south alone, the majority dying from hunger and disease. However, statistics related to Sudan's conflicts are often incorrect and contested and readers must take them with caution.

22 Lisa Blaydesa and Jennifer De Maiob, "Spoiling the Peace? Peace Process Exclusivity and Political Violence in North-Central Africa." *Civil Wars*, Vol. Number 1, Pages 3–28, June 28, 2010.

23 Long-time observers such as Alex de Waal, and media outlets in the western world, have since had the mistaken idea that secession was imposed by the allies of South Sudan at the last minute and that these allies made a mistake in rushing South Sudan to separation before it was ready to run itself. In an interview with al-Jazeera Television in April 2015, de Waal made his disdain for South Sudan's independence very plain. But nothing could be more false than he supposed.

24 See Jok Madut Jok, Berghoff Foundation.

25 See Jok Madut Jok, 2015, "The Comprehensive Peace Agreement and the Nuba Mountains were Left Out." In *Conflict in the Nuba Mountains:*

From Genocide by Attrition to the Contemporary Crisis in Sudan edited by Samuel Totten and Amanda F. Grzyb. London: Routledge.

26 Thomas, 2015.

27 Anthony Wanis-St. John and Darren Kew "Civil Society and Peace Negotiations: Confronting Exclusion." *International Negotiation* 13, 11–36, 2008.

28 See Alex de Waal and Julia Flint, 2005, *Darfur: A Short History of a Long War.* London: Zed Books.

29 See the BBC's James Copnall's recent assessment of whether Sudan will ever resolve these conflicts in a peaceful manner. "Will Sudan ever Find Peace in Darfur, South Kordofan and Southern Blue Nile?" BBC News, December 6, 2014.

30 Bekoe, 2008.

31 Jok Madut Jok, 2015, "Sudan's Comprehensive Peace Agreement and How the Nuba Mountains was Left Out." In *Conflict in the Nuba Mountains: From Genocide by Attrition to the Contemporary Crisis in Sudan* edited by Samuel Totten and Amanda F. Grzyb. London: Routledge.

32 "South Sudan and its unending bloody conflict: No power-sharing without political reform." Mahmud Mamdani, *The East African*, February 15, 2014.

33 Many people argue that if it had not been for the commitment of the United States, the United Nations and some European countries, South Sudan's referendum would not have taken place.

34 There have been many independent reports about and analyses of these groups and their relationship with Khartoum, some by independent researchers and others by human rights groups or think tanks such as the International Crisis Group and the Small Arms Survey.

35 "The panel is of the view that as matters stand, it is impossible to bridge the chasm between the parties and will therefore refer the matter back to its mandating principle, the AUPSC, for further guidance," the AUHIP said in its statement.

36 "South Sudan: Raising the Flag." *The Economist*, July 15, 2011.

37 A group of pro-South Sudan activists in the United States released the text of a letter sent to President Salva Kiir Mayardit and other senior officials in Juba expressing concern over what they described as the "increasingly perilous fate" of the new state. The letter, signed by former US State Department special envoy to Sudan, Roger Winter, Sudan researcher, Professor Eric Reeves, co-founder of the "Enough Project," John Prendergast and former congressional aide, Ted Dagne, said that

they concluded that "without significant changes and reform," Sudan "may slide toward instability, conflict and a protracted governance crisis."

38 "Promise and Peril in Sudan: South Sudan may get independence in 2011, but could start life as a pre-failed state." *The Economist*, June 13, 2009.

39 J.J. Messner, "South Sudan Replaced Somalia as Most-Fragile State." *Fragile States Index*, June 24, 2014.

40 Daniel Howden, "A failed state before it's born? Inside the capital of the world's next nation." *The Independent*, January 7, 2011.

41 I was once viciously attacked by some security agents of the SPLA in Wau town, an incident I could only explain as punishment for having been critical of some of the behavior of public officials and security agents.

42 For some of these warnings, see a December 3, 2013 policy brief by the Juba-based research center, the Sudd Institute, in which the researchers alerted the government that its actions had reached a level of "playing with fire."

43 The latest liberation war period is awash with stories and jokes about what the SPLA soldier said to the civilian about his food needs and what the civilian replied.

44 See "South Sudan and the Risk of Unrest." *Sudd Institute Policy Brief*, December 3, 2013. Juba, South Sudan.

45 This is a phrase many politicians and other public figures put forward as an excuse for lack of services or any other shortcomings in governance.

46 For an analysis of the causes of violence in Lakes state, see Jeffrey L. Deal's "Torture by Cieng: Ethical Theory Meets Social Practice among the Dinka Agaar of South Sudan." *American Anthropologist*, Vol. 112, Issue 4, 563–575, 2010.

47 An anecdote circulating around the country was that Governor Matur Chut Dhuol, in response to popular perceptions of him as an illiterate military bully who had no business being a governor, suggested that he might not be a lawyer, doctor, engineer or expert in any other field of learning which his critics claim he lacked, but that he was well-educated in the field of violence and if people wanted to challenge him in his chosen profession, they should meet him in the field.

48 In late 2014, South Sudan was ranked the fourth most corrupt country of 172 ranked by Transparency International, a global watchdog.

49 These elections, which took place in 2010, were dubbed "mid-term" because they took place during the CPA's interim period. They were aimed at rallying the support for the unity of the country just one year before South Sudan's referendum.

50 Tim Costello, "South Sudan anniversary is no cause for celebration." *Sydney Morning Herald*, July 8, 2014.

51 Paul Collier has written extensively on why this is the case.

52 See for example, Jok Madut Jok, 2007, James Copnall, 2014, and Douglas Johnson, 2003.

53 Since the north-south war the re-division partially triggered has resulted in South Sudan's independence, it may be argued that the re-division had positive unforeseen consequences and should therefore be seen as having contributed to the liberation.

1. THE TWO SUDANS AND THE DEFEAT OF THE CPA REFORM PROJECT

1 As some speculate about the potential for the two countries to reunite in some distant future, such social relations are envisioned as the building blocks of new unity.

2 Jok Madut Jok, "Sudan's Comprehensive Peace Agreement and How the Nuba Mountains Was Left Out." In *Conflict in the Nuba Mountains: From Genocide by Attrition to the Contemporary Crisis in Sudan* edited by Samuel Totten and Amanda F. Grzyb. London: Routledge, 2015.

3 Jok Madut Jok, "Nationality and Citizenship in the "New Sudan": A Legal or Moral Issue?" *Middle East Law and Governance Interdisciplinary Journal* 6, 225–249, 2014.

4 The word "independence" is in quotes because of the debate about whether South Sudan gained independence, which suggests that it was a colony of the north, or seceded, which means a single country split.

5 It is worth noting that the slogan "free at last," was one of the most displayed slogans in the days leading up to July 9. It captured the countdown, but was pregnant with expectations for a better life.

6 The phrase "final walk" is a caption on a billboard showing the picture of John Garang that dotted the roadsides of major towns throughout South Sudan in the days leading up to July 9th.

7 These, often referred to as "the three areas," were part of the liberation war on the South's side and had a special arrangement in the peace agreement, but this was unfulfilled when South Sudan gained independence, leaving them intrinsically in a state of war with Khartoum.

8 See Alex de Waal, "Making Sense of the Protests in Khartoum." *African Futures,* October 11, 2013.

9 Examples of security challenges in South Sudan are numerous. See *Sudan*

Tribune, August 19, 2011. See also Edward Thomas, *South Sudan: A Slow Liberation*. London: Zed Books, 2015.

10 Center for Strategic and International Studies, *Negotiating Sudan's North-South Future*. Washington, DC: CSIS, 2010.

11 See Jok Madut Jok, "Insecurity and Ethnic Violence in South Sudan: An Existential Threat to the State?" *The Sudd Institute,* August 20, 2012.

12 Klemens von Metternich made this statement in reference to Italy around the time of its unification in 1861. It has since been used in relation to many emerging post-colonial states that were linguistically and culturally diverse, such as Nigeria and other African countries. It is an important concept for South Sudan, as it will be needed to answer the question about what it is that makes it a nation.

13 *See* "The Birth of South Sudan: Managing Expectations." *The Economist*, July 11, 2011.

14 See for example, International Crisis Group, "Politics and Transition in the New South Sudan." ICG, Washington: *Africa Report No 172*. April 4, 2011.

15 A year before independence *The Economist* opined that South Sudan was a pre-failed state. See "South Sudan's Biggest Ethnic Group: On your tractor, if you can." *The Economist*, May 26, 2010 and "South Sudan: Are they Heading for a Crash?" September 23, 2010.

16 A blog sponsored by the Bill and Melinda Gates Foundation, which issued a report a month after independence describing the reality of the daunting development needs facing the world's newest country in no uncertain terms. *Poverty Matters*, August, 2011.

17 See "South Sudan: Promise and Peril in Sudan." *The Economist*, June 13, 2009.

18 See "Diversity, Unity and Nation-Building in South Sudan." *United States Institute of Peace Special Report*. Washington, DC: USIP.

19 See "Violence in South Sudan: their own worst enemies." *The Economist*, February 16, 2011.

20 After the signing of the CPA, and because most South Sudanese were determined to vote for secession, every political leader was aware of many south-on-south problems; no one missed any opportunity to sound caution and plead for unity among southerners.

21 This is the notion that the future of Africa is bleak because of the multitude of problems faced by the continent. See George Ayittey, 1992, *Africa Betrayed*. New York: St. Martin's Press, and 1998, *Africa in Chaos*. New York: St. Martin's Press. Also see Dorothy Hammond and Alta Jablow,

1970, *The Africa that Never Was: Four Centuries of British Writing about Africa.* New York: Twayne, and Beverly G. Hawk (ed.), 1992, *Africa's Media Image.* New York: Praeger.

22 See Zachary G. Pascal, "After South Sudan: The Case to Keep Dividing Africa," *The Atlantic,* July 11, 2011. Also, Jonathon Temin, "Secession and Precedent in Sudan and Africa," United States Institute of Peace, *Peace Brief,* November 2010.

23 "Sudan" in the context of this paper refers to the Republic of Sudan, both before and after the split, whereas "South Sudan" refers to the Republic of South Sudan only after the split.

24 As noted throughout this chapter, South Sudan's secession meant that Sudan lost 75% of its oil reserves, but South Sudan, having no access to the sea, had to continue to deal with Khartoum to export its oil through Port Sudan on Sudan's Red Sea, which entailed specific arrangements for fees to be paid to Sudan.

25 The 1998 Ethiopia–Eritrea war and subsequent continuing confrontations, although initially triggered by disputes over territory, have revealed serious issues about how to separate people who have long lived on the other side. Ethiopia deported more than 75,000 people of Eritrean descent and denationalized thousands of citizens of Ethiopia suspected of supporting Eritrean Independence. See John Campbell, 2013, *The Role of War and the Uses of Law in (Re)Defining Nationality in the Horn of Africa*, Citizenship Rights in Africa Initiative.

26 Jok Madut Jok, "Nationality and Citizenship in the 'New Sudan': A Legal or Moral Issue?" *Middle East Law and Governance Interdisciplinary Journal* 6, 225–49, 2014.

27 "Anti-Christian Backlash After South Sudan's Secession," *Christianity Today,* October 29, 2011, http://www.christianitytoday.com/ct/2011/octoberweb-only/sudan-secession-backlash.html

28 "*Muslim Extremists in Sudan Threaten to Target Christians : Pastors in north fear increased persecution from local and foreign Islamic extremists,*" World Watch Monitor, September 13, 2011, https://www.worldwatchmonitor. org/2011/09-September/article_120231.html/

29 Soraya Sarhaddi Nelson, "Christians Flock To South Sudan, Fear Future In North," *National Public Radio,* January 20, 2011, http://www.npr. org/2011/01/20/132930349/christians-flock-to-south-sudan-fear-future-in-north

30 Christina Haneef, *Return to South Sudan, the building of a new nation, a place to call home: an exploratory study into the sustainability of voluntary*

repatriation of South Sudanese refugees, (MA thesis, Centre for Development and Emergency Practice, Oxford Brookes University, 2013).

31 James Copnall, "Dispossessed: the South Sudanese without a nationality," *BBC News*, April 6, 2012, http://www.bbc.co.uk/news/world-africa-17624075

32 Mike Sanderson, "Statelessness and Mass Expulsion in Sudan: A Reassessment of the International Law." *Northeastern Journal of International Human Rights* 12, no. 1, 2014.

33 Mike Sanderson, "The Post-Secession Nationality Regimes in Sudan and South Sudan," *Journal Of Immigration, Asylum and Nationality Law*. 27, no. 3, 2013.

34 Copnall, 2014.

35 This statement was reported in many media outlets, including the *Citizen* newspaper and Arabic dailies in Khartoum.

2. INDEPENDENT SOUTH SUDAN AND THE BURDEN OF LIBERATION HISTORY

1   This quote is from an interview with an experienced local observer, and sums up the growing suspicion that the new country would not succeed in meeting the expectations of its citizens.

2   See John Ryle, "Not saving, but drowning." *Times Literary Supplement*, October 15, 2004.

3   He did not make his true move until the 2013 war started and he joined Riek Machar in the ongoing conflict.

4   Jok Madut Jok, "Insecurity and Ethnic Violence in South Sudan: Existential Threat to State?" *Sudd Institute Special Report*, August 20, 2012.

5   For more detailed documentation of Jonglei's conflict dynamics, see Edward Thomas, *The Unfinished Liberation*. London: Hurst Publishing Co.

6   See M. Mwagiru (ed.), 2008, *Human Security: Setting the Agenda for the Horn of Africa*. Nairobi: Africa Peace Forum.

7   See Copnall, 2013.

8   International Crisis Group, "Sudan's Spreading Conflict." ICG, June 18, 2013.

9   Bekoe, 2008.

10 Jok Madut Jok, "Nationality and Citizenship in the 'New Sudan': A Legal or Moral Issue?" *Middle East Law and Governance Journal* 6, 2014, 225–249.

11 Young, 2012, and Johnson, 2011.

12 Young, 2012.

13 See Julie Flint, 2011, "Return to War in Sudan's Nuba Mountain." *Peace Brief 112*. Washington, DC: United States Institute of Peace.

14 See the *SPLM Manifesto*.

15 At the end of the first round of war (1955–1972), Nimeiri was generally seen as a hero in South Sudan for his brave move to end the war and grant the south autonomy. But his decision to apply Shari'a law in 1983, reneging on the Addis Ababa Agreement by dividing the south into three weak provinces, and a host of other issues including his political marriage with Hassan al-Turabi's National Islamic Front, began to feed the southern rebellion against him.

16 See Deng Akol Ruay, 1992, *The Politics of Two Sudans, North and South*. Uppsala: Nordik Afrika Institute.

17 "Marginalization" has entered Sudan's political lexicon and is probably the most popularly used political term.

18 The letter, written by John Garang to General Joseph Lagu, in January 1972, came two months before the accord was signed. It spelled out the fundamentals of the "New Sudan," which he wanted the southern negotiators to emphasize in their negotiations with the north. Though it was never published, this letter remains in circulation among the South Sudanese.

19 See John Garang, 1987, *John Garang Speaks*. London: Kegan Paul International, and Garang, 1990, *The Call for Democracy in Sudan*. Foreword by Mansour Khalid (ed.). London: Kegan Paul International.

20 Gatluak Gai was killed in July 2011 in mysterious circumstances, after signing a peace deal and amnesty with the SPLA and the governor of Unity State, Taban Deng Gai, a deal that offered the rebel leader and his soldiers a program of absorption back into the SPLA.

21 This was a phrase commonly used by the South Sudanese when commenting on the liberation wars.

22 The southern rebels fighting for separation were popularly known as Anya-nya. When it became clear that the south was going back to war, the first people to put up a front called the movement Anya-nya II, in recognition of the previous war and to project the notion that this war was a continuation of the struggle for the same ideals.

23 The historical details of this episode are well documented by many researchers and there is no need to revisit them. See for example Douglas Johnson, 2003, *The Root Causes of Sudan's Civil Wars*. Oxford: James Currey.

24 See Jok Madut Jok and Sharon Hutchinson, "Sudan's Prolonged Second Civil War and Militarization of of Nuer and Dinka Ethnic Identities." *African Studies Review.* Vol. 42(2): 125–45, 1999.

25 See Alex de Waal, "Counter-Insurgency on the Cheap." *London Review of Books.* Vol. 26 (15), August 5, 2004.

3. SUDAN'S WARS: THE EXPERIENCE OF ONE VILLAGE

1 Although the village is real, the name is fictional. It literally means "dark forest," to imply not just the remoteness of such villages from the centers of power and decision-making, but also how they have to suffer and live with the consequences of decisions made elsewhere. The concept of darkness in Africa has taken on another meaning in more recent years, that of the lack of electrical power.

2 "Basic Education and Gender Equity in South Sudan." UNICEF, Juba, South Sudan, 2008. http://www.unicef.org/southsudan/education.html

3 See the World Health Organization, "South Sudan: Country Cooperation Strategy." http://www.who.int/countryfocus/cooperation_strategy/ ccsbrief_ssd_en.pdf

4 The Dinka practice *lahot*: "levirate" or "ghost" marriage. In this tradition, a woman can be "married" to a deceased man, whose family then assign her to a male relative to father children for them. Even though most of the soldiers from Ror Col were too young at the start of the war to have had children, this tradition considers them to have posthumous children.

5 Jok Madut Jok and Sharon E. Hutchinson, "Sudan's Prolonged Second Civil War and the Militarization of Nuer and Dinka Ethnic Identities." *African Studies Review.* Vol. 42(2): 125–45, 1999.

4. POLITICAL RIVALRIES, THE NEW WARS, AND THE CRUMBLING SOCIAL ORDER

1 See the BBC's Karen Allen, "South Sudan: Women Raped Under the Noses of UN Forces." BBC, June, 2014.

2 The Sudd Institute, "South Sudan and the Prospects for Peace Amidst Violent Political Wrangling." *Special Report*, The Sudd Institute, January 2014. Juba, South Sudan.

3 There is still debate about whether the wars have always been for separation or for reforms within a united Sudan. The number of the dead in the

course of the two liberation wars of 1955–72 and 1983–2005 also remains a matter of extrapolation.

4 Mohamed Omer Beshir, 1968, *The Southern Sudan: Background to Conflict.* C. Hurst & Company.

5 Jok Madut Jok, "Diversity, Unity and Nation Building in South Sudan." *Special Report Number 287*, United States Institute of Peace, October 2011.

6 Douglas Johnson, 2003, *The Root Causes of Sudan's Civil Wars.* Oxford: James Currey.

7 Martin Plaut, "Background to South Sudan's crisis: warnings ignored." wordpress.com December 17, 2013.

8 See al-Jazeera English series, "Sudan: the Break up," the portion on South Sudan, "*Fight for the Heart of the South.*" July 9, 2011.

9 Thomas, 2015.

10 Lesley Warner, "Armed-Group Amnesty and Military Integration in South Sudan." *The RUSI Journal*, December 2013, Vol. 158 (6): 40–47.

11 Jok Madut Jok, 2013, "South Sudan and the Risk of Unrest." *Sudd Institute Weekly Review*, December 3, 2013.

12 At a well-attended lecture given at the University of Juba, the former minister of finance of Afghanistan, Professor Ashraf Ghani, made a strong case about why such countries seem to always return to war. He listed reasons including weakness of institutions, security sector issues and the entitlement felt by "liberators."

13 Collier, 2007.

14 Jok, 2012.

15 Scott Straus, *The Order of Genocide: Race, Power, and War in Rwanda.* Ithaca, New York, Cornell University Press, 2006.

16 *Sudan Tribune*, May 16, 2013. The interview was conducted during the annual celebration that commemorates the martyrs of the past liberation wars. By "two people," he was referring to the two leaders, the president and the former vice president.

17 Jok Madut Jok and Sharon E. Hutchinson, "Sudan's Prolonged Second Civil War and the Militarization of Nuer and Dinka Ethnic Identities." *African Studies Review.* Vol. 42(2): 125–45, 1999.

5. REPORTING SUDAN'S WARS: THE MEDIA AND THE BLURRED LINE BETWEEN INFORMING AND INCITING

1 See Hilde Johnson, 2016, *South Sudan: The Untold Story, From Independence to Civil War.* London and New York. I.B.Tauris.

2   Some people suggest that the Juba incident exacerbated the conflict by turning a political conflict, a struggle for power among the élite, into a war with an ethnic hue.

3   Jok Madut Jok, "Militarism, Gender and Reproductive Suffering: The Case of Abortion in Western Dinka." *Africa: Journal of International African Institute.* 69 (2): 195–212, 1999.

4   Jok Madut Jok, 2005, "War, Changing Ethics and the Position of Youth in South Sudan." In *Vanguard or Vandals: Youth, Politics and Conflict in Africa.* Jon Abbink and I. van Kessel (eds.) Leiden and Boston: Brill.

5   Jok Madut Jok, "Violence and Resilience: Women, War and the Realities of Everyday Life in Sudan." *The Ahfad Journal: Women and Change*, Vol. 23, No. 2, December 2006.

6   Jok Madut Jok, 2012, "Negotiating Security: Gender, Violence, and the Rule of Law in Post-war South Sudan." Howard Stein and Amal Fadlalla Hassan (eds.) *Gendered Insecurities, Health and Development in Africa.* New York: Routledge.

7   Jok Madut Jok, 2013, "Power Dynamics and the Politics of Fieldwork under Sudan's Prolonged Conflicts." In Dyan Mazurana et al (eds.) *Research Methods in Conflict Settings: A View from Below.* Cambridge, UK and NY: Cambridge University Press.

8   "Understanding the Bentiu Massacres in South Sudan." *Radio Tamazuj*, May 1, 2014.

9   "UN Confirms Massacres in South Sudan, says FM being used to Broadcast Hate Messages." *Radio Tamazuj*, April 21, 2014.

10 See Report of the Secretary General to the Security Council, Report (S/2015/203) issued on 23 March 2015.

11 Ibid.

12 Human Rights Watch, https://www.hrw.org/africa/south-sudan, 2014.

13 http://www.voanews.com/content/south-sudan-women-children-sexual-violence-united-nations/2482221.html

14 4 Amnesty International. Nowhere Safe: Civilians under Attack in South Sudan, May 2014.

15 Human Rights Watch, https://www.hrw.org/africa/south-sudan, 2014.

6. MIXED ECONOMIES, CORRUPTION AND SOCIAL DISPARITY

1   Lise Grande, UN resident coordinator and country director of UNDP in South Sudan presented this view in a public lecture *How to be*

Humanitarian? UN Intervention in Post-Conflict Societies, given at the London School of Economics in 2009, in which she outlined how these indicators were the worst in the world. See UNDP, Juba, South Sudan, "Scary Statistics – Southern Sudan," November, 2010.

2   Kevin Peraino, "Is Massive U.S. Aid Helping South Sudan?" *Newsweek*, September 24, 2010.

3   The country comprised ten states when it was still part of Sudan, but on October 2, 2015, President Salva Kiir Mayardit issued an executive order to create eighteen more states, making a total of twenty-eight federal states. This sparked an intense debate on the constitutionality of the decree and created a crisis around the peace agreement he had recently signed with the opposition SPLM-IO's Riek Machar. The order remains a subject of controversy; there is huge public support for the content of the order but also opposition, on the grounds of its illegality and unconstitutionality. For more analysis of the impact of this order, see "The Creation of 28 South Sudanese States: Is It Legally and Economically Viable?" Juba: The Sudd Institute, October 6, 2015.

4   If the order creating 28 states remains in effect, these structures will have to be revised and the boundaries redrawn.

5   Oystein Rolandsen, 2005, *Guerilla Government: Political Changes in the Southern Sudan during the 1990s*. Oslo: Peace Research Institute.

6   See the Global Corruption Blog for other examples around the world.

7   See Daron Acemoglu and James Robinson, 2012, *Why Nations Fail: the Origins of Power, Prosperity and Poverty*. Crown Publishing Group. See also McFerson 2009.

7. ETHNIC RELATIONS, THE NEW WAR AND THE (DIS) UNITY OF SOUTH SUDAN

1   "Diversity, Unity and Nation-Building in South Sudan." 2011 United States Institute of Peace Special Report. Washington, DC: USIP.

2   https://www.hrw.org/reports/1999/sudan/SUDAWEB2-01.htm

3   I was present at a town hall meeting in 1998 with people in the Apuk section of Gogrial some years after he had switched sides back to the SPLA. This was exactly what he said in his address to a crowd of people he and his forces had terrorized for years.

4   This is a question that stood out in my notes as a response to an interview in 1998 on a similar topic in another project on the militarization of ethnicity. See Jok and Hutchinson, "Sudan's Prolonged Second Civil War

and the Militarization of Nuer and Dinka Ethnic Identities." *African Studies Review.* Vol. 42(2): 125–45, 1999.

5   Small Arms Survey, Update, June 3, 2011.

6   See Lesley Anne Warner, "Security Sector Reform and Military Integration in Post-Conflict Situations: Armed-Group Amnesty and Military Integration in South Sudan." *The Royal United Services Institute Journal,* Volume 158, 40–47, 2013.

7   International Crisis Group. "South Sudan: A Civil War by Any Other Name," Africa Report 217, April 10, 2014.

8. CONCLUSION: THE FATES OF THE TWO SUDANS

1   Adegboyega Christopher Ariyo, "Sustaining the New Wave of Pan-Africanism: African World Religion." Papers resulting from a workshop held at Windhoek Campus of the University of Namibia, December 6–9, 2010.

2   Jeffrey Gettleman, "After Years of Struggle, South Sudan becomes a New Nation." *The New York Times,* July 9, 2011.

3   Young, 2012.

4   *Christianity Today*, "Anti-Christian Backlash After South Sudan's Secession," October 29, 2011, http://www.christianitytoday.com/ct/2011/octoberweb-only/sudan-secession-backlash.html

5   Jooma Mariam, "Situation Report: Sudan: Eighteen Months After the CPA." Institute for Security Studies, July 17, 2006.

6   Sidahmed quoted in a report: "Can Sudan's oil feed north and south?" by James Copnall, BBC News, Khartoum, July 4, 2011.

7   Marina Arbetman-Rabinowitz, "Power Distribution and Oil in the Sudan: Will the Comprehensive Peace Agreement Turn the Oil Curse into a Blessing?" *International Interactions: Empirical and Theoretical Research in International Relations.* Vol. 34 (4), 2008.

8   Al-Atabani has recently broken ranks with the party, over the regime's killing of protestors in the Autumn 2013 demonstrations against the new economic policies of the NCP. Along with thirty other NCP leaders, he petitioned President al-Bashir, condemning the killing of peaceful demonstrators, for which those responsible were punished by removal from the party leadership.

9   See Ghazi Salahuddin Atabani, "Post-Secession Sudan: Challenges and Opportunities." *African Arguments,* December 17, 2011.

10   This statement was reported in so many media outlets, including the *Citizen* and Arabic dailies in Khartoum.

11 The freedom to work, to own property, to move between borders, and to choose one's residence.

12 "Sudan's Bashir meets Festus Mogae in Khartoum over South Sudan Peace," *Radio Tamazuj*, November 16, 2015.

13 2014 "Nationality and Citizenship in the 'New Sudan': A Legal or Moral Issue?" *Middle East Law and Governance Interdisciplinary Journal* 6, 225–249, 2014.

14 Jok Madut Jok, "The Break up of Sudan and the Links that Connect the People of the two Countries," *Sudan Studies 1*, a publication of the Sudan Studies Society of the United Kingdom, 2014.

15 Belloni, Roberto, "The Birth of South Sudan and the Challenges of Statebuilding." *Ethnopolitics* Vol. 10 (3–4), 2011.

BIBLIOGRAPHY

Anderson, Benedict, 1991, *Imagined Communities: Reflections on the Origin and Spread of Nationalism.* London and New York: Verso.

Bayart, Jean-Francois, 2009, *State in Africa: The Politics of the Belly.* New York, Polity.

Bekoe, Dorina A., 2008, *Implementing Peace Agreements: Lessons from Mozambique, Angola and Liberia.* London and New York: Routledge.

Committee on Foreign Relations, US Senate, 2012, *Sudan and South Sudan: Independence and Insecurity.* Washington: US Senate.

Copnall, James, 2014, *A Poisonous Thorn in Our Hearts: Sudan and South Sudan's Bitter and Incomplete Divorce.* London, Zed Books.

Duffield, Mark, 2001, *Global Governance and the New Wars: The Merging of Development and Security.* London and New York: Zed Books, Ltd.

Ferguson, James, 2006, *Global Shadows: Africa in the Neoliberal World Order.* Durham: Duke University Press.

Hartley, Paul F. and Ronald Bland (eds.), 2012, *South Sudan: Challenges and Opportunities for Africa's New Nation.*

Johnson, Douglas, 2003, *The Root Causes of Sudan's Civil Wars.* Oxford: James Currey.

Johnson, Hilde F., 2011, *Waging Peace in Sudan: The Inside Story of the Negotiations that Ended Africa's Longest Civil War.* Sussex: Academic Press.

Jok, Jok Madut, 2007, *Sudan: Race, Religion and Violence.* Oxford: Oneworld Publications.

LeRiche, Matthew A., 2012, *South Sudan: From Revolution to Independence.* New York: Columbia University Press.

Murshed, Sayed Mansoob, 2010, *Explaining Civil War: A Rational Choice Approach*. Northampton, MA: Edward Edger Publishing, Inc.

Natsios, Andrew, 2012, *Sudan, South Sudan, and Darfur: What Everyone Needs to Know*. Oxford: Oxford University Press.

Reno, William, 1999, *Warlord Politics and African States*. Boulder: Lynne Rienner Publishers.

Savir, Uri, Abu Ala, Shimon Peres and Dennis Ross, 2008, *Peace First: A New Model to End War*. San Francisco, CA: Berrett-Koehle Publishers.

Sriram, Chandra L., 2008 *Peace as Governance: Power-Sharing, Armed Groups and Contemporary Peace Negotiations (Rethinking Peace and Conflict)*. New York: Palgrave Macmillan.

Sriram, Chandra L., Olga Martin-Ortega and Johanna Herman, 2009, *War, Conflict and Human Rights: Theory and Practice*. London and New York: Routledge.

Suhrke, Astri and Mats Berdal, 2012, *The Peace in Between: Post-War Violence and Peacebuilding (Studies in Conflict, Development and Peacebuilding)*. New York: Palgrave Macmillan.

Thomas, Edward, 2015, *South Sudan: Unfinished Revolution*. London: Zed Books.

Tilly, Charles, 2003, *The Politics of Collective Violence*. Cambridge, UK and Cape Town, SA: Cambridge University Press.

Utas, Matt (ed), 2012, *African Conflicts and Informal Power: Big Men and Networks*. Uppsala, London and New York: Zed Books, Ltd.

de Waal, Alex, 2005, *Famine that Kills: Darfur, Sudan*. London: Zed Books, 2nd edition.

de Waal, Alex, 1997, *Famine Crimes: Politics and the Disaster Relief Industry in Africa*. London: Villiers Publications.

Wrong, Michela, 2010, *It's Our Turn to Eat: Story of a Kenyan Whistle Blower*. New York: Harper Publishers.

Young, John, 2012, *The Fate of Sudan: The Origins and Consequences of a Flawed Peace Process*. London and New York: Zed Books Ltd.

Zartman, I. William, 1995, *Elusive Peace: Negotiating an End to Civil Wars*. Washington, D.C., Brookings Institution.

INDEX